D1164451

JAMES JOYCE:

Common Sense and Beyond

Consulting Editor HASKELL M. BLOCK

Brooklyn College of The City

University of New York

JAMES
JOYCE:

COMMON SENSE AND

BEYOND

by ROBERT M. ADAMS

Cornell University

 RANDOM HOUSE *New York*

Studies in Language and Literature

PR
6019
O9Z44
O9Z
2
copy

Fourth Printing, February 1971

© *Copyright, 1966, by Random House, Inc.*

Since this page cannot legibly accommodate all the copyright notices, the page following constitutes an extension of the copyright page.

All rights reserved under International and Pan-American Copyright Conventions. Published in New York by Random House, Inc. and simultaneously in Toronto, Canada, by Random House of Canada Limited

Library of Congress Catalog Card Number: 66-23281

Manufactured in the United States of America by The Colonial Press Inc., Clinton, Mass.

ACKNOWLEDGMENTS

Excerpts from "The Tower," "Who Goes With Fergus," and "When You Are Old," by William Butler Yeats, reprinted from *The Collected Poems of W. B. Yeats*, Definitive Edition, with the author's final revisions (New York: Macmillan, 1956), by permission of The Macmillan Company, Mr. M. B. Yeats, and The Macmillan Co. of Canada. "The Tower," copyright 1928, The Macmillan Company, copyright renewed 1956 by Georgie Yeats. "Who Goes With Fergus?" and "When You Are Old," copyright 1906, The Macmillan Company, copyright renewed 1934 by William Butler Yeats.

Excerpt from *James Joyce*, by Herbert Gorman (New York: Farrar & Rinehart, 1939), by permission of The Society of Authors.

Table from *James Joyce's Ulysses*, by Stuart Gilbert (New York: Knopf, 1931), by permission of Alfred A. Knopf, Inc., and Faber & Faber, Ltd. Copyright, 1930, by Stuart Gilbert.

Excerpts from *Dubliners*, by James Joyce (New York: Viking Press, 1958), reprinted by permission of The Viking Press, Inc. Originally published by B. W. Huebsch, Inc., 1916. All rights reserved.

Excerpts from *A Portrait of the Artist as a Young Man*, by James Joyce (New York: Modern Library), reprinted by permission of The Viking Press, Inc. Copyright 1916 by B. W. Huebsch, Inc., 1944 by Nora Joyce.

Excerpts from *Finnegans Wake*, by James Joyce (New York: Viking Press, 1959), reprinted by permission of The Viking Press, Inc. Copyright 1939 by James Joyce.

Excerpts from *Ulysses*, by James Joyce (New York: The Modern Library, 1961), by permission of Random House, Inc., and The Bodley Head, Ltd. Copyright, 1914, 1918 by Margaret Caroline Anderson; copyright, 1934, by The Modern Library, Inc.; copyright, 1942, 1946, by Nora Joseph Joyce.

06733

For Lucy—

*Teach Floh and Luse polkas, show Bienie
    where's sweet*
*And be sure Vespatilla fines fat ones to
    heat.*

—FINNEGANS WAKE

PREFACE

The book which follows has been written with a very simple purpose: to provide, for someone who wants to read in the work of James Joyce, a handy compendium of necessary background information and to point out the most sensible and economical approaches to his fiction. This limited aim excludes the hand-in-hand, guided-tour-through-Joyce approach; it supposes that, once the major possibilities are mapped out, the interested reader can and will go adventuring on his own. It precludes also any attempt to impose novel interpretations or argue special theses to a conclusion. At this stage in the discussion of Joyce, original work of any merit is almost certain to be detailed and closely wrought; a survey cannot attempt it. The present book aims to supply those materials and suggest those approaches which will enable a perceptive reader to gain a footing in Joyce.

On the other hand, nothing would be duller than a mere recitation of the *idées reçues* about Joyce, a compilation which pussyfooted around the areas where there has been, or might be, controversy. I have committed three or four conscious heresies in the following pages, to which I call special attention here, so that the reader may be properly alerted. Not everyone will accept my low estimate of the epiphanies (pp. 87–89); to others, my qualifications on the ending of *A Portrait of the Artist as a Young Man* may seem excessive (pp. 113-115); and every sound, sensible student who builds his faith on established facts will take issue with my placing of *Finnegans Wake* above *Ulysses* (pp. 214-216). I hope the reader will not be too easily swayed by my persuasive rhetoric on these points—that he will be led to study in the modest bibliography at the end of the book, and grant me his full consent only when he understands the full reasons for my position and the full force of the objections to be brought against it.

It is not easy to write plainly about complex topics, and the common-sense approach to Joyce—within whose life and mind common sense was not always a ruling principle—may easily result in a disastrously truncated view of his work. But it has long seemed to me a mistake to take hold of Joyce, or any other difficult writer, by his complexities. It is like making a man's acquaintance through a detailed account of his neurotic symptoms; after such a recital, who wants to know the fellow? Traditional devices of literary exegesis will go a long way toward making the major work of Joyce both clear and interesting. There is, moreover, a special interest in tracing through his career the line at which they fail. For Joyce was a man who changed immensely during his lifetime and whose change was governed by an inner logic, a personal dialectic as implacable as Ibsen's. One of the most important elements in this development is the growth of a quality which I shall call (without further explanation at this time) visionary writing. Visionary writing begins precisely at the point where common sense leaves off. But I am hopeful that there are ways to describe it and to invoke a sort of sympathy with it, which do not transcend common sense. Meanwhile, the reader may console himself with the thought that large areas of understanding and delight are available to him, this side of the line. Solving symbolic puzzles and seeing deep visions are two of the pleasures of

Joyce, but they might well be seen as the final reward of studies rather than as a formidable preliminary test to be passed.

Because it is introductory and elementary by intention, I have not felt obliged to stud my text with footnotes or those elegant academic qualifications which, as they cover up the author's tracks, also muffle the reader's understanding. Having drawn without scruple on what seemed useful in previous scholarship, and discarded without polemic what did not, I offer the mixture which follows for the benefit of the beginner. Let no man cite me as an authority, or hang me out as a scarecrow, without taking this intention of the work into account.

ROBERT M. ADAMS

A NOTE ON EDITIONS

In quoting from Joyce's books and citing page references, I have used the following editions: Compass Books (Viking) for *Dubliners* (C41) and *Finnegans Wake* (C45); Modern Library for *A Portrait of the Artist as a Young Man* and *Ulysses* (G52), the latter in its post-1961 edition.

The first two of these texts represent acceptable compromises, though they appear without the name of an editor. The *Dubliners* text, though neither critical (in the sense of a fully-worked-out "best text") nor acknowledging the many variants (in manuscripts, serials, and texts published within Joyce's lifetime), is at least easily available. Marvin Magalaner's *Time of Apprenticeship*, in Chapter III and Appendices A and C, sketches some of the variants and reprints of the magazine version of "The Sisters." A scholarly edition of *Dubliners* is being prepared by Richard Ellmann and Robert Scholes.

The text of *Finnegans Wake* has special advantages in that it reproduces Joyce's 1939 edition line-for-line, and is said to incorporate Joyce's corrections. These are good features and to go beyond them toward a really critical edition would involve immense labor with manuscripts and proof sheets, which no one at present seems ready to undertake. So this text, with whatever errors poor half-blind Joyce and his bewildered printers allowed to slip through, will clearly be standard for a long time.

As for *A Portrait of the Artist as a Young Man,* the only edition now in print in the United States is the revised Compass C9 edition, advertised as "definitive." The text is not definitive; it is, in essence, an eclectic compilation, based partly on a holograph which there is every reason to think Joyce discarded early in the process of his revisions, partly on a composite of readings from the various editions. Joyce never in his life saw anything like this text. I have, therefore, preferred not to use it. If one were looking for a reasonably correct text, that put out by Jonathan Cape in 1924 incorporates most, though not all, of Joyce's final corrections to this novel. However, rather than be altogether esoteric in my references, I have turned back to the old Modern Library edition, which (though no longer in print) is likely to be found in most libraries; and I have applied to it Peter Spielberg's list of Errata contained in the last essay of Thomas Connolly's little collection titled *Joyce's Portrait* (New York: Appleton-Century, 1962), pp. 318–328. The Modern Library text has about 300 pages, as opposed to approximately 250 in Compass C9; to translate a reference in Modern Library onto the Compass scale, multiply the Modern Library number by ⅚ and look around. According to this rule, p. 180 in Modern Library should equal about 150 in C9; in fact, the same passage occurs on p. 155. In all such transpositions, one has to give or take a few pages.

Ulysses, in the standard Modern Library text, was originally set from Roth's corrupt pirated edition and never properly corrected, although silent corrections were made, over the years, on the old plates. In 1961 the edition was "corrected and reset"—however, neither the standard nor the basis for corrections nor the maker of them was identified. Whoever the editor was, he improved the text considerably. But the unfortunate mistake was made in the new edition of changing the old pagination, on which such standard works of reference as Hanley's *Word Index* had been founded. This edition contains fifteen more pages than the earlier Modern Library printings; to get an approximate fix on a passage located in the *Word Index* or the earlier text, one must add, for the new edition, about two pages for every hundred in the basic number. Thus a reference to p. 506 in the *Word Index* should be sought ten pages further on ($5 \times 2 = 10$), or on p. 516 of the 1961 edition, and even that is only approximate (in fact, the equivalent passage is on p. 517). Still, since most students will probably be working with this post-1961 text and since it is better than its predecessor, I have made my references to it. However, for textual accuracy, the best available edition is that issued by the Odyssey Press (Hamburg, Paris, and Bologna, 1932); the second and third printings of 1933 and 1935 show increasing correctness.

These problems of rudimentary reference are disagreeable, but the anxious reader can console himself with the reflection that no radically new reading of any of the books depends on minutiae of diction, punctuation, or capitalization. Even the C9 *Portrait*, which represents the most striking departure from a text as Joyce finally approved it, merely clogs the ear with a number of adolescent rhythms and close repetitions; it does not alter the "meaning" of the *Portrait* in any essential way. *Ulysses* in the third Odyssey printing is not strikingly different from *Ulysses* in the old Modern Library version. But if one has the appetite for accuracy, the current available texts of Joyce will hardly satisfy it.

CONTENTS

APPENDIX B

JAMES JOYCE:

Common Sense and Beyond

CHAPTER I

IRELAND AND JOYCE'S HERITAGE FROM IT

Like most men, James Joyce inhabited several different worlds more or less simultaneously and cannot be fully understood without some explanation of them all. Born late in the nineteenth century, in the most backward and ruinous land of western Europe, he inherited the nightmare history of a country which had never in the annals of civilization won a war or endured a century without losing one. Exiled and estranged from his homeland, he wrote his greatest epic during the first international convulsion of the twentieth century, and died in the course of the second. His work was performed amid incessant crises—of language, of faith, of allegiance, of manners, of morals, of style, of vision, of mythology—so that we must, first of all, reach into the dark pocket of Irish history in order to understand some of those energies, resources, and traditions which sustained him, as well as some of the problems which bedeviled him, in the maelstrom of the twentieth century.

The history of early Ireland is shrouded in myth, legend, and uncertainty. It is a scientific fact that the land was inhabited in neolithic times; by whom and under what circumstances is less easy to say. A myth sprang up in the late eighteenth and nineteenth centuries that the Celtic peoples originally covered the greater part of Europe. Under pressure from Franks and Teutons, they were gradually pushed westward, and survive now, amid their epic griefs and frustrations, in the mountains of Wales, the bogs of Ireland, and the misty headlands of Brittany. This is one story. Other myths tell of a race of primitive giants inhabiting Ireland—myths which are less easy to deride since skeletons of enormous men have been found in the Irish bogs, as well as of enormous elk, and a breed of immense wolfhounds which did not die out until the sixteenth century. Giants in the earth—it is a universal myth, and the Irish gift for fantastic mythologizing would be bound to have invented a myth like this, except that it happens to be true. This is a frequent characteristic of Irish myth, especially that used by James Joyce and William Butler Yeats.

In the welter of legends and fables which have descended from antiquity or were engrafted onto it, there is not much point in distinguishing time, place, or order of events. Among the traditional stories of invasion and civil war, there is one, directly opposed to the legend of the giants, which describes the island as being long occupied by a race of contemptible Firbolgs—dwarfish, malicious, and inhospitable skulkers —who were ultimately overcome by a noble race, the Tuatha De Danaan. These in turn gave way to a still nobler group, the sons of Miletus, who are alleged to have reached Ireland from Spain, after leaving Scythia, where they traced their ancestry through Partholon, Fenius Farsaigh, and Japhet, back to Noah. These fabulous lines of kings and fabulous levels of ethnic nobility are worth noting, not for their historicity but because they seem like an effort to explain a striking and recurrent duality in the Irish character. Throughout their history, the Irish have produced heroes and leaders who capture the popular imagination and earn deep devotion from their followers. The captain or chief is surrounded by an aura of almost religious worship; he is a demi-god, whom men will serve with their lives. Yet he is attended, almost inevitably, by the figure of the traitor, the informer, the weakling, who at the crucial moment is always able to strike the hero a disabling blow. Irish history is irresistibly melodramatic and the Irish character has in it a bit of the manic-depressive; the black-and-white contrasts of both are dramatized in the noble sons of King Miletus ruling over a snarling horde of hateful Firbolgs.

Leaving aside now these misty patterns of antiquity —no less interesting for their mists than for their patterns—let us pause a moment to sketch the Irish people as they may be supposed to have existed from roughly the sixth to the twelfth centuries of our era— between, let us say, the conversion of the island by St. Patrick (who landed on the Wicklow coast in 432) and the arrival of Strongbow and his Anglo-Normans in 1169. Primarily they were a pastoral people, raising cattle in the bogs and green fields of their wild, wet island. They had few cities or towns, and these usually were on the seacoast; few major roads, for they usually made do with bridle paths or unmarked trails; and few permanent political divisions. Scattered across the land, the populace dwelt in wicker cabins or huddled within the confines of small earthen forts. The social unit was the clan or family, loosely defined but united under a kind of headship which might be glorified with the title of *ri* or king. The *ard-ri* was the high king, whose power to control a multitude of lesser *ris* was very much a function of his personal strength and astuteness.

Diffused throughout the countryside, and far from the major trade-routes, most of the population kept to itself, living off the land, as represented by cows, pigs, fowl, bees, and some local corn crops. Famous alike for good fellowship and combativeness, this pastoral race passed quickly from merriment to bloodshed; and though legendary for the ferocity of their encounters, they had, even in those distant days, an unaccountable preference for heroic failure over practical success. When they first came up against armor of plate and chain, the Celtic gallowglasses were unable for a long time to persuade themselves that its use was not unmanly; for some generations they continued to go to inevitable slaughter in their light linen shirts, using at most a wicker shield or a leather cap for protection.

Inevitably with a people so fond of combat and so loosely organized politically, the Irish lived in a state of chronic disorder. Their plethora of minor and major kings only augmented the strife; and the record of turbulence is such that in the long chronicles and epic legends it is the rare exception to learn of an Irish king who did not die on the field of battle. Their domestic feuds were augmented by a sequence of devastating invasions and conquests—of which more later. Yet for all this ceaseless bloodshed, it would be wrong to think of the ancient Irish as a savage or uncultured race. Their monasteries housed a learned and much respected clergy; during the Dark Ages, wandering scholars from Ireland were teachers to half the continent of Europe. Thus fiery Columbanus, gentle Fiacre, subtle Duns Scotus, and a hundred other Irish-educated monks returned to the Continent the light which had been brought over by St. Patrick.

Indeed, the importance of the monastery in Irish life is impossible to overstate; it has been the home of poets, saints, and scholars, the center of civilization, the fortress against barbarism. Aside from these positive functions, it dramatizes an aspect of this curious people which is not very easy to explain: its notable suspicion and hatred of the human body, especially that of the opposite sex. There is a broad streak of natural asceticism in many Irish—accompanied, sometimes, by a deliberate vein of bawdry and prurience but having also an authentic existence of its own. Handsome young St. Kevin, a patron of the island (alongside St. Patrick and St. Bridget), was once tempted in his stony retreat at Glendalough by a delectable colleen, but he pitched her unchivalrously into the icy lake—where she drowned, and good riddance to her. Whether religiously, economically, or temperamentally motivated, Irish asceticism is proverbial. It found natural expression in Irish monasticism; and the Irish sense of sexual sinfulness survived to burn brands which need no emphasizing on the consciousness of James Joyce.

But Irish learning of the Middle Ages was not exclusively monastic. Each *ri* or petty king was likely to maintain a private *ollave*, that is, a kind of ceremonial poet-diviner-historian, whose calling was a family tradition and whose authority (perhaps owing something to remembered accounts of Druid bards) was surrounded with awe and reverence. In addition to this scholastic and traditional learning, the ancient Irish were famous for other accomplishments. Their lyric and satiric poetry, which the eighteenth and nineteenth centuries imagined as suffused with misty, elegiac melancholy (after the manner of Macpherson's famous forgery) was in fact hard, chaste, and beautifully specific. As harpers and musicians, the Irish were second to none in Europe. Irish mines (now long exhausted) furnished silver, gold, and copper in modest abundance, and from these materials the craftsmen of the island fashioned jewelry of the greatest intricacy and splendor. The famous Tara brooch and the splendid Cross of Cong are unmatched in the history of the jeweler's art. They combine great simplicity of outline with a highly stylized and exhaustively elaborated pattern, within which tiny naturalistic details lie half-concealed. This wedding of abstract pattern and inconceivably minute detail seems to be characteristic of the Gaelic genius for decoration. It revealed itself most fully in the creation of illuminated manuscripts such as the priceless Book of Kells, now in the Trinity College library. This golden treasury of handiwork, each page of which represents months, perhaps years, of labor by an imaginative and disciplined scribe, served James Joyce as a model and an inspiration for his labors on *Finnegans Wake*. But indeed, we can trace in Joyce's character many specific traits from the ancient Irish.

He was a savage enemy and a man with a passionate concern for personal loyalty; his fascinated fear and hatred of sex was balanced by an equally fascinated fear and hatred of the celibate priest. He had a deep-seated, almost fatal impulse toward heroic failure; he was generous and vain; and he practiced his art with the reverent devotion of one for whom it had magic meaning, magic power. He did not think of himself as a paid entertainer, nor did he think of the work bestowed on his art as an investment which ought to yield a proportional return. He had an immense sense of the presence of the past in every moment of the present. How closely one thinks these traits should be related to the traditions of ancient Ireland is obviously a matter for individual decision; the fact is that James Joyce, growing up in a culture of which many features were shaped by Gaelic scholars, students of folklore, and revivers of ancient traditions, was made abundantly aware of his heritage, even as it worked on him unconsciously.

Last, let us take brief note of the multitudinous invasions and depredations which befell the ancient Irish—this folk so learned yet so primitive, so unpredatory as a group, though individually so belligerent. Of the traditional invasions and conquests, reaching far back into antiquity, we have already spoken. Historically speaking, the year 795 saw the first appearance off the Irish coast of the fleets of marauding Norsemen, who came to harry, burn, rape, plunder, and kill. Finding a divided country and good loot, the predators returned in waves. Raid was followed by counter-raid; the land was submerged by violence. The monastery at Armagh was sacked and rebuilt ten times—three times within a single month. With ax and torch, club and spear, the attacking Norsemen and defending Celts ravaged the entire land, working from the seacoasts inward. An incidental but lasting effect of the invasions was the establishment of many coastal cities, including Waterford, Limerick, and Dublin (Dubh-linn = dark pool) at the mouth of the Liffey. After many seesaws of fortune and interminable bloodshed, Brian Boru won, at the battle of Clontarf (Good Friday, 1014), a partial victory over the Norsemen; henceforth the Celts partially limited their power and influence, though without expelling them from the island. They settled down around the cities, intermarried with the local populations, and added a Norse strain to the Irish ethnic medley.

In 1169, various Anglo-Norman knights—notably Richard de Clare (known as Strongbow), Robert Fitzstephen, and Maurice Fitzgerald—were invited to Ireland by a local chieftain, Dermot MacMurrough, to assist him in his quarrel with Tiernan O'Rourke, king of Breffni. To Ireland they came, bringing with them the Norman systems of warfare, land-tenure, inheritance, and law. Having resolved the quarrel for which they were invited, they settled spaciously on the land, portioned it out among their followers, built themselves castles, and ruled over Ireland—far from their own technical overlord, Henry II—as independent lords over a conquered people. And though, over the years, they became, in the words of the chroniclers,

Hibernis ipsis hiberniores, more Irish than the Irish themselves, they never ceased to be resented by the native population as Saxon usurpers. Claiming descent from the Fitzgeralds, they were known as the line of the Geraldines; their craft, energy, cupidity, and wealth have lived on as legends in the land.

Ruthlessly skipping half a millennium of bestial struggle, violence, greed, and mismanagement—merely mentioning Elizabeth's sixteenth-century policy of planned, gradual genocide and Oliver Cromwell's massive seventeenth-century effort at immediate extermination—let us turn from medieval Ireland to another Ireland which James Joyce carried within his consciousness, and which bulked large in his existence. This is eighteenth-century Ireland, the Anglo-Irish nation which, between the age of Swift and that of Wolfe Tone, provided the island with its first and only interlude of moderate prosperity until the present. Even so late as the eighteenth century, indigenous poetry of no mean stature was being written in Gaelic. Blind Turlough Carolan, the last of the professional Gaelic bards, died in 1738; and that broad, bold Gaelic satire on women, Brian Merriman's "Midnight Court," dates from 1781. But the literary achievements of eighteenth-century Ireland were primarily in English—the English of Swift and Berkeley, of Burke, Goldsmith, and Sheridan. Though all these men had a foot in England as well as Ireland, none of them failed to maintain and to profit by their Irish connection; indeed the fate of being Anglo-Irish was a good deal less pressing in those days, when one found much the same sort of earthy, moneyed, sports-loving, classically-educated squirearchy on both sides of the Irish Sea. To be sure, the gap between the Irish peasant and his Protestant landlord was as deep in the eighteenth century as before or since; and the cultural achievements of the eighteenth-century Anglo-Irish were by no means popular, they were frankly aristocratic. How much

this tradition amounted to at the time and what resources it offers the modern writer are questions which
admit only of individual answers. Yeats was fond of
speaking about his spiritual and physical ancestors as
exemplifying

> The pride of people that were
> Bound neither to Cause nor to State,
> Neither to slaves that were spat on
> Nor to the tyrants that spat,
> The people of Burke and of Grattan
> That gave, though free to refuse—*

For Joyce, with his Catholic background and his
utter indifference to aristocracies, the eighteenth-
century tradition was less immediately available; yet
the clarity, point, and elegance of eighteenth-century
prose and the dignity and proportion of eighteenth-
century buildings were perpetually before him. Dublin
is, as it happens, one of the great eighteenth-century
cities of Europe. Showpieces include the dignified and
impressive law building, called Four Courts, and
Gandon's great Custom-House. On Merrion or Fitz-
william Square it takes little imagination to call up
the sauntering fop, with lace at wrist and throat, greeting the great lady, all patches, powder, and furbe-
lows, as she is handed out of her coach-and-four by a
respectful lackey. Trinity College itself, though an
Elizabethan foundation, is largely of eighteenth-century construction. And in the very slums and back
alleys off the Coombe, one is struck by the vision of
an elegant fanlight, a tattered, filthy, but still ex-
quisitely proportioned doorway. Eighteenth-century
Ireland was before Joyce in Belvedere College, an
eighteenth-century town house converted to a Jesuit
school; it made itself felt in the old buildings of Uni-

* From "The Tower," *The Collected Poems of W. B. Yeats*,
Definitive Edition, with the author's final revisions (New York:
Macmillan, 1956).

versity College on Stephen's Green; in stories of the
Smock Alley theater, White's gambling establishment,
Buck Whalley, and the famous Hell-Fire Club. All
these traditions and many more remained alive and
tangible during Joyce's youth; they made the eighteenth-century world dramatically present before him.

The literary figure of the earlier age with whom
Joyce shows deepest affinities is evidently Dean Swift.
To trace out the parallels and influences in detail
would be a book in itself, but a few broad similarities
can be sketched quickly. Like Jonathan Swift, Joyce
was obsessed with the problem of man's true dimension (one of the pleasant puzzles about Bloom is how
he manages to become Brobdingnagian without ceasing to be Lilliputian); like Swift, Joyce was a clean-
minded man obsessed with nasty, scatological ideas;
like Swift, he commanded an unusual store of "curious
learning" which he used to baffle and defeat as well
as to amuse his reader; like Swift, he was an egotistical
nihilist, whose hard, sharp wit was attracted irresistibly
by soft gullets; like Swift, he could be high and mighty
with "authorities," but playful and familiar with the
humble. These similarities must be qualified by many
and obvious differences, and there is a sense in which
they are almost too deep-seated to be useful in a
literary discussion. Fundamental affinity of personali-
ties is more an odd coincidence than a matter of
demonstrable literary significance. Still, the kinship of
Swift and Joyce is a useful concept for readers of the
latter; and Joyce's reliance on Swift's great example
is felt far beyond the section of *Ulysses* where Stephen
Dedalus invokes him among the spiritual fathers
(*Proteus*).

In the long, tragic history of Ireland, the eighteenth
century appears as a momentary interlude of spacious
and gracious achievement by heroic individual per-
sonalities. Its end is marked by the crashing chords of
social and political disaster. The insurrection which

is associated with the names of Wolfe Tone and Lord
Edward Fitzgerald was crushed in 1798; by the massive application of threats and open bribery, the Irish
Parliament was forced to vote itself out of existence;
and the Act of Union, passed on January 1, 1801,
crushed the unfortunate and passionately unwilling
nation into the arms of their Saxon jailers.

Aside from inflaming long-standing racial, historical,
and religious antipathies, the Act of Union worked to
Ireland's immediate disadvantage in several obvious
ways. The political representation supplied by even
an imperfect Irish Parliament was immensely curtailed
when Ireland's only voice was a small minority group
in the English House of Commons. Since the days of
Dean Swift, no observer of Ireland's social problems
had failed to recommend the establishment of Irish
manufactures; the Act of Union, by placing Irish poli-
cies directly under English control, assured that there
would be no Irish competition for English industries.
Finally, the Catholics (comprising in many districts
90 per cent of the population), who had been disenfranchised since the seventeenth century, remained
disenfranchised under the Union. But as an obvious
majority in Ireland, they had had a potential influence
which they no longer possessed as a small minority
within Great Britain. The first work of recovery after
the Union therefore seemed to be the enfranchising of
the Catholics, but only after more than a quarter-century of bitter agitation and protest was this elementary justice achieved in 1829, under the leadership of
the great orator Daniel O'Connell.

In the meantime, however, the economic position
of Ireland had become steadily more precarious. Tied
to the English economy, its agricultural exports controlled by English needs and subject to English tariffs
and quotas, the Irish economy nonetheless flourished
on the high grain prices induced by the Napoleonic
wars. But while Anglo-Irish landlords grew rich ex-

porting grain and cattle for English consumption, the native Irish population grew steadily larger and poorer. In 1800 the population was estimated at more than 5,000,000; forty years later it was more than 8,000,000. In a land without significant industry other than agriculture, this mushroom growth was perilous. For in fact most of these millions depended for their livelihood on the potato—a miserable crop, known proverbially as "the root of misery." Whatever the crop they raised for the landlord or for export, the Irish peasantry depended for their essential existence on the humble spud, dug from the field where it grew and stored itself, roasted or boiled over a turf fire, and consumed as an entire meal by young and old alike. When a blight struck the potato crop in 1846 and 1847, hundreds of thousands of Irish peasants died of malnutrition and its attendant evils—to be perfectly frank, they starved to death on the threshold of the richest and most powerful nation in the world. Other hundreds of thousands fled the country, migrating to America or England or the Continent, wherever unskilled labor could earn a meager subsistence. Thus, over the latter half of the nineteenth century, while the populations of most European and American nations were growing spectacularly, that of Ireland declined precipitously. By the turn of the century, Ireland had lost fully half the population it possessed in 1840.

To shrink in numbers by 50 per cent in 50 years is a horrifying experience for any nation; in modern Europe only Ireland has undergone it. As one would expect, it was chiefly the young and vigorous who emigrated, the despairing and lethargic who remained. One still sees, in the shambling, tumble-down houses of Dublin and in the deserted countryside, marks of this terrifying depopulation. Yet even amid a populace stunned by misery, despair, and loss of leadership, active underground protest movements continued to spread. Whiteboys, Molly Maguires, Fenians, and Ribbon-men inherited something from the heroic tradition of '98; but without leadership, their revenge was blind. Across the desolate countryside, they fought a lonely, secret guerrilla warfare, with such weapons as came to hand—club, scythe, and torch. But gangs of rural outlaws could scarcely hope to make much impression on the British Empire and the Irish representatives within the English House of Commons were powerless to defend lawlessness, even had they wished to. Under the leadership of mild Isaac Butt, they presented their ineffectual legal protests, and were voted down; while in the countryside a desperate peasantry pursued their ineffectual illegal protests, and were hunted down. Failure to coordinate the legal with the illegal work hamstrung both efforts. Even an attempted invasion by Irish-Americans trained in the American Civil War and desperate for revenge ended in fiasco (1866 and 1867).

Thus the middle of the nineteenth century presents to the surveyor of Irish history an image of unalloyed weakness, misery, and ineffectuality. By a peculiar combination of greed, cruelty, indifference, stupidity, and even an occasional good intention, the English rulers were in the process of wiping out half the population of this island and inspiring in the remainder a hatred so bitter and malignant that it has become proverbial. Yet Ireland's darkest hour came just before her dawn. The start of the movement which was to culminate in Irish independence can be traced back to the founding of the Land League in 1879. The creation of Michael Davitt and Charles Stewart Parnell, the Land League was an organization for linking the parliamentary with the popular struggle; its immediate aim was to better the lot of the Irish peasant, its ultimate aim to secure Home Rule, that is, independence from England. With the help of money from the Irish established and newly prosperous in America, both programs were soon in full swing.

The struggles on the land involved such time-honored tactics as gang violence, mob riots, and rent strikes, seasoned with a certain amount of informal arson and unofficial sabotage; but a tactic first exercised on, and then named after, Captain Boycott, Lord Erne's agent in County Mayo, did much to increase the effectiveness of the popular protest. The boycott simply wiped an offending agent of English rule from existence on this earth. No one would buy from such a man, sell to him, speak to him, perform a service for him or accept one from him; he was declared a pariah by the whole community. The moral force of this wordless, faceless conspiracy of contempt was particularly terrifying in the small, closely-knit towns of the Irish countryside. After a few weeks of this silent, non-treatment, a man might be expected to take a curse or a kick as a gesture of kindness.

Meanwhile, in the English House of Commons, Parnell had taken over leadership of the Irish delegation after the death of Isaac Butt (1879). A consummate parliamentarian and tactician, Parnell resolved to make the role of the Irish delegation in the English House one of deliberate, systematic obstruction. Carefully maneuvering his forces, and resorting to every trick of exasperation and delay, Parnell baited and tantalized the Commons with endless, irrelevant discussions and inopportune questions, until he and his disciplined little band of Irishmen had brought the flow of legislation to a standstill. A colleague remembered seeing him one day when he had deliberately provoked the House to fury. He stood erect and arrogant, his hands clenched by his sides, smiling contemptuously while the full House roared and rained abuse on him. Only when he sat down was it noticed that his nails had bitten so deeply into his palms that his fingers were dripping blood.

The full story of Parnell's tempestuous agitation is too long and complex to be told here. From the beginning, it was a narrow, dangerous path he trod, for if he could be proved to have incited lawlessness, his parliamentary career was over, while if he conformed with the spirit as well as the letter of the law, he would be no more effective than old Isaac Butt. But he held with amazing skill and tenacity to his chosen course, in spite of jail sentences, libel suits, forged documents, and acts of senseless violence by fanatics of his own party. Though not himself a man of violence, Parnell moved all his life in an aura of violence—a violence which his own inflexible will, cold intellect, and mysterious gift for loyalty somehow attracted to him. He fell from his position of power and leadership in the Home Rule movement in 1890, as a result of being named corespondent in a suit for divorce. Upon that pretext, the English Nonconformists and the Catholic bishops of Ireland turned abruptly against him; his former friends and supporters hounded and vilified him throughout Ireland; and within a year of the fateful meeting in Committee Room Fifteen at which he was deposed, Parnell was dead and the Home Rule movement was in ruins.

James Joyce, who was born just three years after Parnell took over from Butt, thought of himself as a literary Parnell, tough, sharp and destructive, taking over from a generation of well-meaning old duffers. He grew up in a house passionately divided by the memory of Parnell, and the image of this magnetic, inflexible man is celebrated somewhere in each of his books. His very first literary effort was a poetic denunciation of Parnell's vitriolic ex-lieutenant, a declamation titled "Et Tu, Healy" (unhappily, no copies survive). It behooves us, therefore, to linger a mo-

ment by the memory of Parnell, to summarize what
his character and example meant to James Joyce. In
the first place, one may cite the strictness of his style.
Parnell was not a florid rhetorician after the traditional
Irish fashion—a man who moved his audience to
tears, but accumulated no votes. Parnell was no
silver-tongued pathos-broker; he was not even a great
persuader. His extraordinary gift was self-possession.
Having bankrupted himself in the struggle for Irish
independence, he was invited to a mass meeting in
Dublin, at which a sum, raised by popular subscrip-
tion and amounting to nearly £40,000, was presented
to him. He put the check in his pocket and spoke
extempore for three quarters of an hour without deigning to allude to it. On another occasion, returning to
Ireland from some parliamentary triumph in London,
he was met at the dock by a brass band, a cheering
crowd, and an enthusiastic navvy, an illiterate stone-
cracker, cheering and throwing his cap into the air
in an ecstasy of enthusiasm. Parnell stepped up to the
man and addressed a single sentence to him, saying,
"Ireland shall be free, my man, and you still break
stones." No other politician of our era would have
been capable of that moment of bitter truth; Yeats
made a poem of it. Finally, Parnell appealed to Joyce
because his career ended in disaster as a result of devotion to a woman. Parnell's great antagonist-col-
laborator Gladstone was for Joyce the archetype of
the prudent, successful hypocrite, who pretends to
work with the hero only in order to stab him op-
portunely and dramatically in the back. Parnell himself embodied the perennial Irish hero, first idolized,
then ruthlessly betrayed; Tim Healy was the pre-
ordained Firbolg to Charles Stewart Parnell's noble
Milesian.

After the drama of Parnell has been played out,
the movement for Irish independence ceases to be of
immediate interest to a student of Joyce, who is in

fact the poet of that quarter-century of disillusion-
ment between Parnell and the martyrs of 1916. His
patriotism, though real enough in certain veins, was
largely nostalgic, and no Irish politician ever replaced
in his affections the figure of Parnell. But for a man
as literary as Joyce, any political movement is interesting chiefly in a literary way, and, in fact, the Irish
national movement had immediate and deep-seated
literary implications, which made themselves felt in
questions of language.

As a result of centuries of English domination, the
use of Gaelic had been gradually relegated during the
nineteenth century to the outlying regions and backward districts of the island. Among the last people
for whom Gaelic was a native speech were the cotters
and fishermen of the Aran Islands, where Synge went
to pick up the idiom of his native land; much of the
peculiar flavoring of his dialogue is said to derive
from its being a literal translation from the Gaelic.
But though Gaelic practically vanished as a living
language, it retained symbolic status; words, phrases,
and constructions survived to influence the dominant
English. And in the late nineteenth century, as an
adjunct to the movement for political liberation, a
program sprang up for the revival of Gaelic. Like
all programs of language reform under political auspices, this one had something doctrinaire and artificial
about it. Joyce mocks its falsity in the opening section
of *Ulysses,* where Haines the Englishman uses Gaelic
to address the old milkwoman, who is symbolically
Ireland herself, Kathleen Mavourneen—all he elicits
from her is a puzzled stare, and the question, "Is it
French you are talking, sir?" Nonetheless, Gaelic
classes were started, using O'Growney's grammar;
patriots insisted on being addressed by their Gaelic
names; and some few works of literature were even
attempted in the ancient tongue. (To this day the
Eire radio broadcasts a brief daily program in Gaelic;

how many people understand it and how many people care what is said, as long as it is said in Gaelic, are other questions.)

Gaelic speech, then, was an adventitious survival, though a threatening one for a prose stylist like Joyce, who had a basic devotion to Newman, Pater, and Oscar Wilde. More interesting and influential was the late nineteenth-century revival of interest in Gaelic mythology and folklore. This revival took place partly as a reaction against the triumph of the industrial revolution. Seeing the ancient folk-culture of England submerged in black smoke and urban squalor, the literary men of Ireland resolved to record and preserve what was left of their ancient heritage. Partly too, they sensed that in the surviving fragments of heroic legend and popular verse, inspiration might be found for renewed struggle against the Saxon usurper. Men like John O'Leary, Standish O'Grady, Douglas Hyde, Patrick Weston Joyce (no relation), and William Butler Yeats took leading roles in the investigation and popularization of the old Irish culture. They translated, they edited, they compiled, they explained, they retold. They strolled into remote villages and inveigled old men into telling them legendary stories or singing half-forgotten ballads in cracked voices. Foreign scholars, such as Kuno Meyer of Berlin and Henri d'Arbois de Jubainville of Paris, lent international cachet and immense erudition to the study. Thus it was no accident that when Patrick Pearse went to his fatal destiny in the Dublin Post Office, on Easter Day, 1916, Cuchulain—the violent god-like boy of ancient Irish myth—was there to watch over him. The movement to revive the national identity in politics went hand-in-hand with a revival of national myths and legends and popular arts. Joyce viewed both developments with fitful interest, but more often with a wary and interested scepticism. Quite properly, he asked of both movements what they could contribute to his art, and at what cost; and he was not quick to strike a fool's bargain.

Indifferent as he was to the Gaelic speech, and dubious of the Gaelic mythology, Joyce could find in the Anglo-Irish writers of the nineteenth century relatively little which might be of value to his developing art. The sort of Irish novel written by Samuel Lover (*Handy Andy*, 1842) used the Irish peasant as a figure of coarse and superficial fun; offensive politically, it had little or no artistic quality, and may be dismissed as one more contribution to the image of that "faith-and-bejabers" comic Irishman who has long bedeviled the race. Charles Lever was a more considerable figure. His long, complexly-plotted novels of life among the hard-riding, hard-drinking gentry (*The Martins of Cro-Martin*, 1856) qualified him for the title of the Irish Dickens. He was an author of great wit, flair, and energy, though of rather less penetration. Lady Morgan (Sydney Owenson), John and Michael Banim, and Gerald Griffin were other novelists of modest merit who described the Irish scene and whose work Joyce knew well. But as they wrote mostly in the degenerate lingua franca of popular nineteenth-century novelists—with theatrical dialogue, long passages of flat, descriptive prose, elaborate plots, and frequent authorial interventions, their work was not a very positive inspiration. Potentially a more various and authentic novelist than any of these, William Carleton also remained a prisoner of his style, while Charles Maturin (*Melmoth the Wanderer*, 1820) and Sheridan Le Fanu (*The House by the Churchyard*, 1863), writers of terror stories, were far removed from Joyce's orbit. Not until we reach a close contemporary of Joyce, George Moore, do we find a writer whose work may have positively inspired in a direct way some of Joyce's. *The Untilled Field* (1903) perhaps owed something to the naturalist school in France, but it owed much more to an acute, unsentimental eye, and a sharp ear for authentic idiom. *Dubliners* can be fairly described as an urban counterpart of Moore's rural studies in *The Untilled Field*.

Among the poets, the record of Ireland's nineteenth century, though bleak, was not quite so bleak as in fiction. Tom Moore, Byron's friend, produced in *Irish Melodies* (1808) one of those books which, without any ugly question of their literary merit ever arising, are predestined to become national classics. The combination of graceful phrasing, smooth melancholy, and easy sentiment made the *Melodies* immediately popular; and popular (in a public-recitation, barbershop-quartet context) they have remained ever since. An obvious tag for any occasion is always to be found in the *Melodies*; it is no wonder that Joyce, with his phonographic memory and talent for punning, made constant use of them for parody and burlesque. Their titles are all, without exception, to be found in *Finnegans Wake*.

The poets of the Young Ireland School—Denis Florence McCarthy, Thomas Osborne Davis, *et al.*—tended to produce a high-flown, political rhetoric dressed in jog-trot meter, which was James Joyce's pet aversion; but in the figure of James Clarence Mangan (1803–1849), he found a kind of Irish Poe whose work and character he consistently idealized. Mangan was a literary artist, not a political journalist; his lyric gift was pure, his critical standards lofty, and his sense of disdainful mockery in frequent evidence. Furthermore, his personal life was wretched in the extreme—he died in a slum, a victim of poverty, narcotics-addiction, and alcoholism; half a century later, the young James Joyce devoted to his memory a bejeweled and intricate essay of appreciation. After Mangan, of course, the next great Irish poet whom young Joyce had constantly before his eyes as a model of literary greatness was Yeats. Toward Yeats Joyce felt a characteristic compound of jealousy, derision, and profound admiration. Their paths were neither the same nor compatible, yet each recognized in considerable measure the talents of the other, and Joyce profited from the study of Yeats' poetic practice, from the range of his unsystematic erudition, and from an awareness of his deportment as an artist in the grand style.

In this abbreviated account of the imaginative worlds of James Joyce, it may not be amiss to add a few words about the Roman Catholic Church and the schools which it operated, as well as about the Dublin stage and the formless, inchoate cosmos of what may be called popular culture. The omnipresence of the Church, or rather the churches, in the everyday life of Dublin is one of those elementary facts that the American reader of Joyce needs to keep steadily before him. The famous church buildings of Dublin are St. Patrick's Cathedral, where Swift lies buried; Christ Church Cathedral, containing the ancient tomb of Strongbow; and St. Michan's, where the bodies of Robert Emmett and Charles Stewart Parnell once lay. But the visitor, as he passes through these noble monuments of antiquity, is struck with the paucity of worshippers. These oldest and most famous churches in Dublin are Church of Ireland, that is, Protestant. The churches which most of the population attend are less striking architecturally, but more numerous. They are the Catholic churches and chapels, many of them built for inconspicuousness in the days when the Roman Church enjoyed only precarious toleration. This division between Catholic and Protestant, once the occasion of murderous affrays, has subsided in ferocity, but it is still present just below the surface of Dublin life. A Catholic boy, though there is no legal reason why he cannot do so, will probably not attend Trinity College—he will go to the National University. A Protestant who dies will have arranged to be buried in Mount Jerome on the south side of town, a Catholic in Glasnevin on the north. A Protestant when he buys a daily newspaper is likely to get the *Irish Times,* a Catholic will get the *Irish Independent.* In these and a dozen other ways, the division of Protestant and Catholic remains open and conscious; and for Joyce, growing up in the Roman Catholic Church, the values and customs of that Church were powerful forces controlling his behavior in every act of his life.

From the time he entered Clongowes Wood, a scared little boy of six, until he graduated from University College at twenty-two, Joyce's intellectual development was in the hands of priests, mostly Jesuits. These were not sly equivocators or subtle diplomats (as the reputation of Jesuits runs) but energetic and disciplined men, dedicated teachers and strict disciplinarians, whose culture at its worst was narrow, at its best erudite and humane. He learned from them habits of clarity, discipline, and intellectual rigor, which lasted all his life. And in the larger sense, the Church (even after he declined its discipline and refused its support) supplied the only intellectual structuring of experience for which he could feel instinctive respect. Whatever faiths he later sought and found were precisely substitute faiths, almost parodies of that from which he had resigned. Even the details of common experience within Joyce's world are impregnated with Roman Catholicism. A barboy is naturally a "curate," napkins in a hotel dining room are folded into "mitres," and among the laundry flapping on a line one may notice a couple of "crucified" shirts.

The Irish parish priest was an especially impressive figure in turn-of-the-century Ireland. Presiding over the regular ritual of the Mass and the intermittent rituals of birth, marriage, and death, his figure carried not only the assurance of a two-thousand-year tradition, but also the immense prestige accumulated by

generations of popular leaders in the national struggle.
The power of the priest was not merely spiritual: Father Murphy had led the pikemen of Wexford to battle
in '98; Father Mathew had redeemed thousands from
their slavery to drink; and the parish priest represented many an Irish family's only source of legal
counsel, economic help, and spiritual guidance. The
priest might easily degenerate in this all-inclusive role
into an easy advocate of spiritual Franklinism (like
Father Purdon in "Grace"), and the hierarchy was
never exempt from the sort of invective leveled
against it by Simon Dedalus at the Christmas dinner
described in the first section of the *Portrait*; but the
Church of Rome always maintained its powerful hold
on the Irish mind. By contrast with the nation's equiv-
ocal political rulers, its religious leaders were generally
figures of supreme confidence and authority. The
Irish clergy were men of great power, and their
power (as usually happens) was admired, envied,
and feared. For evil as well as for good, the shadow
of their authority fell long on the soul of James Joyce.

Turning now from the monolithic Irish Church,
with its wide streak of Puritan moral authority, the
first thing that strikes us in young Joyce's world of
popular culture and entertainment is its extraordinary
variety. At the theaters, opera houses, music halls,
and concert rooms of Dublin, Joyce had access to that
amazing mixture of art and trash which has been
characteristic of the stage in our time. He attended
plays by Shakespeare and plays by Sardou, melodramatic potboilers by Dion Boucicault, and nameless pantomimes and vaudevilles. "Conn the Shaugh-
raun" rubbed shoulders with "Othello," a talking dog
jostled the divine Sarah Bernhardt; and if, momentarily, the supply of professional entertainment failed,
there were amateur performances, to which Joyce lent
an enthusiastic hand—college representations of
Anstey's "Vice Versa," or the humbler exercise of

family charades. Dublin being a busy musical town, he also attended operas by Verdi and Wagner, Puccini, Rossini, Meyerbeer, Flotow, and Balfe. Traveling operatic companies, such as those directed by Carl Rosa or Charles Manners, frequently visited Dublin; and special concert tours were made by leading artists from London and the Continent. Like the Dublin theater, the Dublin concert stage was unabashedly eclectic: one might hear, on the same single program, a few Mozart arias, some sentimental Irish ballads, and a comic recitation. Meanwhile the rural ditties were not mute; barroom renditions of "The Croppy Boy" or "The Last Rose of Summer," such as *Ulysses* describes in the bar of the Ormond Hotel, were everyday occurrences. Beggars and wandering minstrels sang patriotic or pathetic ballads in the streets, and schoolboys declaimed (with gestures) such elderly, high-minded chestnuts as "Who Fears to Speak of '98?" or "The Wearing of the Green."

We are all more or less aware of a world of tags and clichés and hackneyed literary or sub-literary materials—a kind of subliminal verbal trash, which floats around or through our minds without ever attracting our full attention. It is only because Joyce wove much of this material into the texture of his books, and made great literature of it, that it seems necessary to insist on this dimension of his experience. He read, for instance, the early comic strips, following the adventures of a fellow with a funny nose named Ally Sloper; he read sketches of Dublin slum life, published pseudonymously by one "Heblon" under the title of *Studies in Blue;* he went devotedly to the Christmas pantomime shows, where the stories of Sinbad the Sailor and Dick Whittington were enacted, with many rococo variations. In the intervals of reading Ibsen, Rabelais, and Gerhart Hauptmann, he memorized the routines of song-and-dance teams and knockabout comedians. From his father, who was one of the great raconteurs and barroom conversationalists of a city fertile in the breed, he picked up a mass of comic stories and picturesque locutions which figure freely in his books. He read a seedy little London publication called *Tit-Bits* which printed brief paragraphs of useless information and short short stories. He went to magic-lantern shows and Albert Hengler's traveling circus. He read the *Police Gazette*, a notorious early scandal sheet. He sang vulgar comic songs like "Phil the Fluter's Ball" and "Finnegan's Wake." He recited that masterpiece of eighteenth-century thieves' argot, "The Night Before Larry Was Stretched." He picked up fragments from famous Irish orations and learned the legends of his native city— the tragic story of Silken Thomas Fitzgerald, the fable of Giant Finn, who lies buried with his head under the Hill of Howth and his toes sticking up under the hills and mounds of Phoenix Park. He read the eight leisurely Dublin newspapers, with their gossip and editorial columns, their revivals of the Irish past, their occasional literary supplements. And he studied carefully a peculiar Dublin institution, Alexander Thom's annual street directory of all the tradesmen, clergymen, gentry, shopkeepers, and miscellaneous citizens of the city. When he lived in Dublin, he was a constant walker of the streets, an acute and detailed observer of city trivia. In his absence, he was supplied by his devoted Aunt Josephine and other informants with such Dublin treasures as old playbills, used tram tickets, concert notices, and newspaper clippings. His appetite for specific detail, in literature as in life, was insatiable.

He read Dante and George Meredith, Blake, St. Thomas Aquinas, Flaubert, and Defoe, but he also had a special fondness for poetry of outstanding badness, in whose absurdities he delighted. Not much discussed hitherto, but very important in the formation of his imagination, were late nineteenth-century novelists like Gabriele D'Annunzio and J. P. Jacobsen, naturalists like Émile Zola and George Moore, dramatists of expressionist or symbolist persuasion, like Maurice Maeterlinck and Gerhart Hauptmann, a critic like Georg Brandes, an historical sociologist like Guglielmo Ferrero, and a pre-Fascist philosopher like Alfredo Oriani. He read Maupassant and Fogazzaro, Quinet and Gissing, Mérimée and Scribe. He was widely read in the English classics, but also in the popular female lending-library novelists of the late nineteenth century—"Marie Corelli," Mary Cecil Hay, Mrs. Henry Wood, Mary Elizabeth Braddon, and Rhoda Broughton. The worse they were, the better he liked them. His appallingly accurate and detailed memory made this verbal garbage as much a part of his novelist's equipment as the work of more respectable authors. As a knowing and provident writer, should, he read with an eye to his own literary advantage, storing away in his memory or notebooks phrases and words which seemed likely to prove useful later on. Clearly this list of his readings and investigations could be extended almost indefinitely; but even in its present schematic and sketchy form, it makes the point that Joyce was an uninhibited and imaginative reader.

JOYCE'S LIFE

James Joyce was born in Dublin, February 2, 1882; he was the oldest surviving child of a family which ultimately numbered ten children—six girls and four boys. His mother was the former Mary Jane Murray, a devout and patient woman with talents for vocal music and self-sacrifice. His father demands a fuller accounting. John Stanislaus Joyce came from a family in Cork which had good connections and the rudiments of a position in the world. At one time John Stanislaus had studied medicine, but found the grind of schooling too much for him; he had borne some hand in politics, but made no permanent position for himself; he had had (some said) the finest tenor voice in Ireland, but contented himself with amateur performances; he had had an investment in a brewery, but lost it through the defalcation of an unscrupulous partner; he had had an income from properties around Cork, but lost it through drink, mortgages, and improvidence; he held for a while a post in the office of the Collector General of Rates, but lost it when the municipal government was reorganized. At last he became frankly shiftless, and aspired only to odd jobs—peddler of ads for the *Freeman's Journal*, canvasser in minor political elections, collector of bad and doubtful debts—his main occupations being drink, recrimination, sponging, and sentimental talk. He was a foul-mouthed, maudlin, talented, impractical, fierce, comic old reprobate; and James Joyce, who by leaving the country escaped the most depressing scenes of his father's long decline, always recalled him with affection and sympathy. But he never lived in the same house with him a minute longer than he had to.

When James Augustine Joyce was born, the family was living at the respectable, even distinguished, address of 41 Brighton Square, Rathmines—this being a fashionable Dublin suburb to the south of the city. Over the next few years, the family moved repeatedly, but always down the social scale. First they went to Bray, farther out in the southern suburbs, then to Blackrock, then near Mountjoy Square, then to the much less respectable district of Drumcondra in the north of the city, then to North Richmond Street in the center of town, which was not far short of a slum,

then briefly to several addresses in Fairview and Clontarf, and finally to a precarious refuge on the heights
of Cabra, not far from Glasnevin cemetery, on the
northern outskirts of the city. On each of these moves,
generally occasioned by non-payment of rent, the
Joyces were accompanied by the family portraits and
the family coat of arms—emblems of more fortunate
days to which John Stanislaus clung when the substance of his dignity had long since evaporated.
Within a decade, the family moved from comfort to
squalor, without, however, abandoning its meager
pretensions to a sort of connection with aristocracy.

At the age of six, when his family was still comfort-
ably settled at Bray, James Joyce was sent to Clongowes Wood College. It is a school run by Jesuit
priests in the County Kildare, not far from Clane—a
school charging a substantial tuition at the time Joyce
attended, having high intellectual standards and considered, by itself and its rivals, to be a cut or two
above the ordinary day school both socially and cul-
turally. Young James Joyce found it convenient to
invent some uncles with distinguished posts in the
army and the judiciary in order to ward off his snob-
bish fellows.

He was the youngest boy in the school and, though
agile and quick of foot, not an athlete; he was often
homesick and sometimes actually ill in the infirmary.
But he was a good student and popular with his fellows, and triumph of a sort came to him, as it does
to Stephen Dedalus in the *Portrait,* when he was pun-
ished for not doing his lessons though he had a valid
excuse (he had broken his glasses). He appealed to
the rector, Father John Conmee, receiving the kind
but qualified sympathy which is described in the *Portrait;* but his fellow-students hailed him as a successful rebel. He had, indeed, acted precisely according
to his nature. When he felt himself wronged, he was
always to be a fiercely litigious man, and his principle

of protest was always to go straight to the highest possible authority.

But Joyce did not stay at Clongowes after his third year; his father's swift career down the hill of fortune left no money for luxuries like tuition. James spent two years, from nine to eleven, at the school kept by the Christian Brothers in North Richmond Street, and bitterly he resented it. Socially and intellectually, the new school represented a lamentable decline from Clongowes, and Joyce never mentioned his attendance there. He escaped quite by accident. Walking near Mountjoy Square, his father one day met Father Conmee, now prefect of studies at Belvedere College, and Father Conmee offered to arrange for James to attend Belvedere without fees. For the next five years he did so. As he was now older and more formed of character, Belvedere left on his mind stronger and more distinctive marks than Clongowes. Here he practiced his English compositions under the eye of a vigilant and demanding instructor; he studied French, Latin, and Italian; and over the years he earned a series of "exhibitions," national prizes for scholarship, which amounted in all to a very tidy sum. The family was fiercely competitive, and very proud of his intellectual triumphs; he was under great pressure to "do well," and quickly formed the habit of using his brother Stanislaus as a "whetstone" to sharpen his ideas and his rhetoric. This was hard on Stanislaus, but good for James. In later life, several other persons filled the same role.

About the age of fourteen, James Joyce had his first precocious sexual experience with a prostitute. Further experiments with debauchery were interrupted by a school retreat, in the course of which a vigorous session of hell-fire preaching roused him to a deep sense of fear, shame, remorse, and repentance. For a while thereafter, he seems to have been a model boy and was indeed elected prefect of the college sodality of the Blessed Virgin Mary. But before long the mood of sanctity and the pursuit of spiritual exercises failed. Whether or not he actually declined an invitation to study for the priesthood, he certainly turned away from all the paths leading in that direction, in favor of lonelier and more perilous ramblings. He had long since established with his family and teachers his full right to read anything he pleased and this came to include all sorts of books hostile to or subversive of the established moral code of Dublin. Dublin had not in fact had much experience with rebellious young men who read books. Rebellious young men *tout court* the town knew well and had successfully managed according to an ancient formula. Allowed to sow a good many wild oats when young, rebellious young men could be pretty well counted on to marry when a bit older, to settle down and return—perhaps a bit restively—to the fold. But Joyce was indulging in a more far-reaching revolt; it included plenty of wine, women, and song, but some other ingredients as well. From his extensive, heterodox readings, he was acquiring the assured judgments of an artist, and he had suffered that obscure, inward hurt known as "losing the faith." This loss is not easy or obvious to define. A man may riot in drink and debauchery without losing the faith, he may be violently opposed to some priests or to all, he may fail to attend Mass; his position is perilous, but he has not necessarily lost his saving faith. That comes from denying in set terms the efficacy of the sacraments and, by consequence, the divinity of Christ. That step or one very close to it the young Joyce took. Like Lucifer, he said, *"Non serviam,"* I will not serve; and in something like a diabolic frame of mind, departed Belvedere for the Catholic University of Ireland.

The University which Joyce entered in 1898 had been founded less than half a century before, with John Henry Newman as its first rector. Gerard Manley

Hopkins had been one of its teachers, but at the time he was an obscure and unpublished Jesuit, and the College was a meager, undistinguished little place which occupied two Georgian houses on the south side of Stephen's Green. A half-mile or so down Grafton Street was Trinity College, with its splendid library and its famous professors—Dowden, Mahaffy, Salmon, Tyrrell—each with a reputation fit to crush the entire University College. But Joyce did not enter the University with the intention of learning much in its classrooms or contributing anything to them. He had read far more widely than his fellows, he was clever and could pass his courses without much difficulty, so he had no real need to work. His professors of French and Italian were amusing and congenial, but the rest of the staff were bores, so he neglected their lectures and snubbed their opinions. Most of his education at University College was acquired on his own, at the reading room of the National Library on Kildare Street or in conversation with his fellow students. Among his close friends were Francis Skeffington (represented as McCann in the *Portrait*), George Clancy (represented as Davin), Vincent Cosgrave (represented as Lynch), John Francis Byrne (represented as Cranly), and Tom Kettle (not represented at all).

This was an interesting and lively group of young men to grow up with. Though each died before the age of forty, Skeffington, Clancy, and Kettle all managed to make their political influence felt—Skeffington as a radical socialist, Clancy as a somewhat naïve and idealistic nationalist, and Kettle as a man of letters as well as a statesman. But it was no accident that the two men of the group who achieved least on their own were most useful to Joyce. Cosgrave and Byrne took over, in effect, the old role of Stanislaus: they became Joyce's "whetstones." Byrne was taciturn and secretive, Cosgrave sardonic and cynical. Neither was

a person of what Dublin considered "background";
taken as a group, in fact, Joyce, Byrne, and Cosgrave
exemplified nicely the sort of thing J. P. Mahaffy had
in mind when he said it was a disaster to found a
college for boys whose traditional occupation was to
hang around street corners and spit into the Liffey.
But Joyce's genius knew how to turn his friends' and
his own limitations to account. With Cosgrave he
sharpened a certain instinctive outsiders' gutter-wit;
to Byrne, who had an inscrutable manner and a gift
for keeping secrets, he confessed. Confession was particularly good for this arrogant, self-conscious, and
guilt-ridden soul. All his life he was to choose his
confessors with particular care and Byrne in his own
way was a remarkable discovery in this line.

In the fall of his second year at University College
(1899) Joyce delivered before the Literary and Historical Society a paper on "Drama and Life." It was
considered a daring and heterodox paper for it up-
held the writer's obligation to deal with modern life
in modern terms, and it cited no less a heretic than
Henrik Ibsen as a model. Though few people in Dublin had read more than one or two of Ibsen's plays,
they knew him as an "advanced" thinker. Joyce's
paper was almost censored by the president of the
Society and the president of the University, and when
delivered, it met with lively attacks from the students.
Joyce defended himself ably—though it may be
doubted if he convinced anybody—and in the first
months of the new century, he followed up his advantage by publishing a review-essay on Ibsen's last
drama (*When We Dead Awaken*) in the *Fortnightly
Review*. It is unusual at any time for a college sopho-
more to publish in a major magazine; it is particularly
unusual for a student in a third-rate provincial university to publish in a metropolitan review. Few or
none of Joyce's teachers had, or could have, pub-

lished in the *Fortnightly Review*. Ibsen himself, then in his seventies, read the article in remote Christiania and asked his English translator, William Archer, to convey his gratitude to the young author. Joyce, barely turned eighteen, felt as if he had received, at the very opening of his career, an apostolic benediction.

The next year he wrote for the college literary magazine an attack on the Irish Literary Theater, which he denounced for putting on plays which were too Irish, that is (in Joyce's terms), too provincial in theme. As against the intransigent Gaelic enthusiasts who held that Ireland, to become independent of England, must live on her native traditions, he was always to uphold the view that Ireland must become more European. But this essay was altogether too bold in its rejection of the patriotic orthodoxies; the editor of the college magazine and its faculty adviser concurred in rejecting Joyce's essay, as well as another on women's rights by his friend Skeffington. Denied official outlet for their thoughts, the two young men had their essays printed privately, and distributed copies on their own. Joyce's contribution was called "The Day of the Rabblement"; it expressed lofty disdain for the cheap popularity to be won by Irish patriotic drama and sentimental peasant themes. Joyce's own effort at a play, unpublished and unperformed, was called "A Brilliant Career"; it was thoroughly Ibsenite in feeling and construction, but too ambitious by far for his limited skills, and he soon abandoned it. Then in his final year at University College he delivered before the Literary and Historical Society that elaborate and ornate prose poem on James Clarence Mangan, which has already been noted. It praised an Irish poet who was safely dead; therefore its condoning of his immorality and its quoting from Ibsen in the Norwegian could be overlooked. "James Clarence Mangan" was roundly heralded as the best paper ever delivered before the Society, and was reprinted without censor-trouble in the college magazine.

Joyce's progress through University College is measured not at all by his success in passing courses, nor even by his performances for the student societies and publications. Judging in its own terms, the college may well have considered his attendance there a complete waste of everyone's time. But Joyce's own remote and lofty program was making good headway. During his years at University College he was quietly and determinedly preparing an artificial personality which he would use as a major element of his creative strategy. The mask of Stephen Dedalus, distinguished esthetician and recorder of vagrant lyric inspirations, fitted only loosely over the features of Jim Joyce. But the mask gave him esthetic distance and a sort of hauteur which was to prove precious. While arguing with his schoolmates on the steps of the National Library, assisting at a jollification in a pub, or wandering through the squalid purlieus of Mecklenburg Street, in Dublin's Nighttown, he stood above and outside experience, preparing it for the use of his art. When in his cups, he was known to stare contemptuously at his companions and threaten to write them all down in a book, with their sins upon them, as Dante had done to *his* contemporaries. One would not think these threats likely to enhance his popularity as a drinking companion, but his social life did not suffer noticeably.

One of his instructors at University College, irked by the young man's open disdain, had suggested that he might try upon graduation for a clerkship in Guinness' brewery as a way of getting back to earth. In fact he graduated (in 1902) not to any practical employment at all, but to a period of vague literary adventures and vaguer efforts at a career in medicine. He made the acquaintance of George Russell, theos-

ophist, painter, agricultural journalist, and poet (under
the pseudonym of Æ); he was introduced to Yeats
and Padraic Colum and Lady Gregory, all of whom
found him remarkable enough, but who could do little
in a practical way to forward his career. He enrolled
in the St. Cecilia Medical School, but pursued his
work at so desultory a pace that within a month it
was already obvious he would never finish. Then,
abruptly, in December of 1902, he departed for Paris.
Behind this decision lay a whole series of disillusions
and aspirations. In Paris he hoped to be able to live by
giving English lessons to Frenchmen; he hoped to find
a medical education that was less exasperatingly humdrum than the one in Dublin; he hoped to do some
literary journalism; and he hoped, like Ibsen, to gain
a perspective on his homeland and his quarrel with
it. Only the last of these expectations was ever to be
fulfilled.

Whatever the pretexts under which it was begun,
the flight from Ireland answered a deep need in
Joyce's nature; it was a flying as well as a fleeing, and
became a condition of his creative life. After leaving
in early December, Joyce returned to Dublin for
Christmas, 1902, left again in mid-January, 1903, and
remained until April, when he returned home in answer to an urgent telegram, and left again, to all
intents permanently, in October, 1904. From the practical point of view, both of his tentative expeditions
to Paris were foolish to the point of ruination. Joyce
learned no medicine in Paris; he acquired one student,
whom he tutored in English; he wrote a few reviews
and poems, which he might just as well have written
in Dublin. He met a remarkable man, J. M. Synge,
but only to quarrel with him—though amiably
enough, for that matter—over literary questions. And
on his second sojourn particularly, Joyce very nearly
starved to death, subsisting for days at a time on
boiled macaroni and watery cocoa. But, practical or

not, exile from Ireland was his destiny; like Ibsen, he never lived spiritually anywhere but in his homeland, and never lived fully there except when physically somewhere else.

The cable which cut short his second journey to France announced the imminent death of his mother. He returned immediately to Dublin, and stood helplessly by while she died, slowly and in great pain, of cancer of the liver. The inevitable end came in August, 1903, but it did not seem to release him. Instead, he lingered in-and-around his father's house in Cabra, doing an occasional review, teaching briefly in a boys' school, loitering, arguing, studying voice, drinking, and drifting. His father's household, grim while Mary Jane Joyce was slowly dying, grew positively chaotic afterwards. The men of the house were drunk, surly, and idle; the hapless girls struggled to bring some order out of increasing disintegration. Books were pawned, the piano sold, shillings cadged from every conceivable source, the house was allowed to fall to pieces—and yet, on many occasions, there was nothing to eat. James and Stanislaus, convinced unbelievers, had refused to pray at the bedside of their dying mother; their father, with his special gift for obscene, vitriolic vituperation, lashed out at them, while they snarled back. The black cloud of guilt and helpless loathing which envelopes Stephen Dedalus at the opening of *Ulysses* evidently mirrors faithfully the mood of this period. Underneath its spell one can feel, in *Ulysses* as apparently in reality, the cruel reach and stretch of a mind preening and preparing itself.

Having quarreled with Byrne and wearied of Cosgrave, Joyce found himself a new friend, rejoicing in the euphonious name of Oliver St. John Gogarty. He was a gay and witty young man, prosperous, cynical, and aggressive, who had graduated from Trinity College, was studying at Oxford, and expected to go on to medical school. Gogarty had a (literally) fascinating flow of conversation; perfect strangers, coming within earshot, were mesmerized by the quicksilver fluency of his chatter. He was a poet, with a special talent for cheerful blasphemy and inventive obscenity, he was a rake and a Wildean esthete, and on the score of all these sympathies, he became Joyce's friend. And yet it was an uneasy relationship, involving a number of qualifications. Gogarty loaned Joyce money, which did not rankle, for in the code of the Joyces a loan, which one had no intention of repaying anyhow, was no more than a form of tribute. Gogarty also loaned Joyce items of second-hand clothing—and this transaction did rankle. Both young men talked freely of the future of the island, which Gogarty wanted to Hellenize and Joyce to Europeanize. Against the solemn disapproval of the clergy and the Dublin bourgeoisie they were, for the moment, allies. Joyce helped Gogarty try for the Newdigate poetry prize at Oxford; Gogarty cured Joyce of a minor venereal infection, picked up in Nighttown. They read, wrangled, joked, fornicated, and wrote poetry together. Each was the most remarkable young man the other had ever known. And if there was a streak of latent hatred in their uneasy friendship—Joyce despising Gogarty as a shallow snob, Gogarty fearing Joyce as a cruel, mistrustful man—this difference constituted only one more bond of unstable attraction. Neither wanted to quarrel until he was sure the moral advantage lay, or could be made to seem to lie, on his side.

During the winter of 1903–1904, therefore, Joyce was idle in his father's house, or on the streets, or in the pubs and brothels of Dublin. His friends were disreputable scoffers, young men of known immorality. He had no money, nor any prospect of getting any. He was, by turns, defiant, suspicious, resentful, and theatrical. Some of his friends felt that he was deliberately throwing his abilities away; many others said simply that he was insane. Then one day, for a new literary and philosophical magazine called *Dana,* he wrote a short, allusive, stylized sketch called "A Portrait of the Artist as a Young Man." * *Dana's* editor, John Eglinton, took the honorable, limited position that he would not print what he could not understand, and rejected the piece. Joyce set to work immediately to expand it into a novel. Working with remarkable speed and persistency, he managed ultimately to compose almost a thousand pages. The title was contributed by Stanislaus: *Stephen Hero.* (The book which has been published under that name represents the surviving third of the original MS.) Unfortunately, the book was not a finished literary work in either of its first forms. As a short sketch, it was complex and dramatically expressive, but obscure; as a novel, it was prosy and prolix. But Joyce was suddenly working, and the opening out of his literary career may have helped him to cut short a musical vocation which was just beginning to bud. With the encouragement of John McCormack, he had entered the national singing contest (*Feis Ceoil*), and on May 16 took part in the competition for solo tenor voices. The two set pieces he sang beautifully, and seemed assured of the gold medal; but he declined even to attempt the simple piece which was to be rendered at sight, and stalked from the stage. Possibly he could not have passed the test, for he was never a good sight reader; in any event, he would not sing a work for which he had not prepared, and took his stand on artistic principles. Thus he was given only the third-place medal, and rejoiced perversely in the apparent ruin of still another career.

Some time in early or mid-June, 1904, James Joyce —to everyone's astonishment—fell in love. The girl

* Reprinted in Robert E. Scholes and Richard M. Kain, *The Workshop of Daedalus* (Evanston, Ill.: Northwestern University Press, 1965), pp. 56–74.

was, from one point of view, a perfectly ordinary, even commonplace, young woman, from another, she was the most remarkable choice he could possibly have made. When Joyce first met her, Nora Barnacle was in service as a chambermaid in Finn's Hotel. Born in Galway, the daughter of a drunken and irresponsible baker, she had attended convent school there, had had two temporary admirers, Sonny Bodkin and Harry Mulvey by name, but had come up to Dublin in consequence of the strictness of her uncle. She was not altogether illiterate, but neither was she very far from it; her surviving letters display a bold devotion to spelling by ear and an innocence of punctuation reminiscent of Molly Bloom. But she was a girl of strong character, strong feelings, and supreme fidelity. Joyce soon came to feel (in words which echoed, doubtless unconsciously, Ibsen's words about his wife) that she had "made a man of him." Their association is one of the great love stories of our time. Many of Joyce's personal relations with people consisted of testing, in various ways, their fidelity to him; these tests, however unreasonable and demanding, Nora Barnacle never failed—yet somehow she managed to remain, in her own right, a person of great dignity and integrity. For James Joyce she was exactly right. A bluestocking would have provoked him in a minute (he ranked lady artists with female priests, as abominations in nature); an aristocratic lady would have been disgusted by him. But Nora Barnacle sauntered into his life and took him as a man, never deigning to realize that it was his art that made him special. More secure in her simplicity than he was behind his arrogant façade of learning, she sometimes referred to this most intricate and tortured intellect as "simpleminded Jim." He, in turn, identified her with Ireland itself, confessed to her, outraged her, adored her, and made after her image, in his two greatest books, his portrait of femininity itself. Old John Joyce, hearing

her name, said simply, "She'll stick to him"; and she
did, to the end of his life. At the time, however, people who recalled Joyce's aristocratic, artistic arrogance
were nonplused by his new interest; and Dublin
tongues, never discreet, were set to malicious commentary.

On June 16, 1904, James Joyce and Nora Barnacle
had their first date. It was to be, in Joyce's personal
history, a crucial day, and he devoted nothing less than
the full eight hundred pages of *Ulysses* to describing
it. But impressive as it was in retrospect, June 16 did
not seem to mark any special turning point in Joyce's
outer life: he was no more continent in his behavior,
no closer to finding a career for himself or a way of
supporting the ménage he was about to set up. He
sang in the Antient Concert Rooms, the night of
August 17, his name standing on the program above
that of J. C. Doyle and John McCormack himself. He
wrote three short stories, later included in *Dubliners*
("The Sisters," "Eveline," and "After the Race") and
got Æ to print them in *The Irish Homestead*; but at a
guinea apiece, this was scarcely a highroad to fortune.
Moreover, Joyce was so ashamed of appearing in "the
pigs' paper" that he published under the pseudonym
of "Stephen Daedalus," so there was not much fame
in it, either. For some time he had been living in a
series of furnished rooms—one or two he rented, the
others he borrowed from friends. In September he
was invited to join Gogarty and an Englishman named
Samuel Chenevix Trench, who were camping pic-
turesquely in the old Martello Tower at Sandymount,
on the coast, some miles south of Dublin. Built as a
gun-emplacement by Pitt in the days when a Napoleonic invasion was feared, the tower left a good deal
to be desired as a residence. Its walls were eight feet
thick and its door ten feet off the ground (access was
by a rope ladder). Within, it was dark, unheatable,
and lacking in even the most primitive amenities. One

could camp out there in summer, but only bohemian young men, more interested in picturesque economy than in comfort, would have tried to do so. Joyce moved in and stayed about ten days. One night Trench the Englishman had a dream about a black tiger and woke up shouting in terror. Gogarty reached for a twenty-two rifle he had handy, and half in jest, half in malice, fired a shot in the dark that brought a tin frying pan down from a shelf onto Joyce's head. Joyce, feeling himself mortally insulted—besides, he was afraid of firearms—withdrew, wordlessly, to the house of his Aunt Josephine and Uncle Willie. Writing to Nora from that address next morning, he said nothing of the nocturnal japes in the Martello Tower, only that he had been thinking of her a great deal and had hardly slept a wink the night before. Taken individually, both remarks were certainly correct.

Three weeks later, on October 6, 1904, having scraped together every last penny they could borrow, James Joyce and Nora Barnacle left Ireland by the midnight boat. Their destination was Zurich, where Joyce had, or thought he had, the assurance of a position in the Berlitz school, but they had just enough money to get to Paris via London. The remainder of the trip would have to be financed by a loan raised in Paris. As for the prospect of Berlitz teaching, widely known as the lowest form of academic peonage, it held no terrors for Joyce. Carrying his own stimulations within him, he welcomed the idea of a monotonous, unstimulating job. In the single valise which he shared with Nora reposed the already-immense manuscript of *Stephen Hero*, a collection of short lyrics, *Chamber Music*, and a growing group of dry, ironic little sketches, of which there were first to be ten but which wound up as fifteen under the title of *Dubliners*.

The resupply operation in Paris ran into some anxious moments, but Joyce managed to raise the wind, to the extent of trainfare to Zurich. Once there, however, he found that the position on which he had counted did not exist. His position was suddenly perilous in the extreme. Amid rage, recriminations, and despair, he finally managed to gain some assurance that there might be an opening for an English teacher at Trieste; and the bedraggled couple set off—only to be once more disappointed. The position at Trieste had evaporated, if it ever existed, before Joyce's arrival. But the friendly chief of the Trieste office, Almidano Artifoni, cast about in Joyce's behalf, and finally discovered that a job might be found at Pola, a naval port on the Adriatic in what is now Yugoslavia. Weary and penniless, James and Nora thus settled in Pola at last; for once, the position which had attracted them was not a delusion but involved live pupils and a meager but actual stipend of two pounds a week. They moved into a room, furnished it sparsely, and began housekeeping.

Though they went through a ceremony only 27 years later, chiefly for testamentary reasons, and were therefore technically "living in sin" at Pola, James Joyce and Nora Barnacle fell automatically and unhesitatingly into a pattern of domesticity which could not have been more bourgeois had twenty ceremonies been performed over them. Nora was somewhat surprised, and on the whole not pleased, to find that her husband made sentences all day; it did not seem as if there could be so much in sentences. Joyce scrutinized her anxiously but vainly for signs of the betrayal he always anticipated. They made friends, accumulated a few domestic comforts, renewed their wardrobes, had Joyce's crumbling teeth repaired, and exchanged language lessons with fellow teachers on the Berlitz staff. In March, 1905, Artifoni arranged an opening for Joyce on the staff of the Berlitz school in Trieste. The town was larger, more cosmopolitan than Pola, and less disturbed politically; the Joyces moved

there, and promptly settled in for a long stay. Shortly
after their arrival, it appeared that Nora was pregnant.

The sort of life the Joyces made for themselves in
Trieste reflected precisely their natures and interests.
Neither had much concern with the domestic niceties,
and Joyce had an active mania for getting into debt
which kept life from degenerating into humdrum. He
drank too much now, consistently and compulsively.
Trieste is a city of cafés, as Dublin is a city of pubs,
and the local wine substituted nicely for Guinness
stout. As he could afford only the poorer, workmen's
cafés, Joyce now began picking up a certain amount
of verbal socialism, to go with his fierce anticlerical-
ism. On the other hand, his comic, casual, blasphe-
mous style of teaching attracted to his Berlitz lessons
mostly Trieste intellectuals and Trieste aristocrats.
As a *déclassé* artist, he had a gift for mingling the top
of society with the bottom. For himself, though his
salary was paid regularly and amounted to more than
he had ever earned before, shiftlessness was his chosen
way of life and Nora, who had begun to pick up
enough Italian to help her husband along, followed
his lead. They ate out in restaurants, splurged on
luxuries, and neglected necessities so systematically
as never to be out of range of insolvency. On July 27,
1905, Nora gave birth to a son, named Giorgio in
memory of James' younger brother George who had
died three years before. A story ran about Dublin that
Joyce's cable to his brother Stanislaus announcing the
birth read "Son born; mother and bastard doing well";
but this was apocryphal. Joyce, who had had a rather
rum time being a son, was deeply moved by the experience of becoming a father. And anyhow, as Richard Ellmann remarks, he was in no position to pay
cable rates on five extra words merely for the sake
of a joke.

Meanwhile, Joyce's literary career seemed gradually to be looking up. After being worked over for

years, *Chamber Music* was making the rounds of publishing houses in England; *Stephen Hero* had accumulated to more than five hundred pages; and twelve of the stories which would later make up *Dubliners* were completed. That was enough for a volume, and Joyce sent it off to Stanislaus for criticism, which proved favorable indeed. At twenty-one, Stanislaus Joyce had a cool, tough literary judgment and an impersonal, outspoken bluntness which would later win him the nickname of "Cato." When he spoke of "masterpieces," it was not just the sentimental adulation of a younger brother. Warmed by Stanislaus' enthusiasm, Joyce proposed that he too come to Trieste and teach in the Berlitz school. James would thus have the benefit of his criticism; Stanislaus would escape from Dublin and the sordid clerkship which awaited him there; there would be economies. . . . Without much reluctance, Stanislaus allowed himself to be persuaded. Then the manuscript of *Dubliners* was duly packed off to the publisher Grant Richards, toward the end of 1905. Richards and his reader were impressed; they sent back a contract, which Joyce signed, and all was proceeding fairly when Joyce decided fatally to add "Two Gallants" to the collection. Richards merely glanced at the story and sent it on to the printer, who had already set up the others. But under English law the printer is equally responsible with the publisher, should they be found guilty of issuing "objectionable" material. Richards' printer felt that his security would be jeopardized by certain words and phrases in "Two Gallants." Alerted by these passages to the perils he was running, he now went back over the entire manuscript—this nameless, censorious, nerveless artisan—and wherever he looked for it, sure enough, he found immorality. The word "bloody" could not be allowed to appear; ladies could not be allowed to shift position; it was very suggestive indeed to have them brush against gentlemen, as they passed by. And these fantastic scruples multiplied endlessly. The more Grant Richards was drawn by his tyrannical printer to look at the manuscript he had accepted so blithely, the more hidden perils he discovered. Before long, Joyce found himself embroiled in an exasperating, interminable altercation over the entire nature and method of the stories in *Dubliners.*

Under these tense circumstances, a momentary crisis in the affairs of the Berlitz school in Trieste determined Joyce to seek employment elsewhere. With his wife and infant son, he moved to Rome and took a job as the English correspondent in a German bank. The experiment quickly proved a disastrous failure. Joyce loathed clerks and clerking, despised banks— and because this bank, by an unhappy accident, paid its employees by the month instead of the week, improvident Joyce was perpetually in debt. He begged and extorted loans from Stanislaus, still in Trieste; he tutored in English after his long hours in the bank; he scraped and hauled. But all this work and worry only made him more unhappy, and being unhappy he began to drink in excess, and there went all the results of his skrimping. Literary work was out of the question, under these circumstances. Back in England, *Chamber Music* (which Joyce no longer thought very good) was accepted by the publisher Elkin Matthews, while *Dubliners,* after many arguments, was finally rejected by Grant Richards, or rather by his printer. Joyce thought briefly of suing for breach of contract, but was dissuaded. Finally, after less than half a year, the Roman adventure came to a sordid climax one night, when Joyce was knocked down while drunk and robbed of an entire month's pay. Thereupon, the squalid little ménage turned away from the Eternal City and fled back to Trieste, despondent and penniless. Joyce had written next to nothing in Rome; he had lost his position in the Berlitz school at Trieste; Nora was pregnant again; and Stanislaus, weary of coming over and over again to the rescue of distressed genius, had turned openly truculent.

But Joyce always responded well to his own self-created crises. He wheedled and threatened his way back into the Berlitz school; he did some articles for a local newspaper on the state of affairs in Ireland; he delivered a series of public lectures on literary topics; and he wrote the last, longest, and greatest of the *Dubliners* stories, in which many of the major themes of his existence are richly interwoven. "The Dead" was by all odds the most sustained and complex piece of fiction he had yet produced. Its artistry augured well for a new story, the germ of which had occurred to him in Rome, but which so far had come to nothing. It was to be a story about a Jewish advertising man named Hunter, whom Joyce remembered from Dublin, its climax was to be his cuckolding, and its title was to be "Ulysses."

Joyce was seriously ill of rheumatic fever in the summer of 1907, and his daughter Lucia was born, in July of that year, into a debt-ridden and appallingly disorganized household. But self-assurance was one quality Joyce never lacked, and no sooner was he out of the municipal hospital than he resigned from the Berlitz school and set up on his own as a language instructor. As an independent teacher, his profit on each lesson was of course greater, but his lessons were fewer; this, however, left him more time for literary work. Thus, while the augmented *Dubliners* continued to circulate vainly from publisher to publisher, Joyce set about rewriting *Stephen Hero* into *A Portrait of the Artist as a Young Man*. His problem in essence was to compress, and by rendering the story less episodic to make it more taut thematically. A first step in this direction was to reduce the number of chapters from the originally-projected 63 to no more than five. Then the last remnants of plodding explanatory prose must be purged from the story, it must be cast in an idiom rich in imagery and rhythmically expressive—the idiom of a finished and conscious artist. This work of revision and rewriting occupied Joyce through 1907 and early 1908, while he recast his first three chapters. He had the advantage, in doing it, of a critic and fellow-craftsman whom he had discovered, altogether unexpectedly, among his own English-language pupils. Signor Ettore Schmitz, owner and successful director of a large marine paint factory, confessed one day that he had written and published pseudonymously a couple of unsuccessful novels. Joyce asked to see them, read them, and discovered, to his amazement, that "Italo Svevo" was a novelist of great talent, perhaps even genius. In later years he was to rescue Svevo from oblivion.

But the immediate effect of Joyce's work on the autobiographical novel was to increase his anxiety and curiosity about Dublin. Never at a loss for pretexts to do what he wanted instinctively to do, Joyce decided that Giorgio should make the acquaintance of his Irish relatives; that *Dubliners*, which had been submitted to the Dublin house of Maunsel & Company, might profit from the explanatory presence of its author; and that, in view of the recent reorganization of University College, he might get himself considered for a professorship in Romance Literature. But a major, unstated impulse drawing him back to Dublin was artistic. Before he could finish the portrait of the artist as a young man, he had to see how things had turned out—what had happened to Byrne and Cosgrave and the little society of friends which had been so close seven years before. He had also an old score to settle with Gogarty. For all these reasons James and Giorgio went to Dublin for August and a few days of September, 1909.

If one is out to round up old Dublin acquaintances, the only time to go is during the August Horse Show. James and Giorgio went to the house which old John

Joyce and his five daughters were renting on Fontenoy Street, where they were welcomed and made much of. Joyce's father had been so furious over the elopement as even to feel constrained about borrowing money, but now, in the glow of family feeling and the presence of an authentic grandson, his anger melted away. Joyce meanwhile trod the streets of Dublin warily, menaced alike by former foes and friends. Skeffington and George Russell admitted that he had changed, and not as noticeably for the worse as they had anticipated. Gogarty, now plump, married, and prosperous, with an automobile and established positions as surgeon and raconteur, was effusively hospitable; Joyce (at least in his own account of the meeting), ironically distant. But after circling one another with wary distrust, they agreed that Joyce would probably write something in which Gogarty would figure—of which Gogarty asked only that it be literature. The specification was quite unnecessary, but evinced a good deal of uneasiness; and on this uneasy note they parted.

The encounter with Byrne was more agreeable; time had worn off the edges of their original, trivial disagreements, and they spent a pleasant afternoon in Byrne's house at #7 Eccles Street. But then an encounter with Vincent Cosgrave opened the very pit of hell within Joyce's mind. For what Cosgrave told him, on the afternoon of August 6, was that during the summer of 1904, when Joyce had been wooing Nora Barnacle, she had secretly been "walking out" with Cosgrave himself. Here at last was the betrayal for which he had schooled himself to look, but to uncover it in so intimate an ally was a shattering experience. At once he sent off a bitter letter to Nora at Trieste, and followed it next morning with one still more anguished. For a day and two nights he tortured himself, and then at last turned for consolation to his old confessor Byrne. At #7 Eccles Street he poured

forth the whole story; and Byrne, in the hour of
crisis, showed himself not only a friend, but a shrewd
judge of character. He began by saying outright that
the story was a "blasted lie." And then he made the
whole episode comprehensible to Joyce by explaining
it as a conspiracy between Gogarty and Cosgrave with
the deliberate, malicious intention of breaking Joyce's
spirit. A less melodramatic story would have answered
worse the immediate purpose. Joyce lived in a world
of enemies and conspiracies; among other things, an
insidious tangle of plots and counterplots appealed to
his Celtic instinct for decoration. Before long, his
emotions were under control and, then, the letters
started to come in from Trieste. Nora seems to have
written quietly and with great dignity that she was a
simple and ignorant girl, to whom he had already
been too kind, and that he should now leave her. But
Stanislaus, to whom she had talked in her misery and
bewilderment, had concrete evidence that Cosgrave
was a malicious, pathological liar. He detailed it, explaining how Cosgrave had indeed once tried to cut
Joyce out with Nora, but had been sent packing; and
he added that Cosgrave had himself told this story,
under pledge of secrecy, in a pub, in 1904.

Joyce's letters to Trieste now changed to abject
apologies and pleas for forgiveness—which in due
course was forthcoming, and indeed led on both sides
to a rediscovery and passionate renewal of the love
which had been so deeply shaken. More than many
lovers, or at least more frankly than most, Joyce experienced in sexual passion the extremes of masochism
and sadism. Because Nora was a sacred figure to him,
he was driven to defile and degrade her; at the same
time he wanted to be before her as a child before, or
even within, its mother, helpless, cherished, forgiven,
and humiliated. Their reconciliation was therefore
vigorous. But the nightmare of jealous suspicion never
really faded from Joyce's mind, *Exiles* explores it at

length, and *Ulysses* includes several full-scale re-enactments of the drama of infidelity which he lived through in August of 1909.

On the outskirts of this drama of sentiment, Joyce's ostensible business in Ireland progressed to his general satisfaction. Giorgio met and was duly appreciated by relatives on both sides of the family. Maunsel & Company agreed to publish *Dubliners*, and Joyce signed his second contract for the book on August 19. The "professorship" at University College collapsed, under inspection, into a much smaller appointment, but Joyce still thought of it as a possibility, and his friend Tom Kettle still hoped to get it for him. And, having come armed with credentials from a Trieste newspaper, *Il Piccolo della Sera*, he took delight in wangling railroad passes, tickets to plays, and other accommodations. He actually did review a Shaw play, "The Shewing Up of Blanco Posnet," which was appearing in Dublin to escape the London censor. His review, in Italian, in *Il Piccolo*, enriched the international flavor of the occasion, but scarcely augmented the play's attendance. Finally, Joyce spent a good deal of his free time loafing around the offices of the *Freeman's Journal*, where there was always a good deal of congenial company, none of it oppressed by an urgent sense of work. The "Aeolus" section of *Ulysses* is evidence of Joyce's sharp eye and ear for this scene.

A serio–comic aftermath of the 1909 visit to Dublin was Joyce's effort to become the proprietor of a Dublin movie house. Noting that there were no cinemas in this city of half a million, he raised the matter with the Trieste movie syndicate and persuaded the four Slovene partners to send him back to Dublin to start one. After working himself half to death over electrical connections, licenses, and publicity, Joyce actually did open the Volta Theater in Mary Street, on December 20, 1909. But he stayed only about ten days to supervise its operation, and then left it in charge of

one of the partners, under whose Slovene taste it
withered and perished without profit or much honor.

Now troubles began again over *Dubliners*. George
Roberts, managing editor of Maunsel's, found a
passage in "Ivy Day in the Committee Room" in which
a character reflected a bit freely, though not altogether
disapprovingly, upon the private life of the late Edward VII. That was a first reason for postponing
publication. Then, like Grant Richards' printer,
Roberts started picking at the book. He guessed that
there was something very immoral about "An Encounter," and before long he was saying that no public houses, railway companies, or any other actual
Dublin persons or institutions must be mentioned by
name. (He stopped short of proposing that the book
be retitled *Anytown*.) Becoming mistrustful of the
very ground under his feet, he demanded to know the
theological definition of that sin of "simony" which is
twice mentioned in "The Sisters." Worse than specific
demands for revision and omission was Roberts' shifty
and unprincipled evasiveness. He refused to commit
himself: in response to questions, he fobbed things
off on his solicitors, who could only be consulted after
long delays; sometimes he did not answer letters at
all, or was so vague as to be incomprehensible. And
the more concessions one made, the more difficulties
he dreamed up. Joyce wrote him letters, alternately
furious and icily patient, threatened to sue for breach
of contract, wrote an open letter of protest to the newspapers, and sought the help of Irish literary opinion,
such as it was. In the summer of 1912, things having
dragged on for three long years, he came to Dublin
for the last time in his life, specifically to cope with
Roberts. Among other things, he offered to go with
Roberts, text in hand, to the various publicans mentioned in the book, to see if they objected to being
named. He raged, implored, threatened; and as a result of his importunity, the book was actually set up

in type and a first edition printed. But then the printer himself, John Falconer, abruptly decided that *Dubliners* was unpatriotic, distributed the type, and destroyed the entire printing. It is hardly possible that he took this highly unprofitable action on his own initiative; for once, Joyce was probably right in suspecting a deliberate conspiracy of harassment, of malignant bad faith. Leaving Ireland in a cold rage, he fired as a Parthian shot from Holland a raging, obscene verse satire, "Gas from a Burner," which he printed abroad and had distributed broadside in Dublin.

Back in Trieste, he continued to struggle, long-distance, with the exasperating problem of *Dubliners*; his career, so logically and sequentially conceived, could not continue till he had solved it, and even the *Portrait* remained stalled at the end of Chapter Three. But the publishers he tried were all discouraging, and he remained helplessly becalmed until, unexpectedly, late in 1913, he received a letter from Grant Richards, who had been having second thoughts about his treatment of Joyce. Perhaps he had fired that timid printer, or perhaps he guessed that the "climate of opinion" had changed; at all events, he showed unexpected courage in the face of difficulties which had terrified him eight years before. Joyce decided to renew relations. Meanwhile he had received another heartening letter, this one from Ezra Pound, American-born and American-educated but free-lancing in London since 1908. Pound had heard of Joyce from Yeats. At the moment, he was characteristically busy, rousing Western culture to a sense of its own higher destinies; having turned up Joyce, he was on the verge of discovering Eliot. And having discovered genius, he was its indefatigable partisan. Without quite knowing what this might prove to be, he offered to do what he could for Joyce's poetry or prose. His aid turned out to be decisive. Pound printed one of Joyce's poems in an anthology, and paid him for it; he recommended others for the (paying) magazine *Poetry*; he arranged for serial publication of *A Portrait* in a little magazine called *The Egoist*; he got Joyce to send some of the *Dubliners* stories to New York for publication in H. L. Mencken's *Smart Set*; and he lent backbone to Grant Richards' good resolve in behalf of *Dubliners* as a whole. The English printers bent, shuddering, to their task, and printed words from which their sensitive souls had recoiled, years before. On June 15, 1914, *Dubliners* appeared, missing the tenth anniversary of Bloomsday by only 24 hours.

No earthquakes, riots, or public catastrophes were reported; nobody prosecuted Joyce, Richards, or the printer. In fact, the book sold few copies and aroused little critical comment, good or bad. In the final hours before Europe plunged into holocaust, nobody paid much attention to the subtle ironies and polished phrasing of *Dubliners*, or to Mr. Henchy's judgment of the private character of the seventh Edward. Nor could Joyce himself spare much time for relief at the appearance, or distress at the small sales, of *Dubliners*, for when the *Portrait* started to appear serially in *The Egoist*, it was only a little more than half-finished. He completed the novel and mailed off the final installments even as the opening surges of the First World War were breaking over Trieste. Moving swiftly and confidently forward, he laid out and quickly brought to completion a drama based largely on his 1909 visit to Ireland, *Exiles*; and already in the back of his mind there had begun to loom the immense epic structure of *Ulysses*. Transformed utterly from its original short-story form, it appeared on the planning-board as a very long novel, with eighteen episodes, divided 3–12–3, just as in the finished book. Joyce began writing the episodes, methodically and

in order, from the first to the last, reworking some
several times over, but always getting one into recognizable shape before proceeding with the next.

Early in 1915, Stanislaus, who had inconvenient
political views which he expressed vigorously, was
arrested and sent to an Austrian detention camp,
where he spent the rest of the war. By June of the
same year, James had been obliged to leave Trieste.
With his family, his manuscripts, and little else, he
embarked by train for Zurich and there, in exile as it
were from his chosen place of exile, he pushed
steadily ahead with *Ulysses*. Zurich during the war
years was a city of expatriates, and what with the
increased competition, Joyce had trouble establishing
himself as a teacher of English. For a while he did
some translating for a pacifist magazine; an opportune
and unexpected gift from one of Nora's Galway uncles
then insured a few more weeks of survival; and after
a while a number of well-to-do Zurichers, realizing
that they had an author of distinction in their midst,
arranged to take lessons from him. Sometimes they
did not need, and often they did not even take, these
lessons, their avowed aim being to help Joyce out.
Simultaneously, back in London, Ezra Pound kept
after Yeats to have Joyce awarded a grant from the
Royal Literary Fund; Yeats approached Sir Edmund
Gosse, and in midsummer, 1916, the grant of £75
came through.

Other similar windfalls turned up from time to
time. Though various publishers rejected the *Portrait*,
an arrangement was finally reached toward the end
of 1916 for B. W. Huebsch to issue an American edition of *Dubliners* and the first edition of the *Portrait*.
Thus Joyce's second book of fiction finally appeared,
this one twelve years after it was first begun. In both
England and America the book was well reviewed;
and though Joyce's royalty payments were slow to
build toward impressive figures, his work was starting

to arouse interest and sympathy abroad. John Quinn, the New York lawyer and book collector, offered to and in fact did buy several Joyce manuscripts and corrected proof sheets for his collection. Anonymous donors kept turning up, too. Impressed by Joyce's writing, aware (usually through Pound's propaganda) of the opposition he had encountered, they sent small contributions and occasionally, increasingly, large ones. Early in 1918, Joyce received £200 from an unknown admirer; later in the same year an even larger sum was put at his disposal by an American woman residing in Zurich; and early in 1919, the income of a very large sum of money indeed was made over to him by Miss Harriet Weaver, a wealthy Englishwoman who had been editor of *The Egoist*. Joyce was suddenly, through the extraordinary generosity of this selfless admirer, a man of independent means. No destiny could possibly have been more unexpected, but he adjusted boldly, with the aid of a new, a more painful and intimate, set of problems.

Joyce's eyes had been weak since childhood, and he had abused them for a long time by inordinate reading and writing, by occasional spells of malnutrition, and by frequent drinking to excess. In Trieste, when Stanislaus wanted to terrify him into temperance, blindness was his most potent threat. The glasses which were necessary to him grew steadily thicker as his vision grew steadily worse. In 1917, in Zurich, he began suffering sudden atrocious attacks of pain in his eyes, so severe that he nearly fainted. Upon diagnosis, it appeared that he was afflicted with glaucoma, and in 1918 he underwent the first of a series of operations. Despite the best care that could be had, his vision continued to deteriorate, and for the rest of his life he never ceased to suffer, in agony and frightful inconvenience, from the inadequacy of his eyesight. For extended periods he had to live altogether in the dark. The operations were many, ingenious, and terribly painful; they invariably left his eyes a little worse than they had been before. Sizable portions of *Finnegans Wake* were written in a darkened room, where Joyce scrawled with a thick red crayon single words on big sheets of yellow paper; over the last twenty years of his life, he was never far from blindness, and the psychological strain alone was evidently horrible.

For the composition of *Ulysses* he was still able, intermittently, to see. The first three episodes had been written and, under the guidance of Ezra Pound, the book was steered toward serial publication in a New York magazine, *The Little Review*, edited by Margaret Anderson and Jane Heap. In March, 1918, therefore, the book started to appear, very much as the *Portrait* had done in *The Egoist*, a little bit at a time. Readers were shocked by the very first episodes, and even Pound took the liberty of censoring some passages. But printers in New York (especially Serbo-Croatians who knew no English) seemed to be hardier than those in London; at least, when passages wounded their sensibilities, they merely botched the type into nonsense, instead of throwing up the task altogether. As for Joyce, the challenge of serial publication was beneficial; he had congenial friends in Zurich, and fresh reason to feel assured of his powers. Even events which other men might have found distracting and upsetting served as grist to his mill. Having joined with a number of other exiles to form a group for putting on English-language plays, he became involved in a violent quarrel with several members of the British consular staff. Altercations, lawsuits, harassments, complaints, and petty acts of spite and revenge multiplied on both sides. But Joyce throve on them, and with joyous malignity wove the names of his chief adversaries (Rumbold, Carr, Compton, Bennett, and Smith) into *Ulysses* in uncomplimentary contexts. For several months he also indulged a sentimental and platonic admiration for Marthe Fleisch-

mann, a Zurich engineer's mistress, with whom he
exchanged vaguely romantic letters and visits—and
who promptly became Leopold Bloom's pen-pal in
Ulysses, under the name of Martha Clifford. Joyce's
trick of making use of whatever materials came to
hand in the course of composition was always notable;
it grew, in part, out of his mosaic method of composition, and was consistent throughout his career. He
wrote no imaginative prose which was not deeply
rooted in specific fact and experience.

After a brief unhappy return to Trieste (late-1919
to mid-1920), Joyce, encouraged by Pound, moved to
Paris; and there, between attacks of eye trouble, he
brought *Ulysses* slowly to completion. But even as he
was working on the final episodes, *The Little Review*
and its publishers were being haled into court to answer charges of circulating obscene material. Despite
ingenious defenses and an odd atmosphere of hilarity
in the courtroom, Miss Anderson and Miss Heap were
convicted in February, 1921, fined fifty serious dollars
apiece, and nearly jailed. Martyrdom was perfectly
to their taste—they thought the penalties assessed
were, if anything, too trifling—but the trial had the
serious effect of scaring off possible publishers of
Ulysses. No New York publisher would print, and
English publishers were a lost cause; Joyce was rescued only by the courage and enthusiasm of Miss
Sylvia Beach, American proprietor of Shakespeare &
Company, a Paris bookstore. She arranged for the
book to be set up by French printers in Dijon. Joyce
augmented it richly in proof, and a devoted little
circle of friends and admirers proofread it for the
half-blind author. Finally it was released, in an ex-
pensive edition limited to one thousand copies, on
Joyce's birthday, February 2, 1922.

As usual with Joyce's writing, the responses were
mixed. Some readers found the book dull, others said
it was incomprehensible, still others called it obscene.

On the other hand, there were many for whom its enchantment was immediate and magical. The very violence of reaction, whether favorable or unfavorable, was testimony to the book's power. This spread of critical opinion is not altogether surprising. The book placed unusual obstacles before the reader, and a novel of epic dimensions and epic quality was unusual in itself. On the whole, Joyce's fellow-craftsmen were the best, as they were the most generous, judges of his achievement. Even Virginia Woolf, who spoke of the book with dismay and disapproval, was not above profiting by its technical lessons, and *Mrs. Dalloway* (1925) was one of the first novels to pay *Ulysses* the sincerest of all tributes, that of imitation.

Of the last 19 years of Joyce's life, 16 were occupied in the composition of *Finnegans Wake*, a book which, apart from being fiendishly difficult to write and furiously difficult to read, almost all his literary advisers and sympathizers warned him to abandon. On the difficulties which attended its composition, it is useless to dwell at length; Joyce's failing eyesight, his increasingly suspicious and domineering temper, his ennui and *taedium vitae,* and the at first neurotic and then increasingly psychotic behavior of his daughter Lucia, all conspired to render his last years miserable. They would have done so had he been engaged on the most flaccid of potboilers. But the design of *Finnegans Wake* involved inconceivable elaborations and complexities; each individual word had to be "composed" several times over, to squeeze every last coincidence and complexity into it. At the same time, its patterns of reference aimed at being nothing less than universal. All the mythologies, languages, proverbs, folklore, history, and geography had to go into it—along with a biography and defense of James Joyce, a catalogue of children's games, sundry choruses of old men, and an interesting letter from Boston, dug up by a hen on a dunghill and partially deciphered for the edification of mankind. Structurally,

the book was tightly and complexly controlled; but its
pattern was so elaborate that almost anything could
be, and was, made to fit into it. Joyce always professed
extreme disdain for the raw materials of his fiction.
Any old junk or garbage would do. The value of the
finished product lay entirely in the workmanship.
Thus he struggled on, wrestling with his great monster of a tragi-comic book, overcome by despair at its
failure to win readers, but altogether and intuitively
convinced that this book and no other had been imposed on him to write. A little cult of admirers and
enthusiasts, such as those who helped with the final
stages of *Ulysses,* gathered around to render Joyce
homage and practical support in the work of composition, and he was never loath to take advantage of these
helpers. For the work on *Finnegans Wake,* his assistants consisted mostly of a small group centering
around the magazine *transition.* Pound was openly
hostile to the new book, Stanislaus Joyce hated it, Miss
Weaver was uncomprehending and on the whole un-
sympathetic. Thus, little of the humor which fills the
book seems to have accompanied the making of it;
this great and strange book was written, not because
its author felt it a prudent and appropriate book to
write, nor even because he as a person wanted to write
this way. The book imposed itself on him, despite his
personal wishes, and continues to impose itself on
readers; how to give it its head without allowing it to
ride roughshod over us is one of the thornier critical
problems of our time.

Meanwhile, the biography of Joyce hurries toward
its conclusion. On July 4, 1931, he went through a form
of marriage with Nora Barnacle in London, so that
she and their children could officially inherit his property. On December 29 in the same year, his father died
in Dublin; though distressed, Joyce did not revisit
Ireland for the funeral. His "enemies" there, he was
afraid, would turn upon him as Parnell's enemies had
turned on him, and destroy him before he could finish

his climactic work. In New York on December 6, 1933, Judge John Woolsey provided Joyce with an occasion for celebration by issuing a court order admitting *Ulysses* to the United States. This was a victory indeed in Joyce's long battle with the world; but a crushing defeat followed less than three months later when Lucia's mental illness took a pronounced turn for the worse. Joyce had taken her from doctor to doctor, had tried to cure her himself, had encouraged her to the limit of his power in several careers, had struggled as hard as he could against the common judgment that she was an incurable lunatic. Now at last he had to stand by while she was taken off to a sanitarium. During the first years of her confinement, she was allowed to venture forth on occasion, in the custody of an intimate and for short periods only, but as her condition grew irregularly worse, these occasions grew less and less frequent. Joyce suffered bitterly over the slow degeneration of his daughter's mind, but at least her departure from his immediate vicinity freed his spirit for the final effort of bringing *Finnegans Wake* to a conclusion. The immense task was brought to completion and shepherded through the ministrations of amazed printers by early 1939. In the fall of that fateful year, the Second World War burst into the open. The Joyces lived uncomfortably and fearfully in Paris during the first quiet stages of the conflict, but when the Germans overran France (spring, 1940), they were forced to flee once again. Painfully, through the toils of official connivance and official negligence, they made their way south in France, crossed the border into Switzerland, and settled once again in Zurich, the city to which they had first come 36 years before. Joyce survived his last perilous journey by less than three weeks. He died unexpectedly of a perforated duodenal ulcer on Sunday, January 12, 1941. He died as he had lived, among strangers, and without the consolation of a creed.

CHAPTER II

DUBLINERS

We have seen, in our brief sketch of Joyce's biography, something of the process by which *Dubliners* came into existence. We note that until he was 22 or 23, Joyce wrote no fiction of any sort. He was an occasional dainty poet, an occasional critic with a good deal of general disdain and some highly special enthusiasms, but fiction he did not undertake until that short semi-autobiographical sketch which he tossed at the editors of *Dana* and they tossed back at him. Some detailed account of this first effort will be in order later, but for the moment let us say simply that "A Portrait of the Artist as a Young Man," in its original form, was less a piece of fiction than a lyric cry. It scorned to give its hero a name, a family, or an appearance; it concentrated entirely on the development of his more exquisite inner attitudes; its style was so allusive and mannered that it could scarcely be thought to intend any dramatic effect at all. It was an intensely personal, almost narcissistic document; and while Narcissus may

well have his place within a story, he is not likely to
have the range of sympathies necessary for an author.
Certainly this first bit of Joycean fiction is too pre-
occupied with haughty withdrawal to augur well for
his future as a novelist.

Joyce's next fictional effort took the form of three
stories first published in Æ's *The Irish Homestead*
under the pseudonym of Stephen Daedalus, and later
incorporated into *Dubliners*. They are "The Sisters,"
"Eveline," and "After the Race" and could not possibly
be more different from the "story" he had submitted
to *Dana*. There is nothing precious about the subjects
or the prose—quite the contrary, both the scenes
selected and the treatment imposed on them are (in
the author's later words) "scrupulously mean." From
two of the stories the narrator is absent altogether—
they are impersonal, third-person story-telling; while
in "The Sisters" there is a narrator, but he is no aloof,
self-conscious artist, he is a confused and quite un-
literary boy. One feature of Joyce's previous writing
continues here: there is little or no exterior action. A
public event threatens to occur in "Eveline," but it
does not; and nothing even looms on the horizon of
the other stories as a possible action. This is not to say
that nothing happens, only that the story is committed
from the beginning to an inward action, an action of
understanding or recognition. But it is time to turn
from a general discussion of these first three narra-
tions, and to grapple with their specific particulars.

"After the Race" does not offer very many knotty
particulars. It is a study in weakness and humiliation
—Irish weakness and Irish humiliation—in the face
of Continental assurance. Jimmy Doyle is a light-
weight carried along by a swift current of factitious
excitement with perhaps a suggestion of sharp practice behind it. All the consequences of his folly are
hinted at rather than spelled out. We have the suggestion of a frightful hangover, the assurance that his

father the ex-butcher will be furious, and that carefully undefined and so all the more ominous cloud—how much money has he really lost? The story boils and bubbles along until all these awful consequences have begun to impinge on Jimmy Doyle's wretched consciousness, and then, as if shrugging off what is already obvious enough, closes on a tableau.

How much contempt does Joyce feel for Jimmy Doyle? How much liking is mingled with this contempt?—for the two emotions by no means exclude one another, particularly in Joyce. The wild oats which Jimmy is sowing are familiar and unimaginative enough; they do not seem even to involve any real pleasure for him, being hectic and gassy, as it were. Joyce as an old Dublin reprobate knew the wisdom of the world on this score: let a boy run a bit wild in his youth because he is bound to settle down later on. The old ex-butcher from Kingstown is clearly following that program and the evidence is that it will succeed admirably with <u>Jimmy who has neither the energy nor the intelligence for any sustained revolt</u>. Indeed, we are reminded that his father was too sensible to play the rebel for long; having "begun life as an advanced Nationalist, [he] had modified his views early." Now he sends his son to "a big Catholic college" in England, and to "Dublin University to study law." Dublin University is of course Trinity College, under its other name, and Jimmy is plainly expected to make friends with the scions of the Establishment. All these little details serve to mark out Jimmy Doyle as a characteristic "shoneen," a breed aptly described in "Ivy Day in the Committee Room" as "always hat in hand before any fellow with a handle to his name." Petty squires and successful bourgeois, such people may call themselves "Nationalists" (like Tricky Dicky Tierney), but they can be trusted to want what is best for the business community, i.e., themselves. Young Jimmy Doyle, when he is "under generous influences"

—drunk—feels "the buried zeal of his father wake to life within him." But it is not much life—Joyce never had anything but contempt for muzzy, sentimental, barroom patriotism—and Jimmy is managed out of his sentiments, as out of his money, by "friends" who really despise him.

He is a feeble figure, then, but in his puppyish way, not altogether unlikeable. And there are even grounds for thinking that he may, in certain respects, have a buried relation with Joyce himself. The names, for one thing, are very similar: James Joyce and James Doyle. Joyce had gone to Clongowes Wood, very often referred to, by those not friendly to it, as a school for training up "shoneens." His father was not a butcher, of course, or financially successful, but he had lived at Kingstown, and had he had a few of the butcherly qualities (which in "The Boarding House" for example enable Mrs. Mooney to deal "with moral problems as a cleaver deals with meat") he might have been a financial success like Mr. Doyle. Jimmy Doyle has some of the physical mannerisms which Joyce persistently attributed to characters whom he associated with himself: like Little Chandler of "A Little Cloud," Gabriel Conroy of "The Dead," and Richard Rowan of *Exiles,* he has a soft mustache and innocent-looking —i.e., weak—eyes. Joyce got the idea for the story after going to an automobile race, and when he wrote it he was fresh from a visit to Paris, where he had felt much humiliated by his own poverty and innocence, as contrasted with the sharp and knowing manner of Parisians. He had, further, a persistent notion that when he got drunk with people like Gogarty, they were encouraging him to drink from malicious motives, in the hope of ruining his talent. Finally, Jimmy Doyle rather fancies himself as a turner of phrases, and he makes up a fawning one, in not very good taste, about the Frenchman and the Englishman. Jimmy is not only Joyce, he is all Ireland in this context—which reminds us of that quiet, ironic phrase in the opening paragraph, "the cheer of the gratefully oppressed." The Irish, like Jimmy, are not only fleeced but grateful. The game of cards, which lies between Routh the Englishman and Ségouin the Frenchman, and in which Farley the American and Doyle the Irishman are the heaviest losers, is a thumbnail sketch of Irish history. "It was a terrible game," thinks poor lost Jimmy Doyle. Indeed it was.

Lastly, though with apologies and reservations, I am afraid something will have to be said about Jimmy Doyle's last name. It had a special fascination for the later Joyce, who included a section in *Finnegans Wake* (pp. 574–576)* where a trial takes place in which the defendant, the prosecutor, and all the members of the jury seem to be named Doyle. What is the point of this foolery? Elijah, preaching a degenerate gospel in the brothel scene of *Ulysses,* implies that under the religion of humanity, everyone is Christ—"Florry Christ, Stephen Christ, Zoe Christ, Bloom Christ, Kitty Christ, Lynch Christ" (p. 507). Stephen, speculating what various characters would be called if their names were translated into English (pp. 622–623) concludes that Jesus would be Mr. Doyle (Christ = the anointed = oiled = Doyle). This identification of Christ with Doyle may have been helped or suggested by a well-known Dublin baritone of the turn of the century, who figures in both *Ulysses* and *Finnegans Wake*; his name was J. C. Doyle.† Thus, by making a series of far-fetched identifications with characters in other Joyce books and people from his biography, we may establish still another, rather grotesque ground for thinking that Joyce viewed Jimmy Doyle

---

* See A Note on Editions on p. xiii for the particular editions to which all page numbers refer.

† Cf. also *Finnegans Wake* where the 12 patrons of Earwicker's pub are "doyles when they deliberate but sullivans when they are swordsed" (p. 142).

with secret sympathy, as an aspect of himself, and Christ, and everyman.

Now the reader himself at this point is no doubt feeling outraged; and if I may venture to interpret for him, he is muttering: "But if we have to read even a little short story like this, a bare sketch, in terms of Joyce's entire career, if we have to make such elaborate transpositions and macaronic puns, so that everything is something else and nothing is itself; if we have to do this, well . . . ." Well, what will happen? We shall have an infinite number of possible relationships to investigate; we shall be so busy fighting our way through riddles and cross-references that we shall have little occasion to appreciate Joyce's work as literature. Unhappily, the fact seems to be that Joyce was very often guided in his writings by these private patterns of word-association, these intimate attitudes, so that from time to time, we shall and must have recourse to some rather strained and exotic exegetical constructs. We shall have to bring his often maddeningly private patterns of association, and the peculiarities of his private attitudes, to bear on the reading of the texts. On the other hand, this procedure is chiefly justified where the text by its own peculiarities requires such treatment. In the example at hand, "After the Race," there are some reasons why the figure of Jimmy Doyle is not simply contemptible, contemptible though he doubtless is. Our "esoteric" reason is no doubt unnecessary in view of the many simpler ones; but it illustrates a sort of critical method which cannot be altogether ruled out, and if it has the effect of rendering the story richer, and the final balancing of attitudes more satisfying, it may well have a claim to our serious consideration.

When stories are so smooth of surface, so little disturbed by dramatic episode or authorial comment, a single odd word will set up reverberations, or the suspicion of reverberations. "Eveline," however, seems relatively innocent of these complications. The situation was evidently suggested to Joyce by the situation of his unhappy sisters, particularly Margaret, the eldest. (Her nickname was "Poppie," and Frank has a pet name for Eveline, "Poppens.") In obedience to a promise made to a dead mother, she is keeping a home together, against terrible odds, for a drunken and ungrateful father. But though she wants to run away with Frank, at the decisive moment she cannot, for she thinks that he is dragging her out to sea to drown her. The reader of course senses that if she is stifling anywhere, it is in the meager atmosphere of "the Stores" and her father's house. Some of these maritime ambiguities no doubt derive from Ibsen, who repeatedly—as for instance in "The Lady from the Sea"—used the ocean to suggest a way of life wilder and more vital, but also more deadly, than the limited existence of the town. And there is an interesting parallel in *Ulysses* (p. 243) where Stephen Dedalus, meeting his sister Dilly, feels that she is sinking, drowning, and pulling him down with her. But <u>Eveline, with her undramatized, almost animal fear of change</u>, is a less complex and moving figure, and her story, like that of Jimmy Doyle, is essentially pathetic.

Let us note, in passing, another complexity of texture which can be neither resolved nor overlooked. Jimmy Doyle's last name was a very unobtrusive element in the story, yet it turned out to have an elaborate connection with the whole tonality of the sketch. The dying words of Eveline's mother, "Derevaun Seraun," look very much as if they ought to have a symbolic meaning, but they don't, or at least it has so far proved undiscoverable. They make no sense in any known language or dialect, and are in no sense useful to the story in any corruption of any language known to man. They are a perfect dead end. So apparently there are some things we must learn to neglect, as there are others we must vigorously pursue, and **no**

way to tell which is which except by our successes. It
is this evident vagueness of the ground rules which has
disgusted many people with the exegesis of Joyce. But
we must be patient, and resign ourselves to carrying
a few unsolved Joyce problems around in our pockets,
at least until they become too heavy for comfort.

As for "The Sisters," it has long been recognized as
a story thoroughly recalcitrant to analysis and, under
its drab, uneventful surface, immensely complicated.
It is odd in its title, for though there are two sisters
in the story, one of them does little, says nothing,
seems to fall asleep halfway through the story and is
never heard from again. The fault of the spoiled priest
is curiously specified too; he has dropped and broken
a chalice, which seems to be a literal experience, for
semi-literate Eliza is no one to engage in metaphori-
cal flourishes. (Her references to the *"Freeman's
General"* and the carriage with "rheumatic" tires will
not escape the alert reader.) But the priest is called
a "simoniac" as well, though there is no mention of
this sin in the usual sense of selling ecclesiastical
offices for money. Perhaps the two other unusual
words which keep running through the boy's mind,
"gnomon" and "paralysis," will offer some help. A
gnomon is a small geometrical figure made by extending inward the lines of a large one, and from which
can be calculated the critical angles out of which the
larger figure can be, if necessary, reconstructed. Paralysis is a general condition afflicting Dublin and
Ireland, and which Joyce proposed as the general
theme of his short stories. Father Flynn is a long-
paralyzed and now finally dead parish priest, who is
the gnomon, or the index, to a society long-paralyzed.
We must think of him not simply as a parish priest
but as having something in common with Charles
Stewart Parnell, Tim Finnegan, and Finn MacCool—
as well as, perhaps, John Gabriel Borkman. In the
dimensions of the suburban Dublin bourgeoisie, he

once promised to be a hero, but at some point, strength failed him. The ambiguity about simony works here for the good of the story since, whether he sold an office or dropped a cup, the only point is that he proved unworthy. After a lifetime of helpless remorse, he lies dead, mourned by two ignorant sisters, like a dwarfed Dublin Borkman—over whom, also, two sisters mourn. (One of Ibsen's sisters, the active one, is called "Ella" = Eliza, the other "Gunhilde" which probably does not equal Nannie.) Father Flynn's life-long obsession had been the immense complexity and difficulty of the law before which he failed. Whether priest, hero, or artist (it does not much matter which), he had attempted to live by a law higher than that known to the Dublin bourgeoisie as represented in the story by Old Cotter and "my uncle Jack." The chalice which the dead priest carries in his coffin is not pointedly symbolic, for Irish priests at the turn of the century were often buried, or at least laid out, with a chalice in their hands. But it suggests the flawing of a talent, the gift unfulfilled—one recalls the overt symbolism in "Araby," where the boy carries an un-flawed chalice "safely through a throng of foes" as an emblem of his secret dream.

The bond between the boy and the dead priest is also interesting, and also carefully undefined; we get a hint of it, though, from another unusual word in the story, when uncle Jack refers to the boy, contemp-tuously and affectionately, as "that Rosicrucian there." The insinuation is that he thinks too much and too privately and too seriously. Dublin's cure for this fail-ing is exercise, suspicion, and conformity. Joyce's young boy is attracted to the priest because he is learned, because he is an outcast, because he is a failure. Spoiled priests are as common in Dublin as spoiled poets. A young man haunted by the sense of having chosen a perilous calling might well be dis-turbed by such an image of failure—not malignant, not attractive, but fascinating. And in this mysteriously fascinating figure of disaster, who once again is called James, we may well have an admonitory and, so to speak, tutelary image of Joyce himself. Thus, as with Jimmy Doyle, the story strikes a balance; there is contempt for the failure but sympathy for the qualities that brought it about, a sense that the law governing success and failure is somehow unfairly rigged, and an unfailing disdain for those (Villona, Cotter) who cannot fail because they never try.

Like the other two stories, "The Sisters" is based on scenes and episodes in James Joyce's immediate family. There had been an insane priest in his mother's family; and two of his maternal grandmother's sisters lived together in a house, the sinister aspect of which fascinated him—it appears in "The Dead" as well as in *A Portrait of the Artist as a Young Man*. But, it will be observed, the story which looks so much like a piece of merely external reporting is controlled in mood and imagery by the image of the boy standing before his dead friend, haunted by enigmatic nightmares, surrounded by crass stupidity, hugging his own never-mentioned chalice and terrified of dropping it or having it jostled from his hands.

I have written at some length on these three first stories because their method is that of the stories as a whole. Paralysis is a recurrent theme, suggestion and innuendo often take the place of dramatic action, and the polished mirror of naturalist representation is lit from the side by a cold and frequently ironic light, a long perspective, such as Joyce could only have learned from Ibsen. In the remainder of this section, before offering some remarks on *Dubliners* as a whole, I shall discuss half a dozen selected stories which offer points of particular difficulty or interest.

"Two Gallants," with its broadly ironic title and suspended resolution, is about as close as Joyce allows himself to come to a story with a trick ending.

We are allowed, up to the last sentence, to think that
sexual seduction is to be the prime end of Corley's
enterprise; the story of his previous triumph with the
girl who is now "on the turf" prepares us to think
there may be something adventurously sensual in
Corley, to which Lenehan's admiration—however mor-
bid—may be a tribute of sorts. But the fact of the
"small gold coin" is wonderfully reductive of all these
ideas. The interest of the "gallants" is strictly in cash.
And Lenehan's whole wistful dream of a fireside and
a home of his own—"if he could only come across
some good simple-minded girl with a little of the
ready"—reveals him for what he is. Emptiness and
parasitism are thus the keynotes of this story. A further special interest attaches to its construction. Lenehan, who is a verbal artist, though of a very low grade
indeed, is a kind of virtuoso of the void; he has no
employment, no income, no future, no past, no home,
no first name—he exists by virtue of a talent for words
with which he flatters such as Corley and makes his
way into groups where drinks are to be cadged. His
costume, of sneakers and yachting cap, is one which
Joyce himself, in the days of his drifting around Dublin, habitually assumed and his habit of walking the
Dublin streets aimlessly is both Joyce's and Bloom's.
The track he outlines in the course of "Two Gallants"
is characteristically devious, it twists and turns and
doubles back on itself, aimless, pointless, the path of
a man hung in the void of meaningless and wholly
alien experience. The conversation about Mac in
Westmoreland Street is classically empty and inconclusive. Another of Lenehan's gestures, playing an
imaginary theme on an imaginary harp, with his
fingers sweeping a scale of variations along the railings
of an iron fence, has the fantastic elegance of high
poetry.

An "artist" in Dublin argot is a trickster, a deceiver,
a workman in flimflam. Joyce was not himself an

artist in this sense, nor would he have been happy to have his work dismissed as trickery. But in his heart he cherished a doubt, expressed on occasion to his wife and only to her, that literary artistry did involve mere tricks and façades; he was also haunted, all his life, by a sense of the icy void lying directly behind the thin stream of human experience. In these respects he has something in common even with the abysmal Lenehan; and, perhaps for this reason, "Two Gallants" has overtones rather deeper and more resonant than one would expect in a story simply satirizing the avarice of these young-old men, who think to cover their real motives under the pretense of lust. "Sir," said Doctor Johnson, on a famous occasion, "your mother, *under pretense of keeping a bawdy-house*, was a receiver of stolen goods." Joyce hits Lenehan and Corley with something like this two-handed engine; but he also deals, with one of them at least, a bit more gently.

"The Boarding House" looks for a moment at the dirt under the carpet of Dublin respectability. Mrs. Mooney's boarding house is said to be gaining a certain fame, and the young men refer to the proprietress as "The Madam"; this is enough to make us see that Mr. Bob Doran is being had when he is forced to marry Polly. He is another of Joyce's helpless sensitives; his glasses, his clerkship, his vaguely bourgeois connections and aspirations, his mild, regretted radicalisms, and his present weak affluence, all make him fair game. Polly seduces him, and Mrs. Mooney, with an assist from bulldog Jack, executes him into marriage. As in "A Little Cloud," marriage is assumed to be a trap. The women, without any verbalizing, but with perfect understanding, connive at hooking helpless Bob Doran into it. From the story itself we do not perhaps understand how appropriate Polly's song is to her character; in *Ulysses* (p. 303), we hear indirectly Bantam Lyons' version of the episode, which is that Polly was freely available to all the young men of the house, and we see also the consequence of the forced marriage. Bob Doran has become a periodic, sodden, mindless drunk.

Lastly, there is a hidden anti-religious dimension of the story that *Ulysses* confirms. Though Polly Mooney is said to "look like a little perverse madonna," no reader of "The Boarding House" would ever suspect this metaphor of concealing a full-scale parodic parallel with the Holy Family. But if Polly is a madonna, Bob Doran must be a sort of Joseph, and so he is described as calling himself, in *Ulysses* (p. 314). [Joyce's interest in humiliated husbands is amply evidenced elsewhere in his work,] and the existence of the parallel is confirmed by a letter to his brother Stanislaus. It is hard to describe this sort of game except as perverse—and equally hard to feel that it is very important, one way or the other. Joyce is like a little boy writing a dirty word on a barn door, but writing it very small, on the inside, so nobody will see it. Yet the trick of concealing an entire perspective in a casual phrase, almost as an act of defiance to the reader, is one that will grow on Joyce.

"Clay," about which there has been a great deal of discussion, may perhaps be best described as a study in myopia. The laundry in which Maria works, for example, has certain odd aspects, the oddness of which may not be immediately appreciated. It is run by Protestants, and there are tracts on the walls. Maria lives in, and so apparently do the washerwomen. Under these circumstances, the word "matron" starts to take on an overtone suggestive of durance vile. In fact, the laundry is called the "Dublin by Lamplight" laundry and (as another letter from James to Stanislaus Joyce allows us to see) it is a laundry run by well-meaning Protestant ladies for the reformation of prostitutes, where they atone for their lamplit sins by washing Dublin's dirty laundry snow-white. Maria does not see much of this, or rather she has seen it and absorbed it and put it in the back of her head, where unpleasant facts dwell. She has shuffled off, in much the same way, Joe's quarrel with Alphy, which unfortunately comes up again at the party, but is quickly re-buried—as well as it can be, though unfortunately Joe's oldest boy has been named Alphy, and he remains awkwardly around, memorial to a lost friendship. Maria ignores until the very last instant the fact that the stout elderly gentleman on the tram is in liquor—and then covers it up with the fact that he is a gentleman. She loses the plumcake, but is cosseted into forgetting her loss; in playing the saucer game, she makes a mistake in picking the clay which truthfully foretells her death, but is allowed to pick a comforting falsehood instead. The nutcracker is lost, so she doesn't get any nuts, but protests that she doesn't want any anyhow; and she makes an awkward mistake in singing the Balfe, but everyone covers it up. The story is a little epic of objects misplaced, trivialities endured, the inconvenient truth about things rapidly and ruthlessly buried. Thus one major overtone of the title is "mortality"—Maria will soon be dead, but another major overtone is "plasticity," for even that ultimate, inconvenient truth can be shoved out of the way. Since the story is set on All Hallows' Eve, Maria is pretty certainly a witch of some sort, or perhaps a ghost. Like an unenlightened Mrs. Alving, in Ibsen's very relevant play "Ghosts," she wants things to be nice at any cost. Certainly here Joyce does not lavish much sympathy on the weak and sensitive little person; rather, Maria is an image of death settling over Ireland, a snug little ghost celebrating in sentimentality and pretense the successful burial of every cruel, vital truth.

Three major stories are among the last four of *Dubliners*; they are "Ivy Day in the Committee

Room," "Grace," and "The Dead." Once more all are deeply rooted in Joyce's personal experience, though the actual materials for "Ivy Day in the Committee Room" were sent to him in a letter from Stanislaus. The story is very much of a time and place. Parnell has been dead more than a decade, and the custom of wearing a bit of ivy on the anniversary of his death is starting to die out. Edward VII is due to visit Ireland in the near future, and in fact he did so during the summer of 1903. Home Rule, still technically a popular ideal and not easy to repudiate, is no longer —except in limited radical circles—an active faith; there is a growing tendency to be glad that the stormy age of romantic revolt is over, and to look toward prudent, and perhaps interested, compromises.

"We all respect him now that he's dead and gone," says Mr. O'Connor, with unconscious self-satire; and this is the mood of the story, for sentimentality toward dead Parnell salves a sour, cynical, and opportunist attitude toward the present. The spokesman for this attitude is Mr. Henchy (who is presumed to represent, within the story, the dialect and style of John S. Joyce). Everyone else is gray and sodden and more than a little weary. Old Jack is caught in what is seen as a characteristic Irish confusion, abusing his son as a "drunken bowsy" who has no respect for his elders when they are drunk. Mr. O'Connor is one of Joyce's gray young men, who seems not to have the energy to take a position on anything—he agrees and qualifies endlessly. Lyons and Crofton are hangers-on. But Mr. Henchy brings to the discussion the sharp edge of a personal animosity which respects no consistencies. He praises Joe Hynes for sticking to Parnell, though he has previously suggested that he is a traitor, a spy, and in the pay of the Castle; he sneers at Tricky Dicky Tierney, but is ready to speak well of him as soon as a bottle of stout appears; he is ready

to accuse others of treason and servility, but is himself
perfectly agreeable to the idea of an address of welcome to Edward VII. The parallel is particularly
deadly here, because Parnell was deposed from the
Irish leadership for alleged sexual immorality, while
Edward had some notoriety as a rake. To condone in
an English monarch behavior which had been held
against an Irish patriot leader would be to confess a
double standard in favor of the outlander. But Mr.
Henchy sees no moral problem at all; "what we want
in this country . . . is capital." He is not much of a
capitalist himself—he expects to find the bailiffs in
the hall when he goes home. But he does not mind
being unpaid for his work as long as someone tips
him a bottle of stout and he does not mind sacrificing
his Irish patriotism as long as he can accuse other
people of servility and salve his conscience with big
blarney about the need for capital. An apparently
irrelevant discussion of the Lord Mayor's office under-
lines this Irish trait of surrogate vainglory. Three men,
all on the thin edge of insolvency, sitting around a
cold unfurnished room on a bleak October afternoon,
complain that the Lord Mayor isn't living in sufficient
splendor. The irony is not developed, but it is none
the less cruel.

The appearance of Father Keon, out of the mists of
intrigue and suspicion which crowd the background
of "Ivy Day in the Committee Room" may seem arbitrary and inconclusive; he turns up, looking for the
sheriff, Long John Fanning, and vanishes as quickly
as he came amid a shower of obsequious thanks and
apologies. There would, of course, be nothing odd in
an Irish priest taking part in Irish politics, but what
a spoilt priest is doing in a municipal election is anyone's guess. It would seem that Father Keon serves
chiefly to swell that burlesque ménage imagined by
Mr. Henchy—a badly-damaged church to go with the
badly-damaged state, while old Jack and Mr. O'Con-

nor serve as underlings. Off they roll in a coach-and-four, splendid in their vermin, nothing lacking.*

There is in fact a kind of warmth to this bit of Irish genre-painting, reminiscent in so many ways of a tavern scene by Bouwers or Teniers, which can hardly fail to gratify the reader. The obvious relish with which everyone turns to praising a safely-dead hero, the mawkish rhetoric of Joe Hynes' poem, and Mr. Crofton's prudent critique are all touches of great awkwardness, deftly delineated. Mr. Crofton is particularly fine at singling out for praise exactly that aspect of the poem which will not stand praise; and the fact that, after all the direct dialogue of the story, his final critique is veiled in indirect discourse, is a touch of high art. But an ironic reading of the story must not go so far as to cast doubt on the sentiments behind this ungainly piece of rhetorical gingerbread. Joe is not quite one of the crowd. He not only works for "the other tinker," Colgan, he has some arguments for him deriving from Joyce's short-lived socialism of this period. Thus nobody in the Committee Room trusts him. He drifts in and out amid considerable coolness; and Mr. Henchy, reminded that he is clever with the pen, declares, in the true spirit of Old Cotter, that some of these hillsiders and Fenians are a bit too clever. He has the instinctive hostility to intelligence of a crafty, violent man. On all these scores, then, as well as for the balance of the story, it seems clear that we must respect the intent of the poem, while recognizing that "a very fine piece of writing" is just what

* Something may also be going on in the story involving the names and symbols of the four evangelists. O'Connor is Matthew, Lyons is named after the emblem of Mark, Mr. Henchy and the old man are Johns (their special interest the Black Eagle), and the symbol of Luke is a bull, for which Crofton may stand by virtue of his ox-like appearance, or Father Keon by virtue of some correspondence which is not immediately apparent. On these terms Parnell is the dead Christ, a notion which does no particular harm to the story.

it is not. Parnell, though no absolute hero, was as much a hero as anyone visible from the Committee Room. His memory is not mocked in "Ivy Day in the Committee Room."

"Grace" raises us from underwater haunts of semi-derelicts and drifters into the serried ranks of Dublin's middle-middle-classes. Elsewhere in *Dubliners*, it is exceptional for characters to have steady jobs, visible family, or tangible habitations; in "Grace," everyone is carefully defined as to employment, prospects, and domestic status. Mr. Kernan's problem, however, is not one peculiar to his social class; it is nothing less than the curse of drink. Dublin, of course, would not be Dublin without a fair amount of elbow-bending. Joyce, who had a weakness for it himself, consistently represents it as a social problem of major proportions. But Mr. Kernan's downfall is presented from a cool perspective, with a droll, dry sense of humor, far different from the sordid realism of "Counterparts" or the seedy misery of "A Painful Case." A bottle of whiskey is the gift which considerate Mr. Fogarty automatically brings for his sick friend, and M'Auley's is the meeting place from which the gentlemen depart on their pot-washing errand.

The story has been said (by Stanislaus Joyce) to correspond with the three stages of Dante's *Commedia*; Inferno is the public toilet into which Mr. Kernan falls, Purgatorio is the scene by his sickbed, and Paradiso is represented by his final appearance in the exalted respectability of the Gardiner Street Jesuit Church. The pattern is certainly visible. But Joyce's interest in the fall and redemption of man was pervasive, and Mr. Kernan's trajectory parallels that of Adam in Milton's poem, as well as that of Dante's pilgrimage. Surely the scene around Mr. Kernan's bed of pain, if it must have a parallel in the mythologies, relates more closely to the Book of Job than to the Purgatorio.

In reading the story, though, it is doubtless best to
let these phantom parallels remain in the shadowy
background, for the brightly-lit foreground is pre-
empted by a group of solemn, irresistibly droll, clowns.
Mr. Kernan's comforters, like Job's, begin as a group
of three: Mr. Martin Cunningham and Mr. John
Power, of the Dublin Castle police services, and Mr.
C. P. M'Coy, whose connections are less eminent and
less stable. Again like Job's comforters, they are increased to four by the arrival of Mr. Fogarty, the
grocer, who like Elihu thinks he has new light to shed
on the problem, but who is unanimously disregarded.
Their discussion, which rambles solemnly across hills
and dales of which they are all more or less ignorant,
is fuzzy and wrong in most details, but vaguely right
overall. Martin Cunningham is wrong about the "mot-
toes" of Pius I and Leo XIII, but not far wrong; the
scene at the Twentieth Ecumenical Council was not
as Mr. Cunningham describes it; and Mr. Fogarty
is right about the "Italian or American" whom he remembers as the last opponents of papal infallibility,
but he is overridden, and the error does not matter
much. Joyce, with his sharp memory for particulars
(and his special advantage in having recently consulted a library) is having his fun with the tradesmen
who (like Bottom the weaver and his friends) are
meddling with matters above their understanding.
But while they are absurdly wrong, with the special
inefficient absurdity of natural clowns, there is a grand
resonance to the faith in which they humbly, dumbly
dwell. Mr. Cunningham's story about John of Tuam
is wrong in every detail, historically, but it illustrates
an ideal of mental discipline and intellectual consistency, for which Joyce could not have failed to entertain great respect. And it helps out the story's rever-
berance that there should hang over "Grace" the image
of a true and potent church, protective of its inno-
cents, vigilant against its enemies, and armored with

a vast, rigorous philosophy, to which the proudest of its defenders is immediately submissive. Only against this background can the actual betrayal of the church's ideals, which is reserved for the end of the story, strike with its proper impact.

Father "Purdon," to whom Joyce with Voltairean malice assigned the name of a notorious street in Dublin's notorious red-light district, was in real life Father Bernard Vaughan; he is cruelly caricatured here, not only because Joyce found him an inviting target, but for balance in the story. The simple-minded worshippers are dimly in the right: Martin Cunningham and his little troop have come prepared for a religious experience, such as they vaguely perceive to be possible, and they are met with a crass exercise in spiritual arithmetic. If there is not some authentic humility in Martin, a little stunted and wizened imagination in his fellow-penitents, we shall feel no shock of disappointment at the seedy sophisms which descend upon them from the pulpit at the end of the story.

"Grace" is Joyce's imaginative development, transposition, and synthesizing of various materials available from his youth. Mr. Kernan the tea-taster had lived down North Richmond Street; John S. Joyce, when drunk, fell down the stairs of a urinal; he was asked to go to a retreat and accepted, but insisted, like Mr. Kernan, on the right to "bar the candles." Martin Cunningham, John Power, C. P. M'Coy, and Mr. Fogarty the grocer were neighborhood acquaintances and friends of Joyce's father; the material on the Vatican Council he looked up in a public library while in Rome. From all these sources, he pieced together the materials for "Grace" and it shares with "Ivy Day in the Committee Room" a redolence of Dublin and a thickness of detail on which Joyce drew liberally when he created *Ulysses*. "Grace" furnishes more characters, and more important characters, for the epic novel than any other of the *Dubliners* stories.

The last, and by general consensus the greatest, of the stories in *Dubliners* stands somewhat apart from the rest, being warmer in tonality, richer in the writing, and more intimate in its subject matter. For these peculiarities several circumstances are responsible. Joyce wrote "The Dead" when he was feeling particularly forlorn and nostalgic in Rome and Trieste; he celebrated traditions of Irish hospitality which appealed to him as generous and happy qualities, and which he often exemplified. He dealt also with deep ambivalences in his own nature—including love of his country and hatred for it, love of his art and loathing of it, worship of his wife and inferiority before her. Gabriel Conroy, with his glasses and goloshes, his literary career, his indifference to Gaelic and his hostility to Irish patriots, is an aspect of Joyce himself; Gretta Conroy, with her West-country background, her early and passionate admirer Michael Furey, and her slight uneasiness in bourgeois Dublin, has many qualities of Nora Barnacle Joyce. Kate and Julia Morkan who live on Usher's Island with their niece Mary Jane are clear counterparts of Joyce's maternal aunts, Mrs. Callanan and Mrs. Lyons, who lived on the same quay with Mrs. Callanan's daughter Mary Ellen, taught music, and had an annual party for family and friends.

Who are "The Dead"? Most of the persons at the party have about them some aspect of the galvanized corpse, the mechanism going horribly through its prescribed routines. It is a house full of old maids, among whom even Lily the servant is festering far worse than weeds. The available men are intolerable bores or intolerable drunks. Miss Ivors is a malicious propaganda machine. The conversation turns on singers long dead and monks who sleep every night in their coffins; death is everywhere. Caught in these drab circumstances, Gabriel Conroy must play out the ingratiating social role imposed upon him by tradition. With his polite phrases and false manners, he must be what Lily has accused him in advance of being—"all pala-ver." The only hope of a marriage, a rich and re-deeming relation which shall lead out of this wilder-ness of death, lies in Gretta. Thus to learn at the end of the story that in his most intimate life he is less real to his wife than a dead man is to give the lie to all his false rhetoric about going on "bravely with our work among the living." The world of the dead is stronger and more vital than that of the living—it is not simply a collection of old scarecrows. It is ac-cepted, by Gretta and by Gabriel, that Michael Furey had died for love of her; Gabriel goes on to see it as a condition of passionate feeling that one should die for it. "Better pass boldly into that other world," he thinks, "in the full glory of some passion, than fade and wither dismally with age." To live passionately is to die; to live coolly and self-regardingly is to survive. The death of one who was named after the warrior archangel is a reproach to one who was named only after the affable archangel.* Thus "The Dead" calls into question culture, prudence, and civilized sensi-tivity before the deeper and more intimate tribunal of the blood.

One aspect of this procedure (already sufficiently emphasized) is Joyce's hatred and suspicion of his writer's trade; to make sentences out of one's very life, and arrange them for dramatic effect, struck him as false in itself and in its consequences. But Joyce, through Gabriel Conroy, is also calling into question the conscious mind as a whole. Before the ultimates

---

* To think of Milton's conversational Gabriel is to comment less ironically on the protagonist of "The Dead" than if one recalls Gabriel the blower of the last trump; Conroy is a bitterly inadequate resurrection-man. But neither of these as-sociations may be as important as that with the American writer Bret Harte, whose novel *Gabriel Conroy* begins, as Joyce's story ends, in a snowstorm.

of love and death (and to make this charge against him, they link hands indissolubly), all the self-sustaining, ego-gratifying devices of consciousness fade into contemptible tricks. For the first time in Joyce, we see the snob writer, who has usually controlled his long perspective to focus on others, now sitting in doom-judgment on himself. Thus Gabriel's impending journey westward, for which a single sentence in the last paragraph provides unexpected evidence, is a journey of discovery in a double sense: an adventure in search of the roots of his instinctual life, and an imaginative probing of his own mortality. The achievement of the story's last paragraph is to suggest a fusion within Gabriel's mind of these two buried preoccupations—a fusion achieved at the ambiguous moment of his falling asleep, when it is hard to say categorically whether he is rising to the height of a vision or fading off into an uncritical and sentimental revery. One thing, however, is clear: for the first time in Joyce's fiction, a conclusion is reached which is not external, in the sense of involving the reader's sympathies, but internal, in the sense of involving a character's intuitions. Gabriel is cuckolded, so to speak, at the most intimate moment of his marriage, by a dead man; but the real balance is to be struck, not with Gretta or Michael Furey, or with the scarecrow society of Usher's Island, but inside his head. This balance has about it something visionary and transcendent. It cannot be fully expressed in discursive logic, or made manifest dramatically, but only suggested through images, rhythms, juxtapositions, enthymemes. In all the other stories a sort of dramatic evidence accumulates which requires us to pass a judgment—however mixed—on characters such as Lenehan or Maria. But Gabriel's character is not at issue at the end of "The Dead," it has already been judged, by Gabriel himself. We do not see him, we see through him, and what we see can only be

intuited, not demonstrated. The fact that his love–
death equation lies close to the heart of traditional
romantic sexuality, that it was widespread in the late
nineteenth century as part of an informal "religion
of women," should not blind us to the novelty of the
visionary moment in Joyce's work. He spoke with some
asperity of his method in *Dubliners* as that of the
polished looking glass; but in the ending of "The
Dead" we see through that glass—if only darkly—and
are asked to intuit an experience of some dimensions,
whose only dramatic validation lies in a feat of style.

Dubliners has been immensely influential by virtue
of several outstanding individual stories. Whether the
book has an overall plan and how important it is are
secondary questions. That some sort of progression
occurs within the fifteen stories is not to be doubted.
Stories of boyhood, relatively modest in scope, come
early in the book; those involving grownups and social
life, and leading to relatively complex judgments,
come later. But there are few common characters, and
the way in which the stories were added, over a period
of four or five years, even after the book had been
submitted to publishers, even while it was being set
up in type, casts doubt on a rigorous, preconceived
architecture. If one had looked at the MS before "Two
Gallants" was added, I do not think one would have
sensed a gaping void. No, the book consists of fifteen
stories bound together for the most part by a common
theme, some common attitudes, occasional common
moods. But it aims at variety quite as much as, and
perhaps more than, unity; its structure is that of the
theme with variations. That these variations become
ever deeper and richer—that in the final story they
wholly transcend the original theme—is a major element of the book's achievement. But to impose a
mechanical form on the stories (as by dividing them
according to the specific deadly sins studied in each)
or to try to educe from them a systematic symbolic

structure (as of birds, colors, temperatures, moistures, or whatever) is to borrow trouble. They give no sign of being cut to any such pattern. There are little gritty pebbles of private association here and there; occasional fantastic arabesques of parallel and connotation which blossom abruptly; some isolated elements that can be fully understood only by reference to the biography, the letters, or later books in the canon. But most of these difficulties are peripheral. The basic pattern of the stories is, generally, accessible, and a sufficient reading of them can usually be based on the dramatic evidence of the stories themselves—that is, the behavior of the characters, their thoughts, words, relationships, and the things we are told about them. In this sense, *Dubliners* is for the most part a work of classic art.

One last thing to clear out of the way. Joyce spoke a great deal of the impersonality of great art, and indeed developed a theory of "epiphanies" or brief prose sketches which depend on the artist getting out of the way and allowing the inner meaning of the event to shine through without editorial interference. In his young manhood he wrote perhaps as many as a hundred of these epiphanies (of which forty survive),* and after giving up on the idea of publishing them separately, he adapted a number of them, in various ways, to service in his short stories and novels. In this work of adaptation he was so successful that the previously-uninstructed reader can rarely tell where the ex-epiphany begins and ordinary fictional prose leaves off. Notwithstanding their successful absorption, the epiphanies have continued to haunt the critical mind, and considerable critical effort has been put into the thesis that the stories of *Dubliners* as a whole are nothing more than a series of such epiphanies, in which the inner essence of various Dublin

* See Scholes and Kain, *The Workshop of Daedalus,* pp. 3-51.

situations is allowed to reveal itself without artistic contrivance. The stories as we have inspected them do not seem very answerable to this conception. The author does not often intervene overtly with editorials or moral comments; he is not present as a recognized manipulator of puppets. But the stories are nonetheless arranged and contrived with considerable art to bring about a balanced judgment, a dramatically enlarged conception of the point at issue. There are even occasions when Joyce as commentator comes very close to intruding on stage *in propria persona*, for example in his description of Mrs. Kernan's religion:

> Her beliefs were not extravagant. She believed steadily in the Sacred Heart as the most generally useful of all Catholic devotions and approved of the sacraments. Her faith was bounded by her kitchen, but, if she was put to it, she could believe also in the banshee and in the Holy Ghost.

Here we have the classic devices of irony and parallelism, yoked to the simple declarative sentence. There is no epiphany, though we have the essence of an attitude. But indeed the whole notion of "epiphany" as a device useful to literature seems to depend on a special conception of reality which was only intermittently Joyce's. A spiritual order of reality buried within, or hidden behind, a fleshly order of reality, may shine through in a moment of epiphany. But if there is no transcendent reality, merely a moment of evocation, what does "epiphany" amount to? Meredith's characters are apt at revealing their whole nature in a phrase or a trivial action; in *A Room With a View*, Cecil Vye exposes his entire spirit by the way in which he refuses to play tennis with Freddy; are these to be called "epiphanies"? How then do epiphanies differ from what Stendhal used to call, rather less pompously, "petits faits vrais"? I have never been clear what good the word would do us, even if we did decide that it could be applied to the stories of *Dubliners*—how it would make the stories any more or less interesting than they now are, or different in any way.

Estimating the value of *Dubliners* in a rational and measured way, we shall probably find it a very good book of short stories, indeed—far better than Heblon's *Studies in Blue,* a good deal better than Moore's *The Untilled Field.* Despite obvious unevennesses, it is a collection worthy of being discussed with the stories of James, Maupassant, and Flaubert. As the work of a beginner in the art of fiction, it is obviously extraordinary and, viewed historically, it takes some amazingly long, bold steps. Gone is the palaver of the nineteenth-century novelist, the pomposity of his drawing-room rhetoric. (When it turns up momentarily in Joe Hynes' poem and Gabriel Conroy's speech, we smile involuntarily before we recognize what it really is.) Gone too are the labored moralizings by which the novelist directed his reader's reactions in every particular, and even sniffled a bit himself in order to prime the reader's tear ducts. The stories reflect carefully composed elements of reality on their polished surfaces, and most of the reactions are left up to the reader's sensitivity and responsiveness. At their best, the stories are swift and surgical. These are achievements of great historical importance, even if specific stories within the collection are not necessarily achievements of great artistic importance. The flexible, expressive style, now hard, now with lyric interludes; the free range of usage, from gutter to impassioned meditation; and the extraordinary balance of intimate with distant perspectives make the book one of great importance in the history of English fiction. Whether it would bulk quite so large in a history of Continental fiction is another matter; in any event, the authentic and indisputable claims which can be made for it are impressive indeed.

But more chilling and solemn than even the actual achievement of *Dubliners* was the spirit in which the collection was conceived and carried through. That spirit is best represented by an extract from a letter of Joyce's to Grant Richards, dated May 5, 1906:

> . . . My intention was to write a chapter of the moral history of my country and I chose Dublin for the scene because that city seemed to me the centre of paralysis. I have tried to present it to the indifferent public under four of its aspects: childhood, adolescence, maturity and public life. The stories are arranged in this order. I have written it for the most part in a style of scrupulous meanness and with the conviction that he is a very bold man who dares to alter in the presentment, still more to deform, whatever he has seen and heard. I cannot do any more than this. I cannot alter what I have written. All these objections of which the printer is now the mouthpiece arose in my mind when I was writing the book, both as to the themes of the stories and their manner of treatment. Had I listened to them I would not have written the book. I have come to the conclusion that I cannot write without offending people. The printer denounces *Two Gallants* and *Counterparts*. A Dubliner would denounce *Ivy Day in the Committee Room*. The more subtle inquisitor will denounce *An Encounter*, the enormity of which the printer cannot see because he is, as I said, a plain blunt man. The Irish priest will denounce *The Sisters*. The Irish board-ing-house keeper will denounce *The Boarding-House*. Do not let the printer imagine, for goodness sake, that he is going to have all the barking to himself.*

Straight down the line to the not-very-indirect insinua-tion of the last sentence, that the printer and his ilk are a pack of hounds, that is an apologia worthy of Dante Alighieri himself.

* Quoted by Herbert Gorman, *James Joyce* (New York: Farrar and Rinehart, 1939), p. 150.

A PORTRAIT OF THE
ARTIST AS A YOUNG MAN

A Portrait of the Artist as a Young Man
in the form which we now read it is the
product of at least two major revisions.
The first version, written in 1904, submitted to *Dana*
and set aside after its rejection, was barely four pages
long. The second version, under the title *Stephen
Hero*, seems to have run over a thousand pages. The
text we now have is a compromise between the first
two versions, both in length and tone. As we have
seen, the *Dana* essay was lyrical, compressed, and
mannered while *Stephen Hero* came closer to being
stodgy and explanatory than anything else Joyce ever
wrote. The work of the third revision divided itself
into two parts. The first three chapters of the present
book were revised from the MS of *Stephen Hero* by
a process of cutting and concentrating. Joyce, very
much contrary to his usual practice (which was incremental), cut down an existing MS by deliberately
omitting bridge passages, transitions, and explana-
tions. Then, when this material began to be published
serially, he came under pressure to finish the rest of
the book. And there, from what we can tell, *Stephen
Hero* does not seem to have been of much help to him.
The last two chapters—all that material which follows
the great hell-fire sermon—are the product of a different set of circumstances and procedures than are
the first three.

These details would be so much dead wood in the
thickets of biography if they did not seem to have
left their mark on the book, in the form of various
intellectual and literary difficulties. The nature of

these difficulties can be indicated in a single inter-
rogative: How much sympathy is the reader supposed
to accord Stephen Dedalus in his struggles with the
political, social, religious, and artistic mores of his
native land? The range of possible answers is very
wide indeed. Some critics hold that Stephen is derided as a spoiled and petulant brat. Others maintain
that he is a martyr, a mythical figure, and type of
the Christ. It is hard to suppose that all these judgments are right. But of course our question is actually
four different questions, and it is not difficult to see
that answers to them may vary considerably from
passage to passage within the book. These answers
also vary in considerable measure according to the
age at which one reads the book and the attitudes one
brings to it. The *Portrait*, as it describes the rebellion
and self-assertion of a young man at odds with his
elders, is bound to be read with special feeling by
young people at odds with their elders—and by elders
at odds with their young people. It is a more liberating book, I think, for the young than for the old, but
it speaks to both conditions. This may well be because
it was composed at two different periods of Joyce's
life, and often includes the basis for two quite different
attitudes toward the same sequence of events or set
of values.

Let us begin with some prosaic details. The *Portrait*,
as we now have it, is an arranged and selective account of the growth of a consciousness. That it is
literally the consciousness of James Joyce which is
described at every point is too much to say, but that
the broad outlines and many of the specific details of
the story are taken from Joyce's actual experience is
quite apparent. From beginning to end, the book
covers, we may estimate, a chronological "distance"
of a little less than twenty years. It begins in 1885
or 1886, when Stephen Dedalus is three or four, and
ends in 1902, with his departure for the Continent

at the age of 22. Public events, such as the fall of Parnell and the production of *The Countess Cathleen,* are mentioned within the book, providing a sketchy, yet consistent basis for dating it. But though we may easily estimate the total "coverage" of the book, its handling of time, as a matter of interior economy, is very uneven and irregular. Pages 1–2 are 1885–1886, reduced to a few pregnant particulars—we cannot stand very much of the moocow bit. Pages 3–26 are the period at Clongowes from 1888–1890, but they end with a reference to the death of Parnell, October 6, 1891; the famous Christmas-dinner scene (pp. 26–41) is Christmas 1891 or 1892, probably the latter; and Chapter I concludes with the great pandy-bat insurrection (pp. 41–64), which presumably takes place after Stephen's return to Clongowes—no earlier, certainly, than spring 1892 or 1893. Thus, six or seven years of development are covered here, though in fact only a few selected hours and minutes have been described. Joyce's stay at Clongowes, which in real life lasted less than three years, and so ended before the death of Parnell, is protracted to four or five years in the novel, ending probably two years after Parnell's death. An awkward, two-year stay in the school of the Christian Brothers, of which Joyce was much ashamed, is quietly put off to the next chapter, there to be dismissed in an ambiguous conditional clause; and after a few boyish adventures with friends in the suburbs, Stephen is entered at Belvedere. These first two chapters are broken in a number of places by four horizontal stars which stand for a change of time or place; but there are, in addition, a number of unmarked breaks where a period of time, long or short, is understood to elapse. The six years at Belvedere are mainly represented by the evening of the Whitsuntide play (pp. 80–87, 91–96) and the four days of the retreat, which occupy Chapter III entire. Apart from this, we have a short, four-page flashback to an event

of Stephen's first term (pp. 87–91), a visit to Cork
with his father (pp. 97–108), and an account of his
winning and spending prize-money (pp. 108–113)
which fades into the story of his sexual initiation (pp.
113–114).

I have indicated here what is perfectly obvious to
any reader of the *Portrait,* the frequently-broken narrative stream and uneven pace of the story. Appendix
A (pp. 217–220) offers a schematic time-chart of the
novel, estimating both the periods of time actually
described and those understood to elapse between
units of the narrative. But if the scenes of the novel
are as discontinuous as loose beads, what strings them
together? Primarily, of course, the development of
Stephen Dedalus. On the stage of the novel, he always stands front and center. The portrait is of him,
and the other characters are all ancillary; for example, only one of his siblings has so much as a name,
that name is used only once, and as for the other
young Dedaloi, we do not know even so much as
their precise number (on p. 284 we get a very rough
estimate). Stephen's central position is not automatic
evidence that we are to take a favorable view of him;
Sir Willoughby Patterne occupies an equally central
position in *The Egoist.* It does mean, however, that
the word "hero" remains appropriate to him, and that
the virtues or faults we impute to him cannot very
well be mediocre ones. We see things through his
eyes, we see very often only his reaction to things
and not the things themselves, and this sort of focus,
this continuous, detailed interest in the processes of
his brain, renders it most unlikely that he will prove
to be such a flabby, floundering pseudo-artist as
Frederic Moreau, the protagonist of Flaubert's *Sentimental Education* or the puppy who is represented in
George Moore's *Confessions of a Young Man.*

For example, a major theme in Joyce's description
of his literary artist's development is his growing com-

mand of words and sensitivity to them. Even as a
very young man indeed, Stephen is conscious of a
story and a poem; and a momentary rhyme catches
and fixes in his mind a connection of far-reaching importance for the novel. The little boy who crouches
under the kitchen table reciting

> Pull out his eyes,
> Apologize,
> Apologize,
> Pull out his eyes.

is memorizing a connection between guilt, submission, and weak eyesight, which, however irrational,
could sink deep into the mind of a sensitive child. The
power of words to hypnotize and fascinate is the
least of the things demonstrated in this abbreviated
scene, which looks forward to a whole series of demands for "submission," somehow connected with
weak eyesight and a bird which brings punishment
from on high. (Cf. Father Dolan's descent on blinded
Stephen [p. 53]; the demand of Heron that he "admit" [p. 91]; his bitter sense that sin comes through
the eyes [p. 161].)

At Clongowes too Stephen is shown to be permeated
by words and names. His own name is peculiar, and
he does not know "what kind of a name" it is (p. 3);
the word "belt" has a funny double meaning (pp.
3–4); and the word "suck" has ugly, fascinating con-
notations (p. 6). Before long the suggestive power
of words is leading Stephen to compose, within his
imagination, little romantic dramas in which he sees
himself dying, the bell tolling, farewell being said, a
melancholy poem being recited; and by a peculiar
sort of confirmation, the vision of his own funeral
(p. 22) is repeated in the outside world by the funeral
of Parnell (pp. 25–26; cf. also p. 104). This pattern
seems, perhaps, over-ingenious and arbitrary, but we
know from outside sources how strong was Joyce's

identification with Parnell, and within the novel this
pattern recurs often enough and pointedly enough
to have a serious claim on our attention. Words, for
Stephen Dedalus, have a way of creating things; he
thinks of the word, the symbol, first, then finds a
confirmation of its existence, its meaning, in the outside world, or at least in an experience. Note how,
though without the intervention of words, the green–
maroon dichotomy of Dante's hairbrushes (p. 2) is
confirmed in Fleming's coloring the earth green and
the clouds maroon: "he had not told Fleming to colour
them those colours. Fleming had done it himself"
(p. 11). The tolling over and over of the words "dark,"
"cold," "pale," and "strange" produces a vision of
Clongowes ghosts, specifically that Marshal Browne
who had died at Prague in 1757 (p. 16). Or again
the little song Stephen learned as a child:

> O, the wild rose blossoms
> On the little green place.

turns, in the presence of Father Arnall's division of
the class into Yorkists (white roses) and Lancastrians
(red roses) into a distortion, a vision of a new world.

> Lavender and cream and pink roses were beautiful to
> think of. Perhaps a wild rose might be like those colours
> and he remembered the song about the wild rose blos-
> soms on the little green place. But you could not have
> a green rose. But perhaps somewhere in the world you
> could. (p. 8)

The sequence of thought here is deliberately indirect.
Stephen's mind distorts the "natural" song into a pattern of words without referents, and finds in this
world of imagery a sudden refuge from practical reality. Words, we will find if we look a little further
ahead in the book,* are not simply passive or imita-

---

* Cf. p. 194 and the poem "The ivy whines upon the wall"
(p. 208).

tive devices for the artist; they are active tools with which he controls, modifies, and selects the raw materials of his life—and sometimes creating them.

A curious episode, involving another use of words, takes place while Stephen is in the infirmary at Clongowes (pp. 23–24). A boy named Athy points out to the slightly delirious Stephen that his name— Athy—is the name of a town, and then asks a riddle with a foolish answer: "Why is the county of Kildare like the leg of a fellow's breeches? . . . Because there is a thigh [Athy] in it." Then he tells Stephen you can ask the same riddle in another way. Stephen wants, mildly, to know what it is, but Athy won't tell, and he never does tell. Later, when there is trouble in the school because some of the older boys have run away, Athy again has something to say; he has the inside story, and he tells it, bit by bit, always holding something back. They were caught—in the square—with Simon Moonan and Tusker Boyle— smugging (p. 44). The point is not that this final word is a piece of insuperably recondite dialect, though plainly it is esoteric to young Stephen; it is the mysterious way in which language can be used to conceal as well as reveal (and the immense dimensions of a verbal mystery) which fascinates the embryo artist. And perhaps he is made aware, as well, that there are topics which society will not let us talk about distinctly—crevasses of conduct as well as of language, which open under our feet.

A special development of these early pages is Stephen's habit of cradling a traumatic experience in verbal swathings. The hypnotic use of adjectives in the account of Father Dolan's pandying is a small case in point; "hot," "burning," "stinging," "tingling," "crumpled," "flaming," "livid," "scalded," "maimed," "quivering," "fierce," "maddening," all occur in less than half a page (p. 54). Or again, and more precisely, the story of Wells who shouldered our hero

into the square ditch is told on p. 5, retold with more
moral commentary (always as an inner monologue)
on p. 10, and becomes a fantasy about rats, to be
evoked by the touch of the prefect's hand, on p. 19.
The little boy's feverish round-and-round thinking is
represented in this scene by fragments of imagery
repeated from previous episodes in the story, by the
disintegration of grammar itself, and the loss of logical control to the streaming of imagery:

> The face and the voice went away. Sorry because he
> was afraid. Afraid that it was some disease. Canker
> was a disease of plants and cancer one of animals: or
> another different. That was a long time ago then out on
> the playgrounds in the evening light, creeping from
> point to point on the fringe of his line, a heavy bird
> flying low through the grey light. Leicester Abbey lit
> up. Wolsey died there. The abbots buried him them-
> selves. (p. 19)

Placed in a new dramatic context, without grammar
to control it, the simile which had been perfectly
utilitarian and straightforward when used to describe
a flying football (p. 3) takes on a new and somber
coloring; it is the soul, Wolsey's or Stephen's, moving
through mists up and away.

These little details look trifling, but out of them a
number of the traits and attitudes of the fledgling
artist are shown to emerge. Stephen is a fondler, a
collector of words, with which he controls and in effect
creates his own universe (pp. 193–194, 207–208, 265–
266). He is acutely conscious of names and their
emblematic or symbolic import, he is an avid reader
of emblems and omens, through which he endeavors
to penetrate the veil of circumstance. He tends to
find these meanings, or at least to search for them,
in moments of fading consciousness, in dreams,
trances, and visions; his meditations are not ordered
and controlled, as by the *Spiritual Exercises,* they are
always tinged with personal emotion, and the truth

after which they reach is generally dim and fragmentary.

It is useful to see Stephen developing, on an almost pre-conscious level, the attitudes, not simply of an artist, but of a symbolist poet, because his actual artistic production, in the course of the book, is so scanty and dubious that some critics have thought him the butt of bitter ironic mockery. Indeed, he does very little artistic creating. It is a very literal-minded criticism, though, which insists on being introduced within the artist's workshop so that the authentic pangs of authentic genius can be duly studied and appreciated. We get this sort of thing from the purveyors of popular fiction about tormented titans. Joyce had too much sense and too much good taste to attempt such a display; so, for the most part, he limited his study to the development of those preliminary attitudes and affinities which go into the making of the artist. The creative act itself he left where it belongs—largely out of the picture; this is one more evidence of his basic respect for the artist.

A second major theme in the book, which interweaves with the theme of verbal manipulation and invention, is that of religion. From the beginning, the consciousness of Stephen Dedalus is dominated by the presence of the Church and its priests. Priests are kind and cruel, they comfort and they hurt, they bring the conscience to a shuddering state of dread, and they reward it with an ecstatic sense of purity. These are some of the first lessons which Stephen Dedalus learns about the Church, and behind all of them there is an immense sense of ecclesiastical power. Even when they are not physically present, priests dominate the scene, as at the Christmas dinner they decide one's future, they have influence (pp. though very much of this world and at ease human foibles (p. 94), they have immense another world which they use to rack, c order the human conscience. Above all, the Roman Church is for Stephen Dedalus a church of order and discipline; its images are all of control, coherence, perhaps limitation; he sets them against the disorder, misrule, and confusion of his father's house, of Ireland. As for the stages by which he grows into the Church and then out of it, they are not in fact very distinct. The retreat quickens into an overpowering sense of guilt a faith which had been, previously, routine and unquestioning; but the process of loss of faith is more vaguely represented. The devotions described at the beginning of Chapter IV are presented with more than a touch of malice as the manipulation of a gigantic spiritual cash register (p. 171), and seven pages of remote description suffice to bring Stephen through his access of religiosity, to the point where he finds it relatively easy to decline an offer to study for the priesthood. This refusal is made, we note, for peculiarly imagistic and impalpable reasons. The director making the offer, though he speaks gently and thoughtfully, stands against a brown crossblind, in a light that outlines his skull but leaves his face in shadow, and thus makes him seem sinister. At the moment of decision or something like it (p. 187), Stephen has a vision of a lean, embittered priest, "sourfavoured and devout, shot with pink tinges of suffocated anger"—one known sometimes as Lantern Jaws and sometimes as Foxy Campbell. These are scarcely theological arguments, but they are dramatic portents of considerable import to Stephen's intimate dialectic. Not that the theological arguments disappear wholly from view, but they are muffled. Stephen declines to take communion, as Cranly tells him, because he fears "that the host, too, may be the body and blood of the son of God and not a wafer of bread" (pp. 286–287). This seems more like a reason *for* taking the communion than for *not* doing so; Pascal would have interpreted it so. Evidently there

is a good deal of rather willful confusion here. Stephen
is fond of the "vesture of a doubting monk" (p. 205),
the appearance both of a heretic and an ascetic (p.
258), and he cultivates in the austerity of his style,
the dry assurance of his judgments, the manners of
the order whose central faith he has left behind.

This interplay of shadow and substance is particularly difficult to pin down in the *Portrait* because the
book itself is impressionistic in its technique. *Stephen
Hero* is less inhibited in dealing with specific ideas,
and more enlightening. Within its pages, Stephen
loses his faith in the traditional manner of adolescence,
with the aid of specific infidel arguments from Vol-
taire, Shelley, and Robert Ingersoll; he dwells at some
length on the familiar *topoi* of the village atheist. But
in its final form the book smoothed over these developments. Partly, no doubt, Joyce intended to make
Stephen a more remote and fascinating figure by
permitting him merely to enunciate conclusions instead of going through arguments; he is rendered
thereby more distinguished and impenetrable. But
partly also, it seems, Joyce did not want to dwell too
long on purely negative arguments against the Church.
For in this book, which seems so full of rejections (of
Church, family, nation, friends), nothing is ever
really rejected for good. Thus the Catholic Church,
rejected as a vocation for Stephen, is yet retained as
the exemplar of a new and private religion of which
Stephen will be both founder and priest. He will not
be a priest before the altar of the Christian god, but
a priest of the imagination; his ways not those of
order and discipline but those of "error and glory";
the emblem of his faith not the Virgin Mary who is
like the morning star, "bright and musical," but the
bird-girl of mortal beauty and profane joy. His transition from one affirmation to another is made through
an intermediate negation, but the continuity is there,
to be sensed. As we shall see below, a recurrent pat-

tern of the book is alternate expansion and contraction, unfolding and withdrawing.

Central to all the religions of Stephen Dedalus is the figure of a woman; and in the development of the artist, women play many, always important, roles. Eileen Vance is an early example of a girl rendered more glamorous by verbal associations from the Bible (p. 45). Mercedes, or her substitute, will introduce him to the "real world" (p. 71) of the Count of Monte Cristo; but those are momentary passions. The mysterious young lady to whom Stephen writes his Byronic poem (p. 77), who attends the Whitsuntide play (p. 85), and for whom he creates his villanelle (p. 261), but who is never given a proper introduction, has a less shadowy existence in *Stephen Hero*, where she is denominated by her full name, Emma Clery, instead of merely Emma or E.C. But in the *Portrait* proper, she seems very much a *princesse lointaine* whom Stephen does *not* touch (p. 77), does *not* speak to (p. 96), and to whom he does *not* send the villanelle (p. 261). Indeed, she does not, in her own person, say a single word in the book, though Stephen's diary, on the penultimate page of the novel, does record a few of her platitudes. A very ethereal figure, then; but it is by no means a merely platonic relation which Stephen Dedalus envisages with her. She is no Beatrice, and he no Dante. It is true that when he dreams—in an interval between sermons—of forgiveness and repentance, God seems "too great and stern" and the Blessed Virgin "too pure and holy," so he imagines Emma to be there (p. 132). But she is no saint or intercessor; she too has sinned, and they accept their forgiveness together, hand in hand.

Her forgiveness? It is a curious passage, for one had thought Emma too passive, too transitory, too evanescent a creature ever to sin. But perhaps it is partially explained by a late meditation of Stephen's:

A sense of her innocence moved him almost to pity her, an innocence he had never understood till he had come to the knowledge of it through sin, an innocence which she too had not understood while she was innocent or before the strange humiliation of her nature had first come upon her. Then first her soul had begun to live as his soul had when he had first sinned: and a tender compassion filled his heart as he remembered her frail pallor and her eyes, humbled and saddened by the dark shame of womanhood.

While his soul had passed from ecstasy to languor where had she been? Might it be, in the mysterious ways of spiritual life, that her soul at those same moments had been conscious of his homage? It might be. (pp. 261–262)

This odd passage, in which Stephen tries to bind his soul to Emma's through a shared guilt and shame, is confirmed in other imagery. He sees her explicitly as an image, a symbol of something outside herself,

a figure of the womanhood of her country, a batlike soul waking to the consciousness of itself in darkness and secrecy and loneliness, tarrying awhile, loveless and sinless, with her mild lover and leaving him to whisper of innocent transgressions in the latticed ear of a priest. (p. 259)

And in fact he remembers as "distorted reflections of her image" various girls of the country who had briefly attracted him. She is, then, despite or perhaps because of her slender claim on material reality, all the women of Ireland and he feels himself humiliated in her preference for a priest, or for the simple-minded Davin. Indeed, she identifies specifically with the woman of Davin's story, whom he had seen

as a type of her race and of his own, a batlike soul waking to the consciousness of itself in darkness and secrecy and loneliness and, through the eyes and voice and gesture of a woman without guile, calling the stranger to her bed. (p. 213)

And finally, she is the girl whom he imagines in the National Library as having an incestuous affair out of which comes the shriveled dwarf who reads Sir Walter Scott (p. 268). Here, specifically, she is Ireland, from whose corrupt yet innocent amours spring only degeneracy;* and Stephen wonders at one point how he can reach the conscience of the Irish gentry

> or how cast his shadow over the imaginations of their daughters, before their squires begat upon them, that they might breed a race less ignoble than their own? And under the deepened dusk he felt the thoughts and desires of the race to which he belonged flitting like bats, across the dark country lanes, under trees by the edges of streams and near the pool mottled bogs. A woman had waited in the doorway as Davin had passed by at night and, offering him a cup of milk, had all but wooed him to her bed: for Davin had the mild eyes of one who could be secret. But him no woman's eyes had wooed. (pp. 280–281)

Toward womankind in general, then, and toward Irish women in particular, Stephen Dedalus feels an essentially jealous attraction; they belong to, or are attracted to, somebody else (someone like his father, more often than not—the "smiling, welldressed priest" [p. 94] or Davin, who has "a good honest eye" [p. 296]), and he wants them to recognize his own special claims. One of these claims is shared sexual guilt; another is his role as "a priest of the eternal imagination, transmuting the daily bread of experience into the radiant body of everliving life" (p. 260). But these claims the women of Ireland will not recognize; their lives are filled with dark, secretive desires, flitting like bats through the night, and it is precisely his power with words, his impulse to make secret life conscious,

---

* Hence the immediate reference to "the Bantry gang" (p. 269). The implication of an incestuous little cabal is to be contrasted with Flood, Grattan, Bushe, the heroic figures of the past (p. 109).

which is for them his greatest deficiency. Stephen–
Joyce comes in this way to hate his own brain, which is
like an incubus, excluding him from a passionate, pre-
conscious life and world which he longs to enter; we
shall see more of this theme later in Joyce, and will
recognize its many affinities in late-nineteenth and
early-twentieth century literature as a whole.

The one girl for whom jealousy is not Stephen's
chosen mode of feeling is the radiant bird-girl whom
he sees wading in the pools of Clontarf strand; and she
is not, properly, a creature of this world at all. She is
a wild angel who silently invites him "to live, to err,
to fall, to triumph, to recreate life out of life" (p. 200);
and under her auspices Stephen drifts off into that
vision of a flower of light,

> breaking in full crimson and unfolding and fading to
> palest rose, leaf by leaf and wave of light by wave of
> light, flooding all the heavens with its soft flushes, every
> flush deeper than other. (p. 201)

Clearly the experience described in this image is to be
seen as supersensory. In a trance or waking dream,
Stephen is translated to "some new world" where the
blossoming of the rose takes place deep within his
mind. His first baby-song thus comes to fulfillment in
a special world, to be reached only in company with
a special bird-woman, who will fly and fall with one.
This is a mode of visionary writing, of imaginative
reaching out after the inexpressible and transcendent,
which Joyce can scarcely have viewed with much irony
since it directly suggests the path of his own future
literary development.

Though the "religion of women" of which Joyce
developed so idiosyncratic a version does not seem to
be subjected to ironic scrutiny, the lecture on esthetics
which occupies a fair part of Chapter V definitely is.
The genesis of this material reveals something of
Joyce's intentions. He had in fact lectured before the

College Literary Society on "Art and Life"; and *Stephen Hero* describes such a formal lecture, as well as the various responses to it of students and staff. Joyce had also proposed a large treatise on esthetics, which he took seriously enough to allow several years for its completion in an outline of his career. But in the *Portrait*, a public lecture would compromise Stephen's aloof disdain; and instead of heresies about Ibsen (which Joyce sensed would soon be dated), or theories of epiphany (such as he developed in *Stephen Hero*), our hero is allowed to discourse to Lynch on definitions of beauty and tragedy, with texts from Aristotle and St. Thomas. The conservative, almost academic nature of these discussions is the first thing that strikes us. A young man with the ideas attributed to Stephen might easily produce neo-classic tragedy or the chillier poems of Walter Savage Landor; it is hard to imagine him writing the "Villanelle of the Temptress." That poem is out of Swinburne, Austin Dobson, Lionel Johnson, Ernest Dowson, as one will, but it would have amazed the Blessed Thomas, no less than the Stagirite. No doubt there is dramatic impact in having Stephen's armored, critical self so remote from his sentimental self; it lends dramatic tension to his thinking to have it *not* all of a piece. Further, the gap suggests dramatically the degree to which his rational thinking is still tightly knotted in the chains of Catholicism—from which we shall see it, one day, burst forth. Thus, though it is a consistent and even an impressive esthetic, as far as it goes—particularly as contrasted with the cold lethargy shown to prevail elsewhere in Ireland—Stephen's esthetic is terribly limited. We feel it as a façade, and perhaps also as an offensive weapon, with which he does in, among others, the dean of studies. Finally, the discussion of the esthetic theory serves to bring out, between Stephen and his friends Lynch and Cranly, a relationship of which he is vaguely proud. They are his "whetstones"; he uses them to sharpen his ideas. But the felt life of the book is all around the esthetic theory, apart from it at all events; the theory neither contains any felt life of its own, nor offers any guide to the understanding of the life of this book. It is to be seen with a considerable measure of ironic distance, as a wooden sword in the hand of a fledgling artist.

More interesting, in some ways, than the ideas they discuss are the complex personal relations existing among the three young men. Both Lynch and Cranly accept positions of tacit inferiority to Stephen; they listen to his ideas but propose few of their own, advise and consult with him on the problems of his career but raise no question of their own destinies. Of Lynch we have merely a vague impression of something disagreeable—a reptilian look about the eyes, a whinnying laugh, a sardonic, street-corner cynicism. This character corresponds to some of the realities of Vincent Cosgrave and the name "Lynch," to which Cosgrave vigorously objected, adds other disagreeable overtones, for it was the name of a mayor of Galway who hanged his own son. Why then does Stephen select so unpromising a disciple as the vessel of his confidence? Partly, no doubt, to gain the impression of camaraderie among outcasts; Stephen must be shown to associate with the lively disreputables, not the good boys. Partly because of the abyss of tempers itself; Stephen must talk to an unlike in order to emphasize his independence of character. And finally, there is the perverse reason. Stephen is attracted to Lynch, and imposes upon him the relation of disciple to master, because he expects and wishes to be betrayed. It is by no means irrelevant to the *Portrait* that Lynch in *Ulysses* will take the part and perform the crucial action of Judas. This literary parallel is n imposed from the outside, it is consciously planne the characters themselves. Whether this does no the whole performance depressingly arch is question for the individual reader; there seems no doubt that Joyce counted on the parallel being felt and the intention being recognized.

Even more complex is the problem of Cranly, who is almost too elaborate a figure in the *Portrait* to come into clear focus. Stephen makes a habit of confessing to him, as to a priest; he gives no absolution (p. 207), but speaks on occasion as an advocate of convention and compromise, intent on reconciling Stephen to his family and to the Church (pp. 285, 289). At several moments Stephen suspects Cranly of "betraying" him with E.C. (pp. 273, 296); on other occasions Cranly offers an affection and devotion (p. 292), which, eked out with a phrase in *Ulysses* (p. 49, attributed to Wilde but actually by Lord Alfred Douglas), has caused some readers to think of a homosexual attachment.* Finally, Cranly is explicitly presented within the novel as a prototype of John the Baptist: Stephen envisions him as a decollated precursor (p. 207), and thinks of him as the son of Elizabeth and Zacchary (p. 293). All these pointers add up to a renunciation which is more than usually enigmatic (p. 289). Because Cranly felt the "sufferings of women, the weaknesses of their bodies and souls: and would shield them with a strong and resolute arm and bow his mind to them"—therefore "it is time to go." Stephen hears a voice in his lonely heart "telling him that his friendship was coming to an end. Yes; he would go. He could not strive against another. He knew his part." His part is evidently that of the sensitive, suffering outcast, but it seems very much like an elected part. For why Cranly's possession of normal human sen-

nterpreted as a challenge, the effect
Stephen away, is not clear.

not intended to be; for in following
e "strange dark cavern of speculation"
lances (p. 207) and from which he then
rt to tantalize, to suggest mystery with-
ut the grounds for it, is obvious.

by
make
critical

his vocation as an artist, Stephen is represented as committing an act of folly and imprudence (pp. 188, 264) involving not only solitude (p. 292) but the deliberate acceptance of error, failure, catastrophe. This is not simply the conventional worldly wisdom about practical aspects of an artistic career. Literary creation for Joyce (and for Stephen) is an act of self-abandonment, an act of trust in one's intuitions, which goes beyond common sense or prudence. This is one reason why the figure of Simon Dedalus, who seems to be rejected so categorically in the body of the *Portrait*, comes unexpectedly back in the book's final sentence, to be invoked as a patron of flight. (If we are in doubt that he is really meant here, we may turn to *Ulysses* [p. 572], where in a crucial moment of fantasy he is shown encouraging Stephen to fly.) The prodigal bankrupt is for Joyce an emblem of the creative artist; he is bound to be a failure in the worldly sense, because his mind gives itself to lavish, impractical things, rather than to severe, get-ahead concerns. The artist is always winning Pyrrhic victories and the symbolic expression of his over-reaching is an attempt to fly which involves not only the risk, but the certainty, of falling.

The idea that literary creation is a form of mantic prophecy is older than Plato, and was particularly common in the nineteenth century as a reaction to scientism; Shelley and Yeats expressed the idea explicitly, Baudelaire, Nerval, and Mallarmé—among others—accepted it. In Ireland, the memory of the Druids and the social tradition of the bards lent primitive support to it; and Joyce was not alone, or even exceptional, in giving a sort of wishful credence to it. Especially after the Oscar Wilde scandals there was added to it the idea that the artist, because of his prophetic gift, is doomed to be an outcast, a deviant, and ultimately a sacrificial victim. Finally, all these metaphors were sharpened and given new force in

Joyce's mind by the circumstance that acceptance of an artistic calling meant for him rejection of a priestly vocation. The words *Non serviam,* spoken by Lucifer, prefigured his fall; the same words, spoken by Stephen–Joyce out of no less egotistical a pride, point toward an even more conscious catastrophe. And of course, Lucifer's fall, like Adam's, may carry with it the connotation of a sexual lapse. This intricate network of associations, which looks perverse but which is deeply rooted in turn-of-the-century moods, did much to color the idea of an artistic calling, as the *Portrait* presents it, in lurid and almost apocalyptic tints.

The imagery of flight is one of the most apparent and impressive of the devices by which Joyce invokes the great tradition of artistic inspiration. The original Dedalus was a flyer on artificial wings, as well as a maker of mazes; and Stephen, at the moment of his first dedication to the calling, feels his soul "soaring in an air beyond the world" and resolves to "create proudly out of the freedom and power of his soul, as the great artificer whose name he bore, a living thing, new and soaring and beautiful, impalpable, imperishable" (pp. 196–197). The first thing he creates, it will be observed, is a flying soul, an artificial creative personality; flight is thus turned inward, for Stephen is to do no soaring through outer space. The world through which he ventures is himself, and the process of flight suggests also abandonment and immersion. In a famous passage Stephen pauses on the steps of the National Library to take augury of the future with the aid of birds (pp. 264–265). Recalling some verses by Yeats, he finds his omen. The real inspiration here is occult and the deliberately vague, streamy prose (not very remote from the fag-end slackness of the "Ithaca" section of *Ulysses*) suggests a kind of sagging into a world below consciousness, where one

neither believes nor disbelieves but simply accepts
what is found there:

> A phrase of Cornelius Agrippa flew through his mind
> and then there flew hither and thither shapeless
> thoughts from Swedenborg on the correspondence of
> birds to things of the intellect and of how the creatures
> of the air have their knowledge and know their times
> and seasons because they, unlike man, are in the order
> of their life and have not perverted that order by reason.
> (p. 264)

One flies into the world of spirit, thoughts fly through
one, and this whole sequence of reflected, undefined
associations (in which, for example, the mind does not
even bother to catch or define in any way that "phrase
of Cornelius Agrippa") could not be less like the
rigid, categorical Stephen Dedalus of the lecture on
esthetics. The clenched fist of logic has opened into
the nerveless, receptive palm of inspiration; and this,
though it is flight, is also a sort of simultaneous fall.

The flying metaphor is, in fact, a little too ecstatic,
and too incapable of development to serve Joyce very
well as a sustained metaphor for creativity. One notes
that during the composition of the villanelle, flight
largely gives place to incarnation as the central metaphor. But in the crannies and crevices, where it can
appear as metaphoric decoration, the imagery of birds
and flight recurs in a variety of guises which it will
suffice simply to list. "Wild geese" are expatriate Irishmen on the Continent, usually there because of mili-
tant opposition to the English, so Stephen's calling
Davin one of the "tame geese" is an interesting re-
versal of roles, as well as an indirect prophecy.
"Heron" is a potential rival in flight, who not only has
a bird's name but looks like a bird (p. 84). And
Stephen, when stricken with remorse over his sus-
picions of E.C., wonders if her life is not "simple and
strange as a bird's life," her heart "simple and wilful

as a bird's heart" (p. 254). In all these uses of avian imagery, Joyce may be drawing on that notion, which so impressed Yeats, that birds, because they know the songs, nesting habits, and migratory patterns characteristic of their species, even when they have been brought up in complete isolation, are the vessels of a knowledge infused from outside. But again the notion cannot be pushed too far, not because it is inherently improbable (as of course it is) but because in prose fiction it is not dramatically viable.

When we look at the inner structure of the *Portrait,* in fact, we find it controlled less by developing metaphors than by a number of deliberate repetitions and an overall pattern of alternating expansion and contraction. The repetitions are not, necessarily, incremental; if one takes as an example the scene of Stephen's tramway farewell to E.C. on p. 76, one finds several sentences of it and many scattered smaller phrases repeated on p. 261; here Stephen is simply reliving an experience, or recreating it through incantation. (One of its side-effects is to suggest that the original experience was itself largely verbal, as the "day of dappled seaborne clouds" on pp. 193–194 is largely a verbal, rather than a climatological, experience.) Elsewhere, phrases about the "batlike soul" of Irish womanhood, which Stephen first conceives at the end of Davin's story (p. 213) are repeated with reference to E.C. on p. 259, and this not only generalizes her role, but makes us aware that formulas learned in one situation serve Stephen as windows to open upon the truth of another. Still more interesting is the series of variations played on Stephen's experience of celestial music, which he hears in various circumstances, to various effects (pp. 116, 192, 194–195, 254). Sometimes the music is the vehicle of a message, sometimes the prelude of one; it comes from another world, beyond the world, and also from within himself. All this apart from the way in which a vague premonition of failure connected with Mike Flynn (p. 67) recurs in connection with his father's social and business failures (p. 72); or the fact that when he is with that always-interesting E.C., he hears what her eyes say to him and knows "that in some dim past, whether in life or revery, he had heard their tale before" (p. 76). The multiplicity of these repetitions and verbal parallels gives to existence as represented in the *Portrait* the quality of a palimpsest; every experience is written over some other experience, and colors as it is colored by it.

As for the expansion–contraction movement of the book, it has something to do with Joyce's prose style and something also to do with the motion of Stephen's mind. Here as elsewhere Joyce's style varies from a florid, adjectival lyricism to a hard, detailed, unrhythmic prose of deliberate meanness. On the whole, the former rhetoric has not worn as well as the latter, and there is something downright embarrassing about some of Stephen's ecstatics. Some critics have tried to redeem the weak passages by discovering irony behind them. But one can be too kind to Joyce; he does not need this sort of special pleading. There are flaws of taste in the *Portrait,* and one of them, I think, is an occasional over-lushness. But the more basic alternation of the book is dramatic—it lies in the ebb and flow of Stephen's mind, which he himself compares, in an interesting simile, to the spreading and unspreading of an equation, the folding and contraction of a peacock's tail. His soul, he thinks, goes forth to experience, "unfolding itself sin by sin, spreading abroad the balefire of its burning stars and folding back upon itself, fading slowly, quenching its own lights and fires. They were quenched: and the cold darkness filled chaos" (p. 116). The passage is built, by the sort of repetitive expansion noted above, on an earlier one in which Stephen identifies his soul with the cold and lonely cycles of Shelley's moon (p. 108).

There is no problem in applying this passage to Stephen Dedalus' various sentimental ventures—to his successive enthusiasms and disillusions for father, Parnell, Ireland, mother, God, Mercedes, E.C., and the ideal of good fellowship. He is a young man of great enthusiasms and bitter disillusions; and no reader will have trouble tracing the alternation of these moods through the *Portrait*. (We note in passing how this alternation fulfills the image set up by the train passing through tunnels and across open spaces, alternately, in the very first pages of the book.) But for Stephen at least his moods are not just moods. They are part of a process by which the mind journeys to the outermost stars and back, and into the worst corruptions of human nature—both forms of self-testing and self-exploration, variations of perspective which extinguish themselves in "a cold indifferent knowledge of himself" (p. 117). The cyclical motion of his mind is imitated both in the repetitions and the variations of the book—in its spreading out and drawing back and turning upon itself. Always the terminus is that cold indifferent knowledge of self. And under this aspect it is permissible to see not only Stephen's plunges into sin, but his ventures into religion and art—and, of course, *a fortiori* the *Portrait* itself—as attempts at self-confrontation. Narcissus presides over almost all phases of Stephen's career, and under this aspect it is certainly open to more than one ironic glance. (One recalls particularly the way Stephen's first effort at poetic creation, the Byronic verses to E.C., ends with a long gaze into the mirror in his mother's bedroom [p. 78].) So seen, the *Portrait* does not end on a note of triumphant flight at all. Stephen, as he departs for the Continent, all high resolve and abnegation, is more in bondage than ever to his own personality. He is swinging in wider and wider arcs of speculation and self-dissection, alternating like the

moon between "sad human ineffectualness" and "vast
inhuman cycles of activity" (p. 108). But he is just as
much like the "barren shell of the moon" on p. 299 as
he was on p. 108.

It is particularly useful to see the *Portrait* as ending
in this way—if one can do so without casting ultimate
doubts on the authenticity of the young man's calling
—because it prepares us to see, in *Ulysses*, a Stephen
Dedalus still very much in bondage. To what extent
Ulysses is an escape from the dilemma of Stephen's
character and a solution to the problem of self-knowl-
edge, to what extent simply a magnification of it, is a
question to which the reader will no doubt address
himself if he reads the next chapter. Meanwhile, let us
summarize, provisionally enough, the achievement of
the *Portrait*. Though generally classified, on the basis
of its theme, as a *Bildungsroman* (or novel of a young
person's development and self-discovery), it occupies
a position within the genre so peculiar that perhaps it
should not be placed there at all. *Wilhelm Meister*, *A
Sentimental Education*, *Richard Feverel*, and *The Way
of All Flesh* all describe the growth of souls in counter-
point with circumstances—but more or less pica-
resquely, episodically, without the inwardness
achieved by Joyce. They do not, in the end, have anything more than a skeletal similarity with the *Portrait*.
A slightly closer parallel might be found in J. P.
Jacobsen's *Niels Lyhne*, a story of deepening unbelief,
alienation, and ineffectuality, and here too we find a
jeweled, meticulous prose style which points us toward
the major achievement of Joyce's fiction. His prose
narrative is as artfully modulated and richly woven as
a lyric poem. Its psychology is neither crystal clear
nor very profound; its social observation is deliberately
sketchy. But its rendering of crucial instants of experience, its weaving together of mood, circumstance,
and imagery, its skilled control of narrative rhythms

and those shorter rhythms associated with sentences and paragraphs, finally its bold psychological mobility —all these qualities made it essentially a new sort of novel. After half a century, its power to fascinate (especially, I think, the sensitive and the young) has not yet failed.

CHAPTER III

ULYSSES

The germ of *Ulysses* was, as we have seen, a short story projected for *Dubliners*. It would be nice to think that this germ swelled to epic dimensions in the darkness and gloom of World War I, as the equivalent germs of *A la Recherche du Temps Perdu* and *Der Zauberberg* actually did, but this cannot be claimed. The first time we hear about *Ulysses* after it has ceased to be a short story, it is already an epic; it covers one day in the life of Dublin, has two main protagonists, Stephen and Bloom, and is divided into 18 episodes arranged 3–12–3. (The first three are the "Telemachiad," the last three the "Nostos.") In all respects, its outline appears just about as it is in the book we possess. In the seven years of its composition, Joyce filled it out with an extraordinary plethora of details, and this process (for what it is worth) can be traced, but he did not change its skeletal structure in any major way.

Before we attempt to talk about the book's structure or vital energies, it may be well to pose, and try to

answer, a few obvious questions about external oddities—questions which may take a little of the strange-
ness off our approach to it.

How should Ulysses *be read?* In the first place,
boldly, as one reads Milton. One's first time through
there is no reason to stickle or hesitate unduly over
the distinction between what one understands and
what one doesn't. Inevitably, there are hundreds of
thematic interconnections that will be missed, references which will fail to come clear, episodes the full
meaning of which will emerge only later in the book,
if at all. No matter, read on. "Proteus" is about as
knotty a swatch of pages as one will get in the book
until perhaps the end of "Oxen of the Sun." A proper
reader will go over or through or around the passage,
as Milton's Satan, with satanic persistence,

O'er bog or steep, through strait, rough, dense, or rare,
With head, hands, wings, or feet pursues his way.

On the other side of the boggy patches, there is always
relatively solid ground. If one is worried about the
complexities of Homeric and symbolic correspondence, the table from Stuart Gilbert's *James Joyce's
Ulysses* (reproduced below as Appendix B, p. 221)*
is really all the apparatus one needs, and is useful in
setting one's mind at rest. It contains a lot of symbolic
correspondences in capsule form. But one doesn't, and
shouldn't try, to read the book the first time for its
symbolic correspondences. It isn't to be read for its
story either, for it is epic in its leisure and amplitude.
Like Rabelais and Swift, Joyce is enormously fond of
digression as a narrative device. But though it doesn't
lay out a straight story-line, *Ulysses* does grow, expand, move, and so it must be read for a sense of its
spacious, copious, serio-comic invention before it is

* An expanded and not wholly consistent version of this
chart appears in Marvin Magalaner's *A James Joyce Miscellany
Second Series* (Carbondale, Ill.: Southern Illinois University
Press, 1959), facing p. 48.

investigated as a double-crostic. Like all good books, *Ulysses* profits by being read aloud—alas, it is too long and (be it confessed) in parts too dull for a full-scale performance. But parts of "Cyclops," or "Sirens," or "Penelope," or even "Lestrygonians" which looked impenetrable on the page will open up miraculously to the intelligence of the ear. I don't want to promise too much; there are permanent dark spots in the book, requiring not just careful attention but special knowledge. When one is hooked on Joyce, these problems become familiar, everyday preoccupations—when one of them is solved, the experience is like losing an old friend. But that comes later. For the first run through, the rule is: Read boldly on. Look to right and left as much as you can, but without impeding forward progress to the end. Then and only then, go back to what puzzled or distracted you. Mark Pattison said that an appreciation of Milton was the last reward of consummated scholarship; reading Joyce is the last reward of a less-easily-defined education. But it is also— or can be for certain adventurous temperaments—a comic delight, a revelation of the possibilities of the language, and an experience of the world transfigured. This last point will get further explanation.

Why did Joyce use stream-of-consciousness techniques so freely in Ulysses? The stream-of-consciousness method in fiction aims to bring the reader into the direct presence of a character's thought-processes, in all their tumultuous, indiscriminate complexity. There is a kind of realism about it for, as we know, people do not think very much of the time in complete, well-directed, logically-linked literary sentences. On the other hand, no printed record could possibly represent fully the multiple irrelevancies, inarticulate or semi-articulate impulses, and shadings of mood or association which make up a single instant of our conscious life. Joyce's stream-of-consciousness style is a compromise between traditional literary prose (as in

Jane Austen, for example, or Sir Walter Scott) and the absolute chaos which a stream-of-consciousness method would certainly bring about if rigorously applied.

The dangers of the method Joyce averted by applying it inconsistently. We never get so deeply into a consciousness that we do not have available occasional crutches of exterior fact, conveyed to us in the traditional manner of a third-person narrator. There are, moreover, only three or four consciousnesses into which we enter—Stephen's, Bloom's, Molly's, and (briefly) Mr. Tom Kernan's. "Cyclops" takes full advantage of the flavor of a nameless narrator, and uses the inflections of his voice to good effect; but he isn't a full-fledged character so much as an articulate point of view. So too with the "marmalady drawersy" narrative voice of the first half of "Nausicaa" and with the multiple stylistic tonalities of "Oxen of the Sun." Joyce does not allow himself to become the slavish recorder of any consciousness. By moving into and out of consciousnesses, by combining them, attenuating them, and, on occasion, dismissing them altogether, he succeeds in retaining the artist's traditional power to direct, select, pattern, and modify for deliberate dramatic effect the materials of his novel.

The advantages he draws from stream-of-consciousness are, in considerable degree, those associated with the traditional novelist's manipulation of point-of-view. Experience filtered through a special style of mind or quality of vision may take on dramatic values; something as simple as imperception may be revelatory, at the same time, of a character and his circumstances. Conflicts develop easily and naturally, without the need of authorial editorializing. Stephen, Bloom, and Molly, for instance, often have interestingly different views of the same events. Joyce is also able to show, by means of stream-of-consciousness, extraordinary dimensions of experience. Under different cir-

cumstances and in different people's minds, Stephen
Dedalus can be analogous to Telemachus, Icarus,
Charles Stewart Parnell, Rudy Bloom, Harry Mulvey,
a lapwing, a stray dog which Bloom once brought
home, and so on indefinitely. If this complex, analogy-
ridden vision seems to dissolve "real reality" and reduce things—things in themselves—to shadows, types,
analogies, a mere bundle of relationships, that is part
of Joyce's intent. (That the Newtonian universe of
solid matter was dissolving, during Joyce's lifetime,
into the Einsteinian universe of energy and relativity,
may be only a coincidence, but it is an interesting
coincidence.) Joyce saw human history as a perpetual,
cyclical repetition of the same events; on a vast scale,
on a tiny scale, the law of life for him was eternal return. The special advantage of stream-of-consciousness
is that it permits him to describe parallel events from
near and far, from past, present, and future, as simultaneously active in a character's mind.

Why does Ulysses *limit itself to the city of Dublin
and the events of June 16, 1904?* Two reasons, one
public, one private. June 16, 1904 was a perfectly ordinary, commonplace day, and one of Joyce's points
was that in a small, random cycle of life in a single
random city, one could see everything. The modern
epic is not, and cannot be, simply of "heroic" dimensions; it has to be a true epic and a mock epic at the
same time. Joyce, who had a special devotion to the
idea of prophetic insight through a deep reading of
the translucent present and deeply-layered past, chose
to deal with a severely-limited time and place in an
effort to give his materials universal significance.
From this point of view, the more arbitrary his self-
imposed limitations, the better. The private reason for
picking June 16, 1904 was that on this day—as closely
as we can specify such an indefinite event—James
Joyce fell in love with Nora Barnacle. There is a great
deal of Joyce the married man in Bloom and a great

deal of Nora in Molly; more largely, the discovery of a kindred soul, a kindred sinner, and a free, trusting companion "made a man" of Joyce. The shackles which bound Stephen Dedalus in the *Portrait* have twisted even more tightly about him in *Ulysses*; Bloom, however (for good as well as for evil), is free. One of the big differences between Stephen and Bloom is Molly. Hence the radical importance of "her" day.

Why is Bloom a Jew and the center of Ulysses, *whereas Stephen is more or less peripheral?* First, Bloom is Jewish because Joyce, as an artistic outcast and voluntary exile, identified with the Jews; their status as special vessels of divine purpose and their long history of pariah treatment correspond with the conditions of the artist. Second, Bloom is Jewish because Joyce was anti- as well as pro-Semitic, and thought the Jews, because they crucified Christ, were doomed to be wanderers on the face of the earth under a cloud of guilt. Bloom's burden of Jewish guilt was useful in suggesting a burden of personal as well as a much wider human guilt, of which Joyce wanted to make use in his novel. Third, Bloom is Jewish because Joyce, who was passionately interested in the *Odyssey* and its scholarship, knew a book by Victor Bérard offering to prove that Odysseus was a Phoenician, i.e., a Semite, the nearest Dublin equivalent of which would be a Jew. Fourth, Bloom is a Jew because in an eclectic, commercial civilization he represents Everyone. He is not even a real Jew, having long ago left the faith of his fathers, but has picked up scraps and pieces of cultural information, misinformation, superstition, and observance from the entire rubbish-heap of history. He is a fouled well of thought. Finally—though one could go on—Bloom is a Jew because the book is to represent the dialectic of the Greek and Jewish spirits, and Bloom as a Jew is a soft, slack, unknowing vehicle of inspiration, as opposed to Stephen who is a hard, thin knifeblade of rationality. And this distinction brings us close to the reason for the relative positioning of the characters in the book. Bloom's is a gelatinous but translucent mind, Stephen's an inflexible and opaque one. Joyce found he could do more interesting things with Bloom's ordinary mind (through which extraordinary ideas could be allowed to pass) than with Stephen's narrow, unusual one (which was committed to being conscious of its own achievements). And in fact the *Odyssey* had already showed him that Odysseus was more interesting than Telemachus, besides committing him to make his Odysseus a central figure in the story.

Why is Bloom an advertising solicitor? Because John Stanislaus Joyce, Teodoro Mayer (publisher of *Il Piccolo della Sera*), and still another of Bloom's originals, the man whose direct representative in *Ulysses* is C. P. M'Coy, had all been advertising solicitors. Because the art/trade of puff and publicity is a characteristic art/trade of modern society, involving cleverness but not creativity, a cliché-ridden mind and a measure of petty shrewdness, a smattering of all subjects and a mastery of none. Because it is performed under the auspices of the business, rather than the editorial, department. Because it is a peripatetic, semi-bourgeois, sub-literary, pseudo-business kind of a job, entirely suitable for a small-time conniver like Bloom.

Why is the book written in so many different styles, with a new one for each of the 18 episodes and several distinct ones, on occasion, within an episode? Because the essential character of the book is parodic. Joyce saw history as developing in a series of never-ending cycles, each of which picked up, repeated, and transformed materials left over from previous cycles; so that for him parody was the texture of ordinary existence. Consciously or not, life was always parodying its own previous forms. But it was always changing them too, and therefore, this book, in which all human life (according to the epic formula) is to be subsumed, must both change and vary its style, while maintaining a steady ground bass of repetition. Like the *Portrait*, it involves the continual expansion and contraction of an equation, a growth of vision, an exhaustion of vision, things seen over and over again, and at last seen through. Therefore, 18 or 24 different styles—which also (let us be frank) give Joyce a chance to display virtuosity. But now let us start with the book itself.

Thursday, June 16, 1904: it is two years, one month, and nineteen days since the ending of the *Portrait*. Stephen Dedalus has been abroad in Paris, studying P.C.N.—*physiques, chimiques et naturelles*—from which hungry exercise he has been recalled by the news that his mother is dying. He has returned, she has implored him to pray by her bedside, he has refused, she has died; and at the moment of the book's opening, he is lingering in the Martello Tower in Sandymount with Mulligan–Gogarty and Haines–Trench, teaching carelessly in the Dalkey School, idling, drinking, and biding his time. His soul is afflicted with lethargy; he is neither in his father's house nor in a house of his own, and the slow, cold torpor of his inner being is revealed in his languid, sullen gestures. We have a sense of great energy lying dormant. Yeats spoke beautifully of these first three episodes as revealing a cruel, catlike mind, yawning and stretching and getting ready to spring.

On the whole, the prose of the first section is classic, third-person narrative prose. There are occasional sections (for example, p. 7, ll. 21–33) when we disappear into Stephen's mind to trace a stream of his associations and recollections. But these passages are placed within a clearly-defined context of exterior experience, and we have little difficulty following them. Perhaps a little more troubling is a phrase like "agenbite of inwit" which occurs without explanation or preparation on p. 16, ll. 7–8, and again on p. 17, l. 3, as well as later in the book several times. It is the title of a treatise by Dan Michel of Northgate (about 1340); the subject of the treatise and the meaning of the phrase is "remorse of conscience." In *Ulysses* it first occurs in a discussion of washing and is followed by the words "Yet here's a spot," which might well be recognized as coming from *Macbeth,* Act V, Scene 1, the scene in which Lady Macbeth goes through the motions of washing her hands in an attempt to remove the guilt of Duncan's blood.

This passage is a microcosm of many others in *Ulysses.* A discussion which has a perfectly simple literal meaning on the surface develops, in Stephen's mind or on its own, a sudden set of symbolic or at least general overtones. Washing off dirt equals washing off guilt, and because Stephen's conscience is dirty, he refuses to indulge in the exterior rite. (He is hydrophobic for other reasons too but, in the specific passage on p. 16, this one chiefly is operative.) Some critics have complained that a dirty hero does not attract our sympathy in very copious measure; but Stephen is not the hero of this book, and he is not intended to attract our sympathy here. He is dirty, therefore, within and without. Why, then, do the words "agenbite of inwit" recur on p. 17, while Mulligan is rummaging in his trunk after clean clothes? Because, for one thing, he has just returned Stephen's handkerchief, which he has never referred to except as a "noserag" or "snotrag," and is now calling for a "clean handkerchief" for himself. His handkerchief is clean, but Stephen's is dirty, and what has soiled it is "the green sluggish bile" which his mother vomited in her death agony. Not only so, but the sea before him is a "dull green mass of liquid" equivalent to the same deadly stain—that sea which Mulligan had merrily referred to as "a grey sweet mother, the snot-green sea" (p. 5). All this complex of associations, with sea, green, liquid, mother, and dirty handkerchiefs lies behind the repetition of "agenbite of inwit" on p. 17; and while it need not be spelled out in complete exegetical detail as one reads along, the character of the book is partly determined by the sensed presence of this network, and others like it, under the smooth surface.

Let us, then, pick from among the elements of this first episode those which seem to have clear symbolic import—not that any ultimate meaning for the novel resides in them, but simply in order to see some of the ways in which Joyce manages to build up a layered series of surfaces. For instance, Mulligan's bowl of lather on which are crossed a mirror and a razor is surely more than a collection of toilet articles; it is emblematic of the religion of art, the razor for dissection, the mirror for truthful reflection, and the lather perhaps representing the bubbles of soft soap, blarney, fraud, and falsity. The old lady who brings the milk is Ireland, and so specified on pp. 13–14: "Silk of the kine and poor old woman, names given her in old times." There is careful irony in the fact that she does not understand Gaelic, though an Englishman has learned it (p. 14). The tower is said to be the *"omphalos,"* that is, the navel of the world, where all sorts of prophetic insights into its total nature can be obtained. Stephen surrenders the key to the tower at Mulligan's request, against his own will; it is not only the key to his home, and to Ireland, but also the emblem of his own manhood and masculinity. When he has given it up, he turns against Mulligan the bitter and resentful word which closes the section: "Usurper."

Stephen's property relations are symbolically complex; he lends Mulligan money from his earnings at the school (p. 11), he gives him the key to a tower on which he has paid the rent (p. 23), but he accepts gifts of secondhand clothes from Mulligan (p. 6), grubs cigarettes from Haines (p. 20), and submits to being treated as a scrounger at the breakfast table. "You have eaten all we left, I suppose," says Mulligan (p. 17); Stephen will later remember these words with bitter accuracy (p. 214). None of these dealings make much practical sense (you can't borrow money from a man who owes money to you; that transaction is called "repayment"), but the secondhand clothes are emblematic of humiliation, the borrowing of drink-money of parasitism, and the cigarette-scrounging of shameful dependence. Haines, whose name will later be seen to have close connections with the French word for "hate," is an Irishman's Englishman, cold, prudent, a ruler of the waves, wealthy but ungenerous, and ready enough to "make a collection of [someone else's] sayings" (pp. 4, 7, 16, 17, 18–19). His worst crime is a calm, hypocritical "fairness" which robs victims even of their right to hate. His silver cigarette case has a green stone in it, which is of course Ireland (pp. 19–20). The drowned man of whom there is talk toward the middle of p. 21 later becomes, by an act of imaginative identification, Stephen himself, who is afraid of drowning (p. 46), would not risk drowning to save a stranger (as Mulligan did), thinks his mother drowned and his sister is trying to drown him (pp. 45–46, 243), and sees a drowned dog which he refers to by Mulligan's special name for him, "dogsbody" (p. 46).

All this suggests—what is clearly as true of Joyce as it is of Yeats—that the best commentary on any given passage in *Ulysses* is likely to be another passage in the novel. Though it could be made more useful than it is, the *Word Index to James Joyce's Ulysses* is an indispensable tool for the second and third readings of the book because it enables one to trace verbal themes back and forth. This implies, I am afraid, that the book must be read backwards as well as forwards;

there is no way out of this, it is a necessity of full appreciation. The book also demands to be read with an alert eye for the literary reference and the buried quotation. No doubt we shall some day have an annotated *Ulysses*, but in the meanwhile it is every man for himself, and the requirements are considerable. Not only are English, French, and Italian literature laid under frequent contribution, but one must have some memory of popular songs, operas, recitation-pieces, pantomimes, early twentieth-century comic strips, and other bits and fragments of the vulgar culture. Inevitably, one misses a good deal; this is a condition of reading the book; one of the burdens it imposes on its reader is that of patience in the face of incomprehension. On the other hand, a hard-earned comprehension is often particularly exhilarating. Finally, one must be prepared to take the book on whatever level it seems to work best at the moment. It is not a smooth-surface, high-gloss book. Like life itself, as James Joyce saw it, its surface is now rough and pitted, now seamed with chasms, it suggests many meanings, and commits itself unequivocally to few. Perhaps these conditions of approach make the book sound forbidding; *mutatis mutandis*, they hold for one's approach to almost any imaginative universe, Dante's as well as Joyce's; the real way to become free of such a universe is to jump in and start navigating.

Following our own advice, we come to the second section of the book, "Nestor" (pp. 24–36), which is not too unlike the first in consistency. The alert reader will be aware of Mr. Deasy, follower of races, as a Homeric parallel to old Nestor, tamer of horses, visited by Telemachus. He will observe the shells and pieces of old money, emblems of history's abandoned forms. The story of Pyrrhus, scamped over by Stephen's lackadaisical teaching, is one of these shells, a ghost story of the last lost valiant stand of the Greek spirit against Roman materialism. Pyrrhus is in fact a pier, a disappointed bridge which never succeeded in reaching across the flowing nightmare of history. In Mr. Deasy, that ravaged shell of a man, is represented a case of genuine mental imbalance, a set of violent and confused prejudices out of the dead historical past. He is, quite literally, the nightmare from which Stephen is trying to awake. (This is clearly an ironic Nestor—as, it may well be, was Homer's.) Finally, the reader will note the peculiarly opaque riddle offered by Stephen for the entertainment of his class, and will, perhaps, be gratified to know that it is a shaggy-dog riddle, traditionally asked in this form and with no answer other than the one Stephen gives it. This is the first of several Dedalian opacities in the early stages of the book, which set him up against Bloom's translucency, but are not to be understood except as expressions of his own bleakly negative attitudes.

These first two sections establish Stephen as increasingly isolated from friends, from the traditions of his land, from women, family, history, Church, students, work, and from his own powers of independent decision and action. The next section brings us within the lonely tower of his head and as it is more complexly-wrought and elaborately-patterned than the others, it merits a special measure of exegetical attention.

Broadly, then, the third episode of *Ulysses* (pp. 37–51), titled "Proteus" in Joyce's outline though nowhere in the book proper, describes the ruminations of Stephen Dedalus as he walks by the shore of Dublin Bay, south of the Liffey mouth on the beach that stretches toward Sandymount. Stephen's opening thoughts have to do with the nature of perception, and the rather formidable phrase, "Ineluctable modality of the visible" with which he begins is defined nicely on p. 186 by "Space: what you damn well have to see." Objects, as Aristotle tells us in *De Sensu*, must be perceived in space, sounds must be heard in time. But Stephen is thinking not only of seeing objects, but of seeing into and past objects, of things as signatures written by an enigmatic intelligence. A major theme of the section is disguise; things are not what they appear to be on the surface, but have to be sought behind the veil. Physical sight may merely limit and confuse authentic insight. Stephen experiments with this notion on the beach, shutting his eyes in order to intuit reality with his ashplant/augur's wand; the shells he is walking on, in addition to being the forms of history and money, are now words, and the rhythm of his walking across them produces a momentary line of verse. But it is scarcely divination, and he opens his eyes again, to be reassured by the discovery that the world is still there.

The sight of two midwives produces a fantasy of reaching back through time on a chain of linked navel-cords to Eden itself—where one might hold a telephone conversation with Adam and Eve. As the parents of the human race, they remind Stephen of his own parents, and also of the great theological debates between Arius and Athanasius on the relation between Son and Father. (Athanasius held the Son to be consubstantial with the Father while Arius, in a limited measure, denied it). Since Stephen is much occupied with establishing a relation to a father, the topic is of immediate concern. He pauses in his walk, to think whether he is heading toward his Aunt Sara's (she is actually Joyce's Aunt Josephine, who lived in Sandymount with his Uncle Willie Murray), and in his mind's eye relives a previous visit (pp. 38–39). But this actual, seedy family of his is no resource; he thinks of Swift's misanthropy and (via the fact that Swift was a clergyman) of the life of the priesthood as an alternative to the disorder of "his father's house." But after running quickly through a metaphysical joke about hypostasis (where is the Holy Ghost when Mass is said simultaneously at two opposite ends of the same cathedral?), he recognizes, in a parody of Dryden's words to Swift, that he will never be a saint. Among his youthful follies, he recalls the epiphanies; and as if to exemplify the epiphanic method, the present scene intrudes itself—an empty porterbottle stands stogged in the sand, emblem of Irish thirst and paralysis, while the hollow shells of the beach, from which all life has disappeared, are mocked by the reduction of the Christian religion to a pair of crucified shirts flapping on a line (p. 41). It is a dead and empty world of hollow objects.

The next three pages (pp. 41–44) are given over to reminiscences of Stephen's life in Paris. There he had known an Irish exile, Kevin Egan (actually Joe Casey), an old dynamitard, now loveless, landless, wifeless, forgotten but unforgetting. His son Patrice is a pink bunny who laps milk while his father drinks absinthe, and has taken to substitute religions while his father clings to the real one. Fulfilling the theme of disguise and quick change, we hear of "Leo Taxil," who was really Gabriel Jogand, and of James Stephens who escaped from Ireland disguised as a bride. In describing the explosion at Clerkenwell prison, Stephen uses the same phrase, "shattered glass and toppling masonry," which he had used previously of Pyrrhus (p. 24), and which will recur again (p. 583) at the climactic moment of "Circe." Not only does the nightmare of history culminate inevitably in an apocalypse; but Stephen, in his efforts to transcend space and time, is menaced by that premonition of disaster which we saw growing on him in the *Portrait*. He knows also (pp. 44–45) that he is now dispossessed from the tower, and for a moment sits down amid the desolate rocks and sands, the language of the physical universe, the playthings of malevolent "Sir Lout," i.e., God, and also the traditional images of spiritual desolation. Reaching into the past after historic events on the strand (p. 45), he recalls the arrival of the Danes in the eleventh century, a herd of whales which ran aground in the fourteenth century and so saved the city from starvation, an historic occasion when the Liffey froze over. All these cruel and primitive images lead up to the appearance of the gypsies' dog, who runs along the strand and yaps at Stephen. This dog has many different characters. He is an enemy, whom Stephen seems to treat with lofty disdain, but of whom he is inwardly afraid. He is also a fawning, obsequious crowd, who will, like the Irish people, follow any pretender or disguised rascal (such as Silken Thomas, Perkin Warbeck, or Lambert Simnel) till the opportune moment for betrayal. Thinking of false claimants, Stephen is led to wonder if his own claim is not an empty one and in a powerful vision which fuses the drowned man with his mother, he condemns himself bitterly as a weakling. But of course there is no ultimate truth about anyone's character, anyone's identity; and the dog now illustrates this by turning into a multiplicity of beasts as he flops and gambols about the beach; in addition to all his other Protean roles, he is now Stephen himself. At last in the presence of the drowned dog-carcass, he turns back into his own dog-like self; for as Mr. Deasy said on p. 34 and Stephen recalls here, all history moves to one great end, and that end, we see here, is self-recognition and death.

The dream which Stephen recollects at the top of p. 47 is a premonition of his encounter with Bloom, an alien figure, and the beginning for Stephen of a new cycle. Seeing the gypsy woman, and thinking of her strange language, the tide of her speech and the tide of her blood, Stephen is led to compose a poem which will be given to us in full text on p. 132, but which is in fact derived from a stanza in one of Hyde's *Love Songs of Connaught*. (Stephen is very much the plagiarist in this book; the epigram on Irish art, for

which he allows everyone to give him full credit, is
simply dilute Oscar Wilde.) But in composition he
sees himself as a diviner, creating images of the
cosmos and reflecting into outer space the same image
of his own soul; like Berkeley, bishop of Cloyne, he
reduces the whole cosmos to his perceptions of it, but
also conceives the opposite process by which the soul
projects itself into, and gives infinite form to, the
farthest reaches of space. The young lady whom he
thinks of transporting beyond the veil (pp. 48–49) is
thus Psyche, though his imagination lends her some
concrete embodiments.

And now in the fullness of the noon hour, he sees
the swirling water and hears the speech of the tides.
Drawn by the mysterious moon-woman, the waters
writhe and hiss and swirl, moving in endless cycles
of weary, cyclical motion, in a manner familiar from
the *Portrait*. But in the tides of language lies the
drowned man, who is still Stephen himself; introduced
by phrases from *Lycidas* and *The Tempest*, he is
abandoned to the tides and thus absorbed into a cycle
of material and spiritual change. Passing from form to
form through the stages of metempsychosis, he knows
life itself as a continual form of death, a pilgrimage to
nothingness. And this perhaps is how one comes to
know reality, by abandoning oneself to it, and being
absorbed into it. Reflecting this process, Stephen picks
up his ashplant and resumes his walk. His undirected
direction is toward evening, toward a setting of the
sun which is going to take place within him as well as
outside him. He is moving, in a word, toward the dark.
And as he moves off on this cycle of departure followed by inevitable return, he looks back to see another cycle just completing itself, a ship moving up
the Liffey bearing (though he does not know it)
W. B. Murphy, the pseudo-Ulysses whose history will
be irregularly outlined for us in the section known as
"Ithaca."

There are all sorts of details to be added to this rough outline of a chapter which is studded with references, recollections, and innuendos. But, sketchy as it necessarily is, this outline suggests the backbone of Stephen's speculation, as well as something close to a categorical rationale for the method of the novel. It is dense but not impenetrable writing; it is not just random impressions put down randomly. It describes, exemplifies, and prophetically suggests a method of insight into commonplace reality. Like Hamlet, who is never far from his thoughts or the pattern of his existence, Stephen is no passive flute to be picked up and fingered by the first comer. But, unlike Hamlet, he is carrying out a sustained speculation, and his speculation does have a visible conclusion, dramatically as well as intellectually sufficient for the needs of the novel. As for its value outside the novel, each reader must decide that for himself.

With the appearance of Mr. Leopold Bloom, our problems change, and exegesis—even such sketchy exegesis as limitations of space forced upon us in dealing with "Proteus"—is no longer appropriate. Since Bloom is a very scientifically-minded fellow, let us begin by laying down a few scientific facts about him —facts gathered from here, there, and everywhere in the novel. He was born in 1866 (p. 76), named Leopold Paula Bloom (p. 723), and is therefore 38 years old on June 16, 1904 (p. 679). His father, Rudolf Virag, who later changed his name to Bloom, was a native of Hungary, a door-to-door pedlar and small money-lender (p. 336), perhaps a hotel-keeper (p. 101), who committed suicide in the Queen's Hotel, Ennis, County Clare, on June 27, 1886. His mother was Ellen (Higgins) Bloom, second daughter of Julius Higgins (born Karoly) and Fanny Higgins (born Hegarty) (p. 682). Born to a Jewish father who had converted to Protestantism (p. 180), Bloom was converted, on the occasion of his marriage with Molly, to

Catholicism (pp. 682, 716); but he neither understands intimately nor sympathizes essentially with any religion. He is not clear-minded enough to be an agnostic; religiously speaking, he is best described as a cluttered nothing. After dame's school, he attended the Erasmus Smith School in Harcourt Street, leaving in 1880 (p. 703), then worked for Alexander Thom (p. 155), for Wisdom Hely the stationer (pp. 106, 154–155), for David Drimmie's insurance agency (p. 177 and 769), for Joseph Cuffe, cattle auctioneer (pp. 315, 399, 680), and now works as canvasser for ads in the *Freeman's Journal.* On the 8th of October, 1888 (an interesting numerological concatenation), he married Marion (Molly) Tweedy, the daughter of Major Brian Tweedy and a lady of uncertain genealogy known as Lunita Laredo (p. 761). Molly, who was born on Gibraltar, where her father was stationed, on the 8th of September, 1870, was thus eighteen years and one month old at the time of her marriage to Bloom. Their first child Millicent (Milly) was born on June 15, 1889; their second child Rudy was born December 29, 1893 and died January 9, 1894. Since November 27, 1893, complete carnal intercourse between Molly and her husband has not taken place (pp. 735–736); much scholarly speculation here, on whether one should emphasize the adjective or the noun in this declaration. Milly, who turned 15 just yesterday (in the novel's time), had her first period on September 15, 1903—just nine months and one day ago—and this episode has had a curious, unclear, occult effect upon communication between husband and wife.

Bloom's habits and dimensions: he is five feet nine and a half inches tall and weighs eleven stone and four pounds, i.e., 158 pounds (p. 668), wears a size 17 collar (p. 710), and has a full build and olive complexion (p. 727). He abstains from hard liquor, and this is distinctive in a city where everybody drinks; he works at his trade, though it is not much of a trade; he is an unfaithful husband, a chaser of other women, but too shy to get very close to them—rather a voyeur, a tease, and a corrupter of innocence than an active *coureur*. His wife is promiscuous (how promiscuous we are left a little in doubt, but certainly promiscuous by temperament), he is aware of it and humiliated before the present lover, yet curiously eager to push her in the way of other potential lovers, such as Stephen (pp. 652–653). Perhaps it is the principle of fighting fire with fire. Though he does work, Bloom does not make very much money, and his financial statement (p. 723) does not show any impressive quantity of capital reserve. His characteristic path through life is by dodging; he is always trying to get free tickets to something, or to "work a pass" somewhere. He has dreams of an elaborate, and hideous, little house in the suburbs, but only hazy and insubstantial speculations about the way to wealth which will render possible "Flowerville" or "St. Leopold's." He is generous with money, lending three shillings to Joe Hynes (p. 119), being well thought of by Nosey Flynn (p. 178), and subscribing five shillings to the fund for Dignam's children (his behavior here contrasts sharply with the uneasy evasiveness of Simon Dedalus). Yet, perhaps because he is not a treater and a buyer of drinks, Bloom has the reputation of being prudent and a little bit stingy. He is an incurable, uncontrollable projector, full of schemes for municipal improvements, commercial enterprises, small dodges, and big programs. He is vaguely connected with the Freemasons, who are said to have got him out of a jam connected with tickets to the Royal and Hungarian lottery which he once tried to peddle (p. 156). He is acquainted with Arthur Griffith, and is accused by a knowing insider of having inspired Griffith's so-called Hungarian policy (p. 337). He has turned, or is ready to turn, his hand to all sorts of odd jobs; he once wrote a song full of municipal allusions for use in a pantomime (p. 678), he considers the possibility of turning off minute stories for publication in *Tit-Bits* (p. 69), and dreams of organizing a concert tour, with his wife as leading performer, to make a tour of English watering-spots (p. 627). His tendency, we note, is toward promotion, not creation. He is submissive to his wife, preparing her breakfast, bringing her mail, kissing her rear, buying her purple garters and thick cream, and carefully staying out of the house till she has finished entertaining her lover; indeed he has been known to carry sympathy so far as to have menstrual pains (p. 338). Yet Molly respects him as a person of sensitivity, who knows what a woman is, though she despises him because she knows she can always get around him (p. 782)—in any case, he is unlike the insensitive stallion, Boylan, who uses and dismisses her with a contemptuous slap across the rear. Bloom is kind to animals; he feeds the Liffey seagulls, and has a penchant for bringing home stray dogs (pp. 657, 768), one of whom happens to be Stephen. He is nosy, curious about all sorts of personal relations and practical problems, half-informed but never expert, and talkative even beyond the Dublin norm (p. 316). He discourses at length on various topics of general interest, mostly schemes for reform and social progress, he stands up bravely to attack by the Citizen, but is not a believer in violence, and collapses in the face of it (p. 333). In fact, there is something gelatinous and wobbly about Bloom (p. 660) as if he were of a different species. He lives at #7 Eccles Street, a drab house in a drab neighborhood of Dublin, partly because it is drab, partly because that is the house in which J. F. Byrne was living when Joyce came to him, in 1909, with Cosgrave's story that Nora had been unfaithful.

In a good many of Bloom's attitudes, actions, and habits, we can trace elements of Joyce's own experience—these parallels often seem all the more revealing of a silent sympathy as they involve trifling manifestations of behavior. Bloom canvasses for *Freeman's Journal* ads as John Stanislaus Joyce had done, and he hangs around the *Freeman's Journal* offices as Joyce himself had done. He tries to cadge free tickets and work passes on railroads, as Joyce did. He loves to walk the streets of Dublin, and has studied *Thom's Dublin Directory* very carefully indeed, as Joyce did. He associates with Martin Cunningham (Matthew Kane), John Power, and Tom Kernan, all of whom were friends and associates of John S. Joyce. He attends the funeral of Paddy Dignam, which is based on the funeral of Matthew Kane; Joyce attended it in company with his father, heard the sermon of the Reverend Coffey, and watched the setting up of a fund for the five Kane children. Bloom dallies, platonically–erotically and chiefly by letter, with Martha Clifford, as Joyce dallied with Marthe Fleischmann. A central action of the book is his cuckolding, or more properly the drama of his feelings about being cuckolded, after the pattern of that momentous upheaval which Joyce experienced when he came momentarily to doubt of Nora. Bloom even sleeps with Molly (pp. 736, 771) in the same curious head-to-feet position in which Joyce slept with Nora.

Thus Bloom is an aspect of Joyce, as well as a character in a fiction. But he is also a number of mythological characters, narrative parallels, and general principles. As Ulysses, he is an aspect of Hermes and a vessel of hermetic knowledge, as well as a sun-god; he is the Apostle Paul, he is the Wandering Jew, he is Elijah, he is Moses, he is Christ; he is Sinbad the Sailor, Captain Nemo, Everyman and Noman (the hint for this is of course Homeric, for sly Odysseus, in dealing with the Cyclops, gave "Noman" as his name); he is Shakespeare, Dante, and the greatest of all authors, Anonymous. He is a wandering star, a heavenly body, swinging through the cold reaches of interstellar space, out into the void and then back again; he is a husband, a civilizer, and a father—that is, a bringer of order, a bearer of seed, a creative and life-giving force. He is both Brobdingnagian and Lilliputian, both heroic and ridiculous, and oftentimes disgusting. As contrasted with Stephen Dedalus, he is the acquisitive, not the ethical, personality; yet by contrast with the Citizen, he represents the higher moral code. He is the scientific, not the poetic, temperament; yet Lenehan sees, and says, "there's a touch of the artist about old Bloom" (p. 235). He is a pishogue, a weakling, a half-and-half, a womanly man, yet he is also a hero, almost a demigod. He is in some sense a metaphor of the human condition.

In order to put this curious, complex figure in motion, Joyce chose to set him before us first in the state of Odysseus, restless but becalmed on Calypso's island. This first section (pp. 54–70) dwells particularly on his fleshly nature as contrasted with Stephen's rather rarefied intellectuality. Not only does he purchase, prepare, and devour that revolting item of diet, a pork kidney, he is seen moving placidly amid the soiled drawers, twisted gray garters, and dirty linen of slovenly domesticity. Molly wipes her fingers on the blanket, Bloom stumbles over the orangekeyed chamberpot, and finally betakes himself to the jakes, where we are not spared any detail of the usual process. After the rarefied speculations of "Proteus," the sordid specifics of "Calypso" are like a serving of notice on the reader. If Stephen is the sharp knifeblade of intellect, Bloom will be the human, the all-too-human, bowels of compassion. But Bloom's sub-ordinary existence in Eccles Street is not without gleams and premonitions of larger significance. Molly, lying in bed (we never see her anywhere else during the course of the entire book) is Calypso in her cave, and while she doesn't know this, she is puzzled by the word "metempsychosis," which, if she followed it out, would tell her who she once was and why she is playing her present role. Bloom is offered, at the Jewish pork-butcher's, an advertisement of a community in the Jewish homeland, which he and Dlugasz have renounced, but which still attracts him. He is drawn to the East, to the land of the rising sun; as Stephen moves toward evening, he moves toward morning, or yearns to. But in this chapter he is at a standstill and the "stale smell" of incense, "like foul flowerwater" (p. 63) is the odor of Bloom, stagnating. Finally, a number of points indicate that Bloom is in resentful service to Molly, languishing unwillingly in the house of bondage, keyless like Stephen, in a lethargy not unlike Stephen's.

The next section too, known as "Lotus-Eaters" (pp. 71–86), fulfills this idea of languor and becalming. The thought of tea growing in hot Eastern places (p. 71), the sight of the gelded cabhorses (p. 77), the idea of confessing everything to a strange woman like Martha (p. 79), the idea of religion as a stultifying force (p. 81), the Oriental distillates of the druggist (p. 84), and the relaxing atmosphere of the Turkish bath (p. 86) all create in Bloom's torpid mind the dream of rest and tranquillity. But from behind this thick and stultifying veil of physical content, a thin voice calls. "I do not like that other world" writes semi-literate Martha Clifford (p. 77); Bloom doesn't much like that other world either but he hears through the lapse of this ignorant slavey an echo of the cold astral distances he must traverse (cf. pp. 114–115). Again, when asked by Bantam Lyons for a loan of his paper, Bloom unwittingly gives him the tip on Throwaway, the long shot, which actually won the Gold Cup that Thursday afternoon long ago. Bloom does not bet himself, takes no interest in the horses, does not want to get involved; but he cannot help being the vessel of prophecy and inspiration for Bantam Lyons and for the world of the Gentiles generally. Prophetic truth passes through Bloom as light passes through clear glass, leaving no mark of its presence. For in fact Bloom is a kind of personal *omphalos,* and as he contemplates the pleasures of the Turkish bath, he sees his own penis and his own existence as a languid floating lotus, the mystical flower of the East, through which one reaches occult knowledge. In all these ways Bloom, without ceasing to be the opaque and earthy figure of the first episode, is rendered increasingly diaphanous and multi-dimensional. But he has not yet really embarked on his travels, and the next three sections, "Hades," "Aeolus," and "Lestrygonians" serve to get him moving through Dublin. These three chapters are much of a piece; the first two present a broad social landscape with Bloom in it, the third returns us to the inner voice of Bloom as soloist, and in all three the developing image of Dublin life is central.

"Hades" (pp. 87–115) shows Bloom as isolated from and despised by his fellow-mourners in the carriage— this aspect of his Jewishness had not yet been made apparent. He is rudely excluded from conversations, his feelings are ignored, he is systematically relegated to the lower end of the social scale. For the true mourners of Paddy Dignam are the society of good fellows who killed him, the drinking crowd; and among their tribe, Bloom, the prudent imbiber of an occasional glass of luncheon Burgundy has no real standing. Yet the fact of shadowy, scarcely-remembered Paddy Dignam's death challenges Bloom more intimately than it does the other mourners. They have some belief in resurrection; but for him death is a disgusting, commonplace, and terribly final fact, the ultimate shape of which is an obscene fat old rat wedging itself into the rotten earth of the cemetery. The reader will be well-advised, I think, to dodge some of the peripheral puzzles, such as "Who is Mackintosh?" which a perverse mind drew up for the bafflement of literal ones, on the score that a problem like this is better as a problem than as a solution. But the real achievement of the scene is its somber, empty poetry. Paddy Dignam's dead and gone, Parnell will never come back; a flat, empty finality prevails. The words and ceremonies of this perfectly ordinary occasion, worn threadbare by a thousand repetitions, fall hollowly into a hollow and more resounding void. Bloom almost welcomes the snub of John Henry Menton as a return to the familiar world of cruel, everyday snobbery. But though he has escaped the kingdom of darkness, Bloom continues to wear his black suit all day, as Stephen his; and these two figures, seeking each other unconsciously through Dublin all that day and night, bear the visible outward mark of death, as if celebrating the burial of a perished past. The dead, as Gabriel Conroy found out, are not just the people in cemeteries. Ordinary little Paddy Dignam is all souls faded and half-forgotten; and Bloom's visit, so early in his voyage, to the cemetery which is the last term of it, casts dark and interesting shadows over his future.

"Aeolus" (pp. 116–150), on the other hand, seems more in the nature of a *tour de force*. It describes a world full of bumps, gusts, interruptions, and noises, the world of business, though nobody in it is very busy. Soft Bloom, in the middle of things, is pushed one way by Keyes, another way by the business office (Nannetti), a third way by the editorial department (Myles Crawford), mimicking the brewery float on which "dullthudding barrels" are bumped by "grossbooted draymen" (p. 116). He is derided by newsboys, pushed by Lenehan, rebuffed by the editor, and haunted by those keys (the one he has lost, the two he must find, two crossed keys signifying the parliament of the Isle of Man, the crossing of Stephen and Bloom, and also an older cross [p. 120]). Yet against all probability he does effect compromises, make his sale, find his ad, get underway something like the little par he needs—the triumph is seedy enough, but amid bumps, thuds, squeaks, and wheezes, the world's machinery does somehow manage to turn. The story of Ignatius Gallaher and the Invincibles reiterates this theme. Everything is terribly confused about this story—the date of the Invincibles' murder, the way in which Ignatius Gallaher transmitted the story, the reason why he had to use so curious a device. But the point is that he superimposed a specific advertisement on a map of Dublin, and by picking out letters on the advertisement traced the escape route of the Invincibles from the scene of their crime. And this method of superposition, of overlay, not only works within Myles Crawford's story, it is constant throughout *Ulysses*; the present reveals its meaning only when one looks through it to the pattern of the past underneath—"the whole bloody history" (pp. 136–137).

And in fact, the truth will out. It is oozing forth all through this chapter. Myles Crawford, a bird and therefore prophetic, utters much mantic nonsense, raving like a sibyl, but then quietly prophesies World War I (p. 132). J. J. O'Molloy knows about the murder of General Bobrikoff (p. 134) before it actually happened, the professor predicts Bloom will get his ad (p. 129), and Bloom himself prophesies the future election of J. P. Nannetti as Lord Mayor of Dublin (p. 119). Amid these prophecies and bursts of inflated eloquence, Stephen puts forth his version of prophecy in the style of *Dubliners*, the fable of the two elderly virgins on Nelson's pillar. Various emblematic meanings can be found in this little sketch. Prudent, chaste, and beefy, Dublin nonetheless admires romantic adultery, condoning in Nelson what it condemned in Parnell. Commonplace priestesses of Dublin's religion of the ordinary, the virgins emit enigmatic aeroliths—little, hard, true, facts (cf. Moses'

Ten Tablets)—on the uncomprehending city. But though the professor repeatedly claims to "see," one point of the parable seems to be that nobody sees. Even Stephen, though he sees into Ireland with Antisthenes' bitterness, has not yet seen through it; and the parable seems to be a parable of non-vision and negation, a shaggy-dog prophecy to go with Stephen's shaggy-dog riddle.

"Lestrygonians" (pp. 151–183), though it does something to fill out the consciousness of Bloom, his fears, memories, and obsessions, is as close as Joyce comes to having someone wander about and report what he sees. On the cosmic level, Bloom is starting to worry about where he is in the universe, and the interesting word "parallax" is, as he dimly intuits, a possible way of measuring an earthly angle and finding out a cosmic dimension. Celestial and mundane considerations are very closely woven in this section; for through the running stream of Bloom's thought runs an undercurrent of food imagery, expressed usually in the form of metaphors or puns. Molly is out of plumb, constables do the goose step, nonsense is gammon and spinach, and even the provost of Trinity torments poor Bloom by being named, anachronistically, Dr. Salmon. The alternation of depression and desire, which constitutes the rhythm of hunger, links obscurely with the tide of Bloom's erotic life. Dublin looks bleak and horrible on an empty stomach but opulent displays of lingerie create the hope of lunch. Obsessed by cold and clammy thoughts, Bloom takes comfort from the memory of warm and happy days with Molly and Milly (pp. 155–156, 168). Finally warmed by a glass of Burgundy, he promptly recollects his first fervid erotic experience with Molly on the Hill of Howth (pp. 175–176); and this memory, which for him is a beginning, will be seen from Molly's point of view as an indistinguishable repetition of her first affair on Gibraltar with Harry Mulvey (pp. 760–

762), and in a longer perspective still as the love affair
of all masculine mountains with feminine rivers.
(Bloom is not only a mountain but actually a range—
Slieve Bloom in Central Ireland [p. 58].) Bloom's
erotic memories and anxieties deepen as the afternoon
advances (the thought of Boylan is always accompanied with a glance at the clock), and the appearance
of his "rival" for the second time today causes him to
dodge into the National Museum and Library, where
he will later be observed, inspecting marble goddesses
to find out if they have rectums, and looking for keys
in the *Kilkenny People* (pp. 729, 200–201).

As he disappears into the National Museum, Bloom
temporarily disappears from the book, turning up in
each of the next two sections but only at a distance
and in passing, then occupying a little more of the
scene in "Sirens" and "Cyclops," but only resuming
his central position in "Nausicaa." The Library scene
("Scylla and Charybdis") is a showpiece for Stephen,
and Bloom only passes through; "Wandering Rocks,"
the only one of the episodes without a Homeric parallel, is a game of Dublin cross-purposes, and again
Bloom is peripheral to the game. At the "Sirens" concert he is for the most part a silent auditor, and in
"Cyclops" the tides of Dublin barroom conversation
seethe and foam about him, without, however, creating any opening through which we can see his
thought-processes. In fact, it seems to me, we have
seen in his first exposure most of the surface things
there are to see in Bloom. There is a nightmare side
to his existence, but we shall not see it until nighttime;
during the long afternoon, Joyce will allow his novel
—which, if he were building on the conventional scale
would now be starting to close its circles and draw its
lines toward a final resolution—to spread, instead,
lavishly across the Dublin landscape. These four
chapters are beyond doubt the richest, most various,
and most leisurely developed in the whole novel. The

ways in which they forward the central action are less impressive; but as the play of a giant comic fancy richly occupied with the decorative possibilities of a scene, they are incomparable.

"Scylla and Charybdis" (pp. 184–218) shows us Stephen Dedalus making his last appearance in Joyce's fiction as the glittering, unassailable young ideologue. His Shakespeare lecture is one of a series of late nineteenth- or early twentieth-century theorizings about the personality of the Bard. Stephen follows in the footsteps of Georg Brandes, Sir Sidney Lee, Oscar Wilde, Frank Harris, F. G. Fleay, Goldwin Smith, and a swarm of other biographers and interpreters of the biography, on all of whom he draws freely and quietly. His basic inspiration, however, is Freudian; for this reason the only person who makes reference to Freud or Freudian thinking is John Eglinton. As a fictional façade, Stephen's views are to be taken altogether seriously; there are a number of potent reasons within the scene why we should accord our sympathy in special measure to Stephen, independently of whether he is "right" or not. He is making a positive and coherent point, against sloth, convention, and confusion. Other participants in the scene repeat the tags and clichés of previous analysis, without offering any individual view worthy of serious consideration. They slur over details, are vaguely and loftily commendatory; Stephen reaches below the surface to a new dimension of understanding. He has an impressive command of specific facts about Shakespeare, which he sets forth with only occasional ironic reservations. At this feast of reason, he supplies all the pabulum; others supply interruptions, irrelevancies, foolish jokes, and the deliberate rudeness of arranging in Stephen's presence a social occasion from which he alone is pointedly excluded.

On all these scores, then, the Library scene draws our sympathies in the direction of Stephen seen as the heroic outcast. Its connections with the novel proper are by no means exhausted with this aspect. Stephen has all along been seeing himself as a Hamlet, a son and heir whose future has been usurped by wicked uncles. But Hamlet is not the only interesting character in the play; and Stephen is starting to see through the Ghost the figure of Shakespeare, an imaginative cuckold whose manhood has been undermined by conspiracy between corrupt Gertrude and rank Claudius, thievish Ann and sinister Richard. By this view, Shakespeare is simply enacting, in his dramas, the story of a spiritual wound; "his unremitting intellect is the hornmad Iago ceaselessly willing that the moor in him shall suffer" (p. 212), and all his plays are versions of *Othello*. But under another aspect, Shakespeare's artistry is a successful solution of his dilemma. For though Hamnet his physical son and Hamlet his spiritual son cannot successfully reassert his right, through artistic creation Shakespeare becomes not only father of his own characters but also a father and conscience to the race. His meaning to the disinherited Stephen is particularly poignant under this aspect; and in fact he enables us to see the book before us as a sufficient answer to the questions posed within it. The artist creates not only his own family, his own progenitors, grandchildren, and self, but his own universe, which he sees against himself and sees himself against; every adventure into the universe is for him an act of self-discovery, for the universe is only as he conceives it. This dialectic between self and universe resolves the basic contrast of the chapter, in which Stephen must steer between John Eglinton and Æ, the literal rock of Aristotle and the swirling whirlpool of Plato. It is an intricate and impressive set of variations on the central themes of the novel, and fills out to special effect some of the ideas first put forth in "Proteus."

Of "Wandering Rocks" and "Sirens" I shall not try

to say very much because both are the products of a hard and glittering ingenuity which carries its own cachet. The 19 episodes of "Wandering Rocks" (pp. 219–255), within which phrases from one episode are deliberately interlaced with another, combine to give us a shifting panorama of Dublin's multifarious, interwoven existences. All sorts of deliberately enigmatic and consciously unexplained coincidences appear here, along with oddities like Cashel Boyle O'Connor Fitzmaurice Tisdall Farrell, Professor Maginni and Mrs. M'Guinness, the flashing bicycle racers of Trinity College, and Mr. (Joseph) Bloom the dentist. But if we leave the full complexity of these local jokes to the appreciation of elderly Dubliners, the chief contribution of the section is a syncopated technique of swift cross-cutting from scene to scene, and a pair of impressive, contrasted processions which proceed across Dublin. Father John Conmee is on an errand of bland and muzzy benevolence, the Lord Lieutenant on one of cold and glittering display. These two progressions, one heading south–north, the other west–east, pass without intercepting one another, scrawling in a clumsy cross as it were the blessing of the secular and religious authorities on sinful and ignorant Dublin. As for the "Sirens" (pp. 256–291), it involves some of Joyce's most elaborately-wrought prose, and a full appreciation of its musical features is beyond our scope here. But we may admire the way in which songs intertwine with sexuality, during the concert, and reach out beyond the Ormond dining room to make a symphony with cosmic overtones. Boylan, having taken measure of the time on a sex-clock, departs for his assignation with Molly, where his proud knock of arrival is picked up and repeated by the blind stripling's tapping on the earth. As Bloom's unified field theory (developed in the last half of "Nausicaa") will maintain, sex and gravity are both magnetism, and essentially interchangeable. Thus we see Molly growing into her role as the earth, an earth-mother on whom we must all knock for admission and accept-ance, in whom we shall all know ourselves finally. But this theme is only adumbrated in "Sirens," and such touches as Lydia's fondling of the beer-pull are, I fear, no better than adolescent pseudo-Freudianism.

"Cyclops" (pp. 292–345), on the other hand, must be recognized as a major triumph of the novel. The comic contrast of Irish epic legend and Irish seedy reality works beautifully within the framework of Joyce's novel; and the leisured Rabelaisian amplitude of the scene gives occasion for rich comic invention. The shifting cast of characters includes a full set of louche grotesques, climaxed by the incomparable Garryowen; and the gutter-dialect of the nameless narrator—with his snarling, cynical, inventive invec-tive—is a capacious vehicle. Joyce enriched the chap-ter with many of his father's most picturesque ex-pressions, and also included, from sheer creative exuberance, a whole lexicon of expressions for asking another fellow to have a drink and for accepting such an invitation. The episodes of the ceremonial execu-tion, and the parody of the fight between Myler Keogh and Percy Bennett, backed up by images of a lynching and a flagellant's parody of the Creed, add a requisite touch of ferocity; and the fine point of Terry's going to sleep over the Citizen's finest flights of patriotic oratory (p. 328) is not to be overlooked. A tidy mind will complain that the Citizen, who is so much a part of the Sinn Fein movement, ought to be better informed of Bloom's role as an admirer and inspirer of Arthur Griffith, if this latter idea is to be taken seriously at all. But in fact Arthur Griffith's party had its basic confusions, and the tide of feeling against Bloom is shown to rise from a muffled complex of aspirations, frustrations, prejudices, and flat errors. Indeed, Bloom is almost too innocent, his virtue seems almost contrived. Accused of defrauding widows and orphans (p. 337), he is actually on his way to help them; assailed for lack of patriotism, he is shown to be an associate and helper of the ultra-patriotic party; charged with greed and profiteering, he is the only man in Barney Kiernan's who is not on the grift for a free drink; and if he does not stand treat on his earnings from Throwaway, it is for the excellent reason that there were none. Actually, Bloom is assaulted by the Citizen very much as Christ was chosen for crucifixion, rather than Barabbas—because he is mild and peace-loving. We can scarcely be in doubt as to Joyce's attitude when he has the Citizen shout, as he rushes after the biscuit-box, "By Jesus, . . . I'll brain that bloody jewman for using the holy name. By Jesus, I'll crucify him so I will" (p. 342). Before this mindless assault Bloom stands his ground with a modest courage and humane perspective which have not gone unappreciated.

All sorts of lovely details enliven this lively chapter. "Lamh Dearg Abu," the Citizen's motto (p. 325) means "Up the Red Hand," and is the motto of the Red Branch Kings of Irish legend, but in context it refers to the red hand on the label of Allsop's ale; Little Sweet Branch (p. 312) is Douglas Hyde under his Gaelic name literally translated; Bloom's cigar is the glowing stake with which Odysseus put out the one eye of the Cyclops; and Garryowen is a dog who once belonged to the father of Joyce's Aunt Josephine (Giltrap), a champion wolfhound of historic memory, and an anthem of Irish belligerence—as well as the best poet in the book. (The reference to "Lowry's lights" in the last line of his stanza implies that he is fresh from an engagement at Dan Lowry's Music Hall.) The noble twin brothers Bungiveagh and Bungardilaun (p. 299) are the brothers Guinness, Lord Iveagh and Lord Ardilaun, with a brewers' prefix; and the enigmatic postcard which has sent Denis Breen off his rocker by presenting him with the message "U.P. up" implies that he has had it, that he can't get it up any more, and that it's all up with him. The joke is a graveyard joke, and Breen's response to the postcard is typically gigantic—he wants to sue for £10,000 without even knowing who sent the card.

The historic catastrophe which ends the chapter is a specially complex and layered event. It is, of course, the climax of the episode's gigantism; on a semi-serious level, it is also the catastrophe, the thunder-clap, which brings one cycle of history to an end and inaugurates another (Bloom is blown out of central Dublin, southwest by west as far as Sandymount, while most of the other characters present are ex-ploded clean out of the novel). The man who picks up the pieces and gets a new cycle going again is rather a cycle himself. He is called His Royal High-ness rear admiral the right honourable Sir Hercules Hannibal Habeas Corpus Anderson, and there follow a list of 19 titles of honor, 18 of which are serious or at least possible (the exception is S.O.D., which is Distinguished Service Order rearranged to stand for "sodomist"). In addition, Hercules is a Greek name, Hannibal a Semitic one (in English it would translate to John Bull), Habeas Corpus is a Roman expression (implying "You may have my body"), and Anderson (from German *ander* = other as well as Greek *andros* = man) implies that he is the Son of Man, the sacred foundling (Moses, Oedipus, Romulus, and Remus, Christ) from whom emerging civiliza-tions have traditionally sprung. It is, very likely, de-plorable that all these elaborate ideas should be buried in a name which is only an incidental part of a joke; but I am afraid this is the way Joyce's mind was always prone to work, and was now coming to work more and more.

The explosion no doubt transmits Bloom to a higher sphere, in terms of the book's program; but it is hard not to feel in the next two sections, "Nausicaa" and

"Oxen of the Sun," a certain forcing of the imaginative powers. Joyce's stylistic tricks seem to be performed, in these two sections, for their own sake, or for the sake of sheer display. The "marmalady drawersy" manner of "Nausicaa" (pp. 346–382) is perhaps all too paralyzingly successful; but why anyone (least of all Bloom or Stephen) should adopt such a manner at this point is not at all clear. Joyce had, it would seem, an almost hypnotic fascination with this sort of bad writing, and the chapter itself is ample evidence that he had studied it tenderly. But it does not make for anything like the bold comic effects of "Cyclops," and twenty consecutive pages of it are likely to get on a reader's nerves. Far more interesting is the second half of the chapter in which, giving up stylistic tricks, Joyce returns to Bloom's familiar inner monologue as he wanders along the same strand over which Stephen passed earlier in the day. This repetition is surely no accident, for the points of comparison with Stephen's earlier monologue are many and interesting. In many crucial details, Bloom's thought actually parallels Stephen's. We are startled to find him quoting *Hamlet* (p. 372), reflecting on the nature of space and time (p. 373), thinking of historical cycles and the odd way they lead to self-recognition ("Think you're escaping and run into yourself": p. 377). He has a vague intimation of *The Parable of the Plums* (p. 377) which he will hear, but not till later that night (p. 685). And, as night settles over Dublin Bay, and Bloom's mind relaxes into a great black pool of darkness, he even seems to see through the limitations of this space–time world and into another one, as Stephen had thought of doing:

> Tide comes here a pool near her foot. Bend, see my face there, dark mirror, breathe on it, stirs. All these rocks with lines and scars and letters. O, those transparent! Besides they don't know. What is the meaning

of that other world. I called you naughty boy because I do not like. (p. 381)

"O, those transparent!" makes transparent reference to Gerty's alluring stockings; but it is also Bloom reaching through the here and now, into another world of outer space, where he almost achieves and is nearly able to write on the beach who he is. "I AM A"—he is not a naughty boy, but in another world there is another word to describe him, which he almost succeeds in reaching. And as grammar gives way, in his last extraordinary cycling sentence, Bloom is carried away on an endless tide of imagery to a world without end because it is round (p. 378), a world in which Bloom will always be returning to his East, ever rising and setting in new transformations achieved through his absorption in world-women:

> O sweety all your little girlwhite up I saw dirty brace-girdle made me do love sticky we two naughty Grace darling she him half past the bed met him pike hoses frillies for Raoul to perfume your wife black hair heave under embon *señorita* young eyes Mulvey plump years dreams return tail end Agendath swoony lovey showed me her next year in drawers return next in her next her next. (p. 382) *

* Helps to reading this complex sentence: imagine a semi-colon after "saw"; bracegirdle is Mrs. Bracegirdle, seventeenth century actress (p. 370), also a vision of erotic abandon; envision another semicolon after "sticky"; "we two naughty" derives from "you naughty too" (p. 279) with the overtone of naught = zero; "naughty darling" (p. 377) leads to Grace Darling, heroic lighthouse keeper's daughter who rescued a ship in distress, providing an emblem for woman saving man in the shipwreck/disaster of intercourse. "She him" says that in the sex relation she was active, he passive: and "half past the bed" suggests that literally Boylan and Molly went to bed at half past four, but also that the bed was only a stage on both their larger journeys through space and (especially) time; even as she met him in (provocative) pike hoses, they were both metempsychosing, passing from one state to another. Imaginary semicolon. "Frillies for Raoul to perfume your wife"

That woman is the path to another world—not a dead moon-satellite, but an independent and majestic heavenly body with its own field of gravity—is a discovery in which Bloom is wiser than Stephen; it is prophetic of the end of the book, and redeems the first half of "Nausicaa" from its all too authentic tedium.

"Oxen of the Sun" (pp. 383–428) is one of those occasional Joyce episodes which, one imagines, were more fun to write than they will ordinarily be to read. The genesis and development of English prose are described in a series of pastiches which parallel the development of Mina Purefoy's child. Joyce, as much

---

can be read as a single phrase, meaning that what was done in one context will have influence (perhaps by metempsychosis) in another, but it joins two different adulterous intents, that in *Sweets of Sin,* and that in Martha's letter. "Black hair" I cannot easily identify, so would set it apart with some sort of punctuation. "Heave under embon" is adapted from *Sweets of Sin,* providing a transition to the *"señorita"* who is Molly (p. 380) and also the female on one of Bloom's dirty postcards (p. 721). "Young eyes" are an attribute of Molly's (p. 64), "Mulvey" is her first lover (p. 371), "plump" is an adjective repeatedly applied to her (pp. 92, 776); and here once again we had better imagine a semicolon. "Years dreams return" may be paraphrased, "over the years dreams return" as well as "years and dreams return" (p. 377), and "tail end" makes reference to the sailor's return "smelling the tail end of ports" (p. 378), to Bloom's habit of approaching Molly from what she considers the wrong end (p. 777), and perhaps to a sexual or doggy end too; at all events, it leads to Agendath, the homeland, the end of our wanderings. Once again, punctuate. "Swoony lovey" returns us to Gerty, but also to any woman in the act of sexual surrender; she "showed me her"—and Gerty showed just about everything she had, but metaphysically the idea is that woman leads man along the path of metempsychosis, from one return to another, always tantalizing him with the vision of her next form. "Next year in" repeats the promise of return, from the Zionist greeting "Next year in Israel"; and "drawers" are not only the veil of circumstance through which Bloom is trying, mentally, to penetrate, but also the *ewig weibliche* which forever drawers us on, to her next her next—incarnation.

fascinated as Bloom by the intricate processes of embryology, studied medical textbooks as well as manuals of English prose style, in order to write this chapter; and, to paraphrase Mr. Crofton, it is a fine piece of writing. Moreover, there is a good deal of miscellaneous information buried in it, with which one can piece out various other passages of the novel. (For example, the sexual relations between the Blooms are rendered more explicit by a passage in the style of Gibbon than even by the scientific catechism of "Ithaca.") But once more the most interesting part of the chapter, fictionally speaking, occurs toward the end, where Joyce allows the history of English prose to degenerate into a horrible mishmash of pidgin, slang, and jumbled plapper-talk. Metaphorically, there has been some discussion whether this monstrous prose represents the baby or the afterbirth. It is by no means undecipherable writing, however unattractive, and has in fact been very largely deciphered—yielding, along the way, a surprising story about a trick of aloof Stephen Dedalus to intercept a telegram and get, illicitly, a hot tip on the Gold Cup (p. 426, ll. 21–28).* But both "Nausicaa" and "Oxen of the Sun" are more interesting for their mysteries than for their factual clarities. Both seem to slope downhill into the area where language and the formal concepts conveyed by language dissolve, and where images take on a queer, capering, illogical life of their own. Without trying to form or structure them, one simply relaxes and lets them sweep past. We may trace this interest in the passive, "opened" mind back to the early pages of the *Portrait*; in these two chapters particularly one feels it growing on Joyce, and taking over the fore-

* Daniel Weiss, "The End of the *Oxen of the Sun*," in *The Analyst*, X (Evanston, Ill.: Northwestern University), with many additions and commentaries by various hands in subsequent issues.

ground of his mind. The unremitting intellect—narrow, jealous, and negative—is fading, the dark night world is opening up. "Circe" gives it free rein.

The longest and most elaborate of all the episodes in *Ulysses,* "Circe" (pp. 429–609) is also the least structured. We do not know within whose mind it takes place, if within anyone's, for Bloom and Stephen flow together in this section, combining, separating, and complementing one another's nightmares under pressure of the same queer energy that animates the talking cakes of soap or causes a person to appear the instant his name is thought of. The skin of civilization has been peeled back for a witch's sabbath in which any of the properties, persons, or episodes of the book may be summoned up to take part in the riotous review. There is not much formal structure to this chapter, in which actions have neither proper beginnings nor distinct endings, and even if we could find one, it might only have the effect of rendering the nightmare less nightmarish. Still, some rough elements of order can be indicated, most economically by an abbreviated outline:

This outline represents merely an order of succession, and does not even pretend to represent what "happens" in a world where time and space are so extraordinarily flexible. For instance, Bloom on p. 478 makes a lewd suggestion to Zoe, who replies, "Go on. Make a stump speech out of it." Bloom does, with the result that he falls into a full-scale political campaign, achieves vast success and public adulation, is accused, turned upon, hunted down, condemned, and burnt to a crisp, all in an instant of time—emerging from his fantasy just in time to find Zoe saying (p. 499), "Talk away till you're black in the face." The world of private fantasy inspires reactions in that of material reality, as well as vice versa.

Stephen's obsessions in "Circe" are pretty much what they have always been, and do not alter profoundly our picture of his character; but Bloom is a revelation. The hideous variety of his nightmares and the depth of his humiliations give him a whole new set of dimensions, as if all of his qualities had been multiplied by a thousand. When he is the hero of the "New Bloomusalem," he is a full comic panorama of bourgeois Utopias and Utopians. As the maid-of-all-work-plus-overstuffed-chair in a whorehouse, he is the ultimate victim of every atrocity ever imagined by Sacher-Masoch. The great developmental cycles of "Circe" are thus largely occupied with Bloom, expanding and contracting him like an equation. Everyone accuses him (even the watch conjugate his name only as far as the accusative—p. 453), and of such a

kaleidoscopic variety of intimate crimes, that it is evident his real guilt is that of humanity itself. Even
when he might conceivably have some defense against
a charge, another charge is made before he can escape
from the first. And beneath all the specific wrongs of
which he is accused, there lies a profound disgust
which Bloom inspires in himself as well as others, and
which he has no real hope of overcoming. Like Kafka's
hero, Bloom is accused of nothing less than the un-
speakable crime of guilt.

The dance of death, which is the first of the episode's
two climaxes, offers no special points of difficulty. The
dance begins as a dance of the hours, played earlier at
the bazaar dance (p. 69), this time not to Ponchielli's
music, but rather to the tune of "My Girl's a Yorkshire
Girl," which was also played that afternoon—for the
bicycle races (p. 254) and for the hobbyhorses at the
bazaar (p. 578)—thus definitely associated with cyclical, circular motion. Stephen, who, like Bloom, is
subject to accusations which cannot be repelled, tries
to argue that cancer, not he, killed his mother (p.
580). But the "green crab with malignant red eyes
[which] sticks deep its grinning claws in Stephen's
heart" (p. 582) strikes down his uneasy rationality
with unerring symbolism. (Cancer is the Latin word
for crab.) Thus, once again, logic is overridden by a
kind of intuitive association of images, and the way
opens for Stephen's act of comic-Wagnerian destruction, in which the smashing of a lampshade stands for
an end to all history, the ruination of space and time,
and the human race's departure on a new cycle of
civilization.

The second climax, that of the Black Mass, is considerably more complicated. One notes that Stephen,
in the preparatory discussions, twice makes use of
quotations from Blake. Tapping his brow, he says "In
here it is I must kill the priest and the king" (p. 589)
and at the last moment before the Mass he quotes:

The harlot's cry from street to street
Shall weave old Ireland's windingsheet. (p. 597)

It is appropriate that Blake, who stood Newton's world
on its head, should introduce a scene in which religious values are turned upside down. Important too
is Stephen's definition of his own intellectual project
—to kill an inner king and priest, principles of
authority within the mind. These are not, I think,
simply authority-figures, internalizations of external
authority; they are the whole principle of mental control. The Black Mass is a major effort on Stephen's
part to see and reject the whole established structure
of civilization as it presses in on him. His vision is an
apocalyptic one, introduced by vast, vague mobiliza-
tions, swarms of screaming birds, and the resurrection
of the dead, divided properly into innocent white
sheep and bad black goats. The race of life comes to
an abrupt end at a chasm into which the brave volun-
teer Tom Rochford casts himself, followed by everybody. The story of Deucalion, Pyrrha, and the dragon's teeth, which began history, is repeated again at
its end. Legendary Irish antagonists re-enact their
enmity all over the place.

The altar which now rises is at the center of the
earth, the *omphalos*, and therefore the Sandymount
tower, lit by shafts of light from the high barbicans,
as on pp. 11 and 44. It is the altar of Saint Barbara,
patron saint of fireworks—a covert allusion, perhaps,
to Gogarty's firing of that biographical midnight rifle
(see above, p. 43), all trace of which has disappeared
from the novel. Mrs. Mina Purefoy, who is teeming,
poverty-stricken Ireland, forever spawning miserable
children, is the naked woman traditional to the Black
Mass, also the goddess of unreason. She is flesh, not
spirit, irrational, not rational, the reverse of everything
the traditional Mass stands for. Father Malachi
O'Flynn, a transvestite priest in petticoats, celebrates

the holy office. His first name is that of Malachi Mulligan, his second that of Father O'Flynn, the Irish priest celebrated in a popular ballad for his country-cute way of looking out for number one (Bloom thinks of the refrain of this ballad on p. 170). Like Judas Iacchias, the Pig God invoked by Lipoti Virag on p. 520, he has two left feet—left being traditionally a sinister side. His feet are back to front and his chasuble is reversed for the occasion. His assistant is The Reverend Mr. Hugh C. Haines Love, M.A., Anglican counterpart of the Catholic celebrant. Haines is the Englishman visiting the tower, Hugh C. Love is Father Bob Cowley's landlord, who is dispossessing him from 29 Windsor Avenue (pp. 244-245); in real life, he was not a minister but a clerk from Belfast, and the tenant he dispossessed was John S. Joyce. The name Haines Love joins love and hate. Cassock and mortarboard are emblematic of the church and the university; and the open umbrella he holds over the celebrant's head symbolizes the practice of contraception. Father O'Flynn celebrates his Mass in Latin, Mr. Haines Love repeats it in English. As the celebrant announces *"Corpus Meum"*—This is my body, Mr. Haines Love raises Father O'Flynn's petticoats and reveals his "grey bare hairy buttocks"—and this scene is a parody of one in George Moore's novel *The Lake,* the hero of which is a restless priest named Father Oliver Gogarty. Tired of clerical celibacy, Father Gogarty dives into the lake, leaving his clothes behind to suggest that he has drowned, but actually swimming across and emigrating to America where almost anything can happen. As he stands poised to plunge, Moore describes the moon shining on his gray buttocks—a passage which greatly impressed Joyce, and has left its mark on this odious scene, in which public and private elements are inextricably mingled.

"Circe" ends with Stephen supine and semi-conscious, murmuring fragments of that most beautiful and enigmatic of Yeats' poems, "Who Goes With Fergus?" while Bloom stands over him muttering masonic phrases and entranced with the vision of Rudy. Rudy is on the scene because Bloom has found a son. Bloom repeats masonic slogans because they represent a kind of religion of man, an ideal of fraternity, in which both the main characters will be united. And Stephen (whose unconsciousness is more significant than the process which brought it about) murmurs phrases from "Who Goes With Fergus?" because he is commending himself to the guidance of a dark, occult principle who

> . . . rules the shadows of the wood,
> And the white breast of the dim sea
> And all dishevelled wandering stars.*

I am not saying that Bloom is Fergus, only that Bloom and Fergus are both exponents of a hermetic view of life to which Stephen, very much contrary to his previous nature and training, is now becoming committed; and Bloom, as Stephen's spiritual ancestor, an age-long outcast, and the ordinary vessel of extraordinary insights, is the immediate pathway to the final vision.

The three concluding chapters of Joyce's "Nostos," or return, do not make any serious effort to balance the twelve Homeric books in which Odysseus, returned to his home by the kindly Phaeacians, plots the destruction of the wicked suitors and carries his plot into execution. Indeed, the reunion of Stephen and Bloom is so chilly and unenthusiastic, and the return to chaste Penelope so clouded with ironic overtones, that some readers have found the last episodes of the book wholly nihilistic. I shall not try to argue that this view is altogether mistaken, only that it is incomplete. The book is nihilistic and pantheistic; it denies

* "Who Goes With Fergus?", *The Collected Poems of W. B. Yeats* (New York: Macmillan, 1956).

all value and affirms all being, pretty much simultaneously.

The first section, "Eumaeus" (pp. 612–665), takes Stephen and Bloom to a cabman's shelter at the foot of the Loop Line Bridge. As they are both fagged out from the active events of the evening, and Stephen is halfway between drunk and overhung, the prose is as shambling, woozy, and platitudinous as it can possibly be. Bloom, in his doggy, friendly way, makes efforts at Stephen's well-being and tries to engage him in conversation; Stephen is cross and sulky. The *conversazione* in the cabman's shelter rambles inconclusively from topic to topic, with the general theme of return running through it. There is a question of Parnell's possible return, W. B. Murphy the boozy sailor has just returned after a long absence, even the proprietor of the shelter is alleged to be Skin-the-Goat, an old Invincible who has served his time for his part in the Phoenix Park murders and has now returned to the scene of the crime. Bloom's little schemes to cash in on Stephen's various talents do not render him a very attractive figure in this episode ("Gob," as the Cyclops said, "he'd have a soft hand under a hen"); on the other hand, he is shrewd—as Joyce understood shrewdness—in judging the motivation of such as Mulligan (p. 620) with relation to Stephen; and in his own wobbly, uncomfortable way, he is kind. When the sweeping-car horse drops three deliberate turds at the end of the chapter, it is a judgment on the style. Bloom and Stephen then wander off toward #7 Eccles Street to the tune of "The Lowbacked Car," the refrain of which assures us that they are "to be married by Father Maher," and in fact some sort of uneasy alliance–marriage has taken place, for the time being, and on a very low level indeed.

"Ithaca" (pp. 666–737) is the ugly duckling of *Ulysses*, a great long detailed catechism of a chapter, containing little or no dramatic action but vast amounts of relevant and irrelevant information and misinformation. Like all three of the "Nostos" chapters, it is completely indiscriminate. "Eumaeus" is the garbage of indiscriminate existence, "Ithaca" the garbage of indiscriminate thought, and "Penelope"—ah, "Penelope"! But we must not anticipate. The business of "Ithaca" is simple enough. Bloom, having forgotten his key, cannot enter #7 Eccles Street by the front door, but with characteristic resourcefulness climbs a fence, gets in the back door, and admits Stephen. Over a cup of cocoa, they continue their halting and difficult discussion, exchanging miscellaneous bits of lore. Stephen declines an offer to stay the night. They go out in the garden and urinate together, Stephen departs, and Bloom thoughtfully retires. Molly interrogates him on the events of his day, he answers more or less evasively, and they go to sleep.

Why is this little grain of business encrusted in so elaborate a shell of questions and answers? Because the episode is a parody of the scientific, rational mind. Any fact is as good as any other fact to it; put in a question, and you get out an answer—prompt, factual, and unbearably detailed. If it provided simply material facts, the "answering" voice would quickly become monotonous; but its perspective is continually wavering from the concrete and immediate to the remote and mythical. Bloom becomes a wandering star or is reduced by cross-multiplication to the nadir of misery (p. 725); his cosmic guides are heavenly bodies observed through a telescope or a placket (p. 727); a meditation on the possibility of life on other planets turns imperceptibly into a verse of Ecclesiastes (pp. 699–700). These varying but often remote perspectives diminish the stature of the novel and its characters, even as they expand our vision to the outside limits of the universe and contract it to the minutiae of the Dublin waterworks. The inconceivably vast and the inconceivably trivial cast a chill over the whole movement and motive force of the characters; and Bloom, looking back from outer space, sees his cuckolding with something like equanimity— given the conditions of human life, the vastness and apathy of the universe, it simply does not matter. It is with edged, far-darting thoughts like these that Bloom slays the usurping suitors. As for events within the chapter, it is true they do not provide much ground for supposing Bloom and Stephen are to be fast friends. But they have already gone off, arm-in-arm into the sunset, at the end of "Eumaeus"; "Ithaca" must do something more with them. Symbolically (and as we approach the novel's end, all the characters, including the most earthy, are increasingly transfigured by symbolic significance) a good deal happens in this episode, between Stephen and Bloom. They drink that cocoa—"Epps's massproduct, the creature cocoa" (p. 677), and a massproduct is not only mass-produced, it may be used in celebration of a Mass. Moreover the botanical name for the cocoa plant is *Theobromos*, drink of the gods, and whether Joyce knew this or not, the symbolic meaning would have been more than acceptable to him. (He was, in biographical fact, an ardent cocoa drinker, ordering it on occasion sent to Trieste especially from Ireland; he also lived on cocoa while a meager student in Paris.) Stephen and Bloom cross linguistic tracks too; they teach one another a little Gaelic and the first rudiments of the Hebrew alphabet. And as they urinate together in the garden, a star is "precipitated with great apparent velocity across the firmament from Vega in the Lyre above the zenith beyond the stargroup of the Tress of Berenice towards the zodiacal sign of Leo" (p. 703). The fall of a star from Orpheus' lyre into the sign of Leo is a pretty explicit metaphor for Stephen's entry into Bloom's orbit.

Finally, as the machinery of catechism clanks on and on, both questioner and answerer (whoever they are) start to get sleepy and woozy. A lot of the answers involve errors or absurdities—not merely calculated symbolic distortions, but a deliberate crazing of the materials; a lot of the questions are so laconic as to challenge comprehension. Thus the catechism fades off into nonsense gabble. Sinbad the Sailor and Tinbad the Tailor and even Whinbad the Whaler (p. 737) are traditional characters in the children's Christmas pantomime; but the other cognates are dreamy, dim inventions of a yawning mind. The further question, "When?" is answered in a spate of words, but they make no sense at all; and the final question "Where?" is answered wordlessly with a large round black dot. Where does anything happen? Where was Moses when the light went out? The only answer is, In the dark. We are all in the dark. The blackness cannot be expressed in words or type; it becomes blackness itself on the page, a round black hole, down which the conscious mind is poured. This black hole at the end of "Ithaca" is a crucial moment in Joyce; once his mind passed through it, it was never a daylight mind again. We have reached what Yeats would call the end of one gyre and the beginning of another; the conscious mind has run out the end of its rope, and the rest of the book—as well as all future books— belongs to the subconscious and the superconscious. After common sense, there is something beyond; Joyce not only found it, but entered boldly into it, and made it the kingdom of his imagination.

As an imaginative achievement—a sheer sustained act of verbal creation—there is nothing in *Ulysses*, and very little in modern fiction, to compare with "Penelope" (pp. 738–783). Mathematically considered, it is 45 pages of unpunctuated prose, divided by paragraphing into eight sentences (they begin on pp. 738, 744, 753, 754, 759, 763, 770, and 776). We must start by getting the obscenity issue out of the way. Molly is not simply a realistic creation. Her thoughts and her language are not, and are not intended to be, those of every woman or indeed of any woman; she is the principle of fleshly existence, foul, frank, and consciously obscene. She is, specifically, woman as conceived by a man trained to think the flesh naturally dirty, woman with a thousand little inhibitions and delicacies deliberately left out, woman in the raw (as it were), designed to shock. We are not being "sophisticated" or "urbane" when we talk about Molly's "wholesome, gusty *joie de vivre*," we are being silly. She is a slut, a sloven, and a voracious sexual animal as conceived by one of those medieval minds to whom the female can never be anything but a *saccum stercoris;* she is a frightening venture into the unconsciousness of evil, and certainly, deliberately obscene.

But Molly Bloom is not only obscene, she is holy; she is life itself, profuse, repetitive, forever polluting and renewing itself. Bloom is a flower on her opulent, amoral–immoral breast, and so are we all. She is mad for flowers and mad for men, all men, indiscriminately, tramps, bootblacks, lord mayors, Boylan, Poldy, Mulvey—so that "he" and "him" come to refer in the course of her soliloquy, to an almost limitless array of lovers. Everyman loves Everywoman. Though mad for fun and life—something of a harumscarum, as she says (p. 779)—yet she is sensible and bourgeois at bottom. Her judgments are simple and ultimate. In Dublin John Henry Menton is an important established solicitor, but to Molly he is only a big stupoe (p. 739). Boylan was a welcome interlude in her sterile and unhappy cohabitation with Bloom, and her frolic with him will continue in Belfast, but she does not take him seriously (p. 776). Bloom tries to find out what she is thinking of (and whom she is thinking of) in the moment of intercourse, tries, as she says, "to make a whore of me" (p. 740); she tolerates this, with his many other oddities, but thinks him ridiculous. Being solidly grounded on her own sexual bottom, she has a keen, secure eye for the inadequacies of that gallery of sexual grotesques by whom she is surrounded. How many lovers has she had? The list on p. 731 enumerates 25 in addition to Bloom, but it is clearly wrong in some respects and incomplete in others, and the point of the indefiniteness is that she has had a hankering for, and inspired a hankering in, practically every male within her range, and how many she actually slept with we neither know nor can guess. In this matter of lovers she is inexhaustible. But she is inexhaustibly fecund in general—in the last pages of the novel she is still bringing forth new characters of whom we have never heard, treasures from her teeming, bottomless past of whom even Bloom never knew (p. 782). True, she does not spawn children with the prolific abandon of Mrs. Purefoy, but the reproductive drudge is no proper emblem of true fertility. Molly, with her young eyes, is the freshness of an eternal receptivity, the vital responsiveness which contrasts magnificently with languid, pallid Stephen, and exhausted Bloom.

The motion of Molly's prose is, appropriately, circular; she is a globe spinning round and round on her axis, using such specific words as "bottom," "yes," and "because," over and over in various contexts. Neither her mind, as a mundane woman, nor her motion, as a heavenly body, ever ceases spinning; she is wholly unpunctuated, centrifugal as a planet, luminescent, vital, on a predetermined, immovable course, and the sun shines for her. Perhaps the most extraordinary feature of her prose is the perfectly commonplace material of which it is woven. She recalls a good many songs, and works their words into the texture of her monologue, but the general run of her prose is wholly unpoetical. She mixes up things of the kitchen and the nursery with lovers of long ago, plans for new outfits, contemporary murder trials, and bits of neighborhood gossip and scandal. Her most spectacular contribution to the *mise en scène* is Gibraltar, where Joyce (for the first time in the entire novel, or, for that matter, in his career) described a community he had never seen. (There is a Gibraltar directory, as there is a Dublin directory, and Joyce got most of the bare bones for his reconstruction out of that book—the odd names, the stores, the strange streets, the apes and caves and public gardens.) But Molly is not an exotic simply because of her origins; it is what she does with these raw materials that counts.

Her prose is irresistibly in motion—it is resilient and self-generating beyond any other prose in this incomparably well-written book. In each new sentence one feels the spring of energy from a train of thought which has been built up—by comparison with Bloom's thin train of scrappy reflections, Molly's consciousness has the solid impact of a river in flood. Thus Gibraltar fuses with the Hill of Howth, Algeciras Bay with Dublin Bay, Bloom with Mulvey with Gardner with Boylan, and Molly with her immemorial past, to form the final tremendous image of the rock by the river in which masculine and feminine relations are forever typified. In Molly's vision, space is abolished as well as time, sight is finally achieved by shutting one's eyes, and someone flies securely and assuredly through or over the gaping, irrational void which is the condition of modern life. Without knowing that she is doing so, without any fuss or palaver, Molly is fulfilling metaphorically the artistic program of Stephen Dedalus. Why not? As Calypso and Circe and Penelope, in Homer, are all versions of one woman, all cave-dwelling weavers, and so all embodiments of Maya, the first woman and the first weaver—so Molly not only is the texture of this world, but the force which creates it by the spinning of her thoughts. The most intuitive and perceptive of men can respond to only a fraction of her infinite creativity. Jealousy, ambition, resentment, and arrogance are all equally alien

and irrelevant to her splendid, filthy, prodigal existence. Stephen's art and Stephen's creativity, by contrast, are all contrivance and arrangement and pre-
tence. Molly is common as dirt, precious as life,
powerful beyond our approval or disapproval; and
the gush of her vitality makes much of the book
which precedes it look contrived, artificial, mechanical.

The effect is surely deliberate. For with "Penelope"
Joyce had reached the point where the traditional
artistic devices for arranging artistic effects and managing fictional sympathies had become self-defeating.
He had always had, in one part of his nature, a great
impatience of artifice, a sense that one was a charlatan,
an impostor, a pretender when one built up the
façades of literary impression. Not that, with another
side of his nature, he was not devoted to weaving
arabesques of pattern, artificial intricacies of infinite
complexity—but there was usually something separate
and detachable about these decorative exfoliations.
They were distinct and complex but unconnected with
the human content of his fable. One side of him was
Dedalus, the intricate artificer, but the other side was
Orpheus, the visionary seer. (If we want still another
side for the realistic Joyce, we might name it after
Apelles, the Greek painter who imitated those grapes
so nicely that birds pecked them.) The Dedalus,
Book of Kells side of his artistic character (eked out
with the Apelles side) provides a complex overlay
through which one reaches after the Blake-and-
Orpheus side. The special effect which results is fascination. About this fascination, and his own power
to produce it, Joyce had many misgivings—doubts
which he expressed chiefly, in the beginning, to his
wife. Only Nora knew what he was like behind his
literary façades—and it is fitting that in writing of
Nora he came, finally, to cast some of them aside.

Thus "Penelope" is a step in the direction of a vision
so naive and deep, so copious and complex that all

languages, concepts, and personae become mere trans-
parencies—a vision still adorned with infinite relevant
or irrelevant artifice, but in its own essential nature
simple, sensuous, and intuitive. When the shackles of
the conscious, civilized brain are cast off, we can
finally see. This was the inevitable trend of Joyce's
development, which he could hardly have reversed or
altered without becoming a wholly different person;
and a sense of this logic may help to explain the
strength of that compulsion which forced him to write
Finnegans Wake against all considerations of prudence and interest, against overwhelming pressure
from friends and advisers, out of sheer intuitive need.

As for passing a summary judgment on *Ulysses*—
the normal task of a concluding paragraph—it is an
idle and impertinent task. For one thing, the book is
altogether *sui generis*. There are long novels and elaborate novels, but there is no novel anywhere which is
so thoroughly composed to the epic scale and in the
epic manner. Not only is there no novel so vast in plan,
there is none so knotty and complex in its details.
Poems, yes—the *Divine Comedy* is more complicated
than *Ulysses*, and *Paradise Lost* has a vaster scope.
But novels, no. There is no novel so private, allusive,
and enigmatic. There is no novel which offers us so
high and low, so complete and complex a view of
man, not forgetting woman—as comic, as disgusting,
as curious, as vital and inventive. I don't mean that
Bloom and Stephen and Molly are "great" in the sense
of "real" fictional characters. Like Don Quixote and
Emma Bovary, they are real enough to get by, but
our most absorbing interest is not in them, it is in what
can be seen through them. However great *Ulysses*
turns out to be in the long run, it cannot help being
one of the works by which English literature of the
twentieth century is measured. This is not merely a
matter of dimensions, it is a matter of standards.
Ulysses is a work of imaginative literature which de-

mands that we consider it by literary standards. Though the twentieth century has produced an immense spate of writing, very little of it pretends to be literature, and even less approaches the standards of permanence. It does not seem conceivable that *Ulysses* will be dwarfed in the near future, when it has scarcely been approached over the past forty years.

The cosmos of *Ulysses* may very well prove, in the long run, exhaustible. It is a hollow world which the book presents, darker and more brittle than any which English fiction from Fielding to Hardy generally gives us; its technical virtuosity undeniably flourishes at the occasional expense of its "human warmth." But human warmth is not itself a quality of which the modern literary mind can stand a great deal; and the alternatives which *Ulysses* opened up show no present signs of quick exhaustion. The opinion used to be prevalent a few years ago that *Ulysses* was a great landmark standing at the end of the history of the English novel. Either it had done everything there was to be done, or it had led the novel in the wrong direction, into a *cul-de-sac* from which there was no exit, except perhaps backwards—to the early novels of H. G. Wells, say. More and more this gambit begins to look, nowadays, like pure piffle. The influence of *Ulysses* is pervasive, multiform, continuing. It is felt in minor novelists, in major novelists, in playwrights, everywhere. The book is the subject of continuing interest, critical conflict, literary investigation. It is widely read for pleasure, sheer pleasure. And, like all great books, and some few which are not really great, *Ulysses* has wrought a change in our relations with the world, has transfigured the reality into which it was born. I won't say whether this change is for good or for ill, but it is part of the intellectual weather under which we all live. Since the publication of this vast, tough, funny, bitter vision, the world will never be the same again.

CHAPTER IV

FINNEGANS WAKE

The first foundation stone of human wisdom concerning *Finnegans Wake* is the proper spelling, reading, and interpretation of the title. "Finnegan's Wake" is the title of a late nineteenth-century music-hall ballad which describes the fate of a hod-carrier who came to work with a hangover, fell from a ladder, broke his skull, was carried home and duly waked—but who, in the course of a fight that broke out during the wake, was splashed with whiskey (etymologically *usquebaugh*, meaning "water of life"; compare French *eau de vie*), and so rose from the dead. Joyce's title makes reference to this cycle, which he saw as containing in little the history (rise, fall, death, and resurrection) of the human race; but it omits the apostrophe in order to make *Finnegans* plural as well as possessive and *Wake* an imperative verb as well as a noun: Wake up, all you Finnegans! It is an invitation to the general resurrection and the Last Judgment; we the readers are all sleepers in the nightmare of history, who are asked, in the words of the chorale, to wake. But, more specifically, Finnegan and we as readers are Finn-again, reincarnations of Finn MacCool, the great Irish giant who has lain sleeping since prehistory, with his head under the Hill of Howth and his toes sticking up in Phoenix Park. The book asks us to become conscious that in our development as an individual organism from pre-natal growth to dissolution after death we recapitulate within ourselves the cyclical nature of life and genetically contain both the prehistory and future of our race within us. We must wake in this sense to the dead men within us, like Professor Rubek, the hero of *When We Dead Awaken*.

Finnegans Wake as a title further mirrors the structure of the book which follows in comprising a three-syllable word followed by a one-syllable word, to represent three books of eight, four, and four sections each, followed by a *ricorso*, or recapitulation, in one book of one section. The first syllable of the title is "Fin" = "end" in French, and the last one "Wake," which implies resurrection. The first book, though it contains several episodes and many sub-cycles, is devoted to the fall of Finnegan, his end; the last book to his resurrection. So much for the title; now the going gets a little harder.

How should one approach Finnegans Wake? Not by any means boldly; here the bold man is irretrievably lost. Rather, prudently, cautiously, a short bit at a time. This is one of the few books in the world which is by longstanding tradition read collectively. Venturing into it alone may be unnerving, perhaps actually painful. So enter upon it as spelunkers into a cave—in a group, with a lifeline, a steady light good for a couple of hours, and a readiness to probe the second corridor if you don't seem to be making any headway down the first. Friends are useful for comfort and support, to discredit one's rash interpretive enthusiasms, to supplement one's linguistic shortcomings, to share one's appreciation of the jokes. *Finnegans Wake* conventicles are found at many of our major universities; discreet inquiry may uncover or inspire one in your neck of the woods. Among the various guidebooks, summaries, and *vade mecums* presently on the market, the least pretentious and most valuable for a beginning student is Adaline Glasheen's *Second Census of Finnegans Wake*. The elegantly titled *A Skeleton Key to Finnegans Wake*, by Campbell and Robinson, had immense influence and value in its day; but there are a lot of doors in *Finnegans Wake* which it does not open, and some which its assured simplicities prevent one from seeing. By relying so heavily on paraphrase, it presents, in effect, a substitute-*Finnegans Wake*; and it is a very general view that if literature is worth anything at all, it is worth reading in its own original terms. Mrs. Glasheen makes available a lot of information supplemental and preliminary to *Finnegans Wake* without imposing a structure or a substitute-texture of her own. Her book makes admirably accessible to the reader a specific fact for a specific occasion.

There is an immense, elaborate, yet at the same time overscribbled and indistinct structure to *Finnegans Wake* and it would be well to learn something about it before embarking on serious explorations. A cautious outline of some of this structure will be sketched presently; both *A Skeleton Key to Finnegans Wake* and *A Second Census of Finnegans Wake* present (differing) summary views. A very minimum preliminary step would be to assign provisional titles to the various books and sections, to aid one in seeing the structure as a unit (tentative titles, some of them Joyce's, some my own, appear below).

Section headings for *Finnegans Wake*

However, before the inexperienced reader embarks on any major expedition into *Finnegans Wake*, I think he would be well advised to read, as a preliminary experiment, and as superficially as he chooses, a short, relatively self-contained passage of *Wake*-prose. Two or three sections in particular seem admirably adapted to this sampling function. Book I, section 2 (pp. 30–47), for example, offers an historical–mythical account —confused, blundering, mock-heroic, and tragi-comic —of the arrival in Ireland and naming of the hero of the book, who is also the public universal hero. He is Tim Finnegan, he is the ancient Irish giant Finn Mac-Cool, he is a Dublin pub-keeper in the early years of the present century, he is also one or all of those invading Danes or Norsemen who harried Ireland during the Middle Ages. Thus his arrival in Ireland is attended with barbaric grandeur and a heroic clangor of epithets. But the hero-outsider, the Milesian invader, is never really liked or admired by the native Firbolgs; and the section culminates in a malicious satiric ballad (*Hibernicé* = rann)*, sung through the Dublin streets by three villainous semi-characters, habitués of the hero's pub, known as Peter Cloran, (somebody) O'Mara, and Hosty (somebody), to celebrate the downfall of the hero. We note that it is a fall which is celebrated, a defeat not a victory; the spirit of the rann is undiluted malicious gratification. Thus the hero in several of his simultaneous manifestations has traversed within a few pages the inevitable hero-cycle, from triumph to disaster, and the reader has before him a little sub-epic of rise and fall, such as will be repeated again and again, in the maze of the book's larger pattern. Tim Finnegan has risen and fallen once more. If in this sample the jokes appeal, the verbal exercise delights, and the distortions of language don't distress one's patience or sensibilities unduly, then the whole of *Finnegans Wake* may well be for you.

Book III, section 1 of *Finnegans Wake* begins on p. 403 and runs to p. 428; in the course of it, an unnaturally meek and subservient Ass (who turns out to be Shem in disguise) interviews the prosperous and complacent Shaun on the formula for his success. After eating a monstrous dinner, Shaun obliges with a lengthy recital; when it is finished, instead of singing a song of triumph, as requested, he recites the story of the Ondt and the Gracehoper (pp. 414–419). La-

---

* "The wren, the wren, the king of all birds" (*Ulysses*, p. 481) is a little folk-poem sung in many parts of Europe and in many languages as part of a festival to celebrate the downfall and sacrifice of a mythical bird-king. For this reason Hosty composes "the rann, the rann, the king of all ranns" (*Finnegans Wake*, p. 44).

fontaine's fable of the ant and the grasshopper is here transposed into the argument of the prudent bourgeois with the feckless, improvident artist, the argument of the Catholic (who believes in salvation by works and merit) with the Calvinist (who believes in salvation by faith or grace), and sundry other associated topics. None of these portentous overtones prevent the fable from remaining delightfully miniature and elegantly buggy. At the end of the fable, we come across one of the several interesting letters with which *Finnegans Wake* bedevils us. This one is being sent from Shem to his mother ALP, but when Shaun thinks of the wicked and improper messages it probably contains, and of the indescribable sanctities of motherhood, he is overcome with emotion, turns into a tub, and goes bobbing off down the Liffey until he finally seems to disappear "like a popo down a papa, from circular circulatio" (p. 427, ll. 7–8). (But really he is just off to America, his cycle as the Rising Son being around the world from east to west along the lines of latitude—while his longitudinal brother Shem rises and falls on a vertical cycle from pole to pole.) It does not seem likely that Shem's letter will ever get where it is going, any more than will that interesting (perhaps identical) letter from Boston (Book I, section 5, pp. 104–125) scratched up by a hen on a dunghill, variously interpreted or misinterpreted, and finally misdelivered by Shaun the Post. In any event, Shaun's interview, his telling of the "Ondt and the Gracehoper" story, and his attack on his brother constitute a clear and effective unit, perhaps a little tougher in texture than the first sample passage proposed, on which to test one's taste for *Wake*-prose.

Either of these passages from the first and third books will serve as a start on *Finnegans Wake*, and it does not greatly matter which one chooses, for any start can be made only by leaving a lot of questions in abeyance. The rest of this essay will be devoted to considering complexities of language and structural pattern, and ways to absorb or overcome them; but even without explanation or help of any sort, it will, I think, be encouraging to find that quite a bit can be accomplished. Despite all its blurring and distorting of verbal forms, the language of *Finnegans Wake* is relatively orthodox syntactically; subject, verb, and objects are generally arranged in the classic pattern of an ordinary (though frequently cumbersome and over-modified) English sentence. Characters do fade, combine, recur, their identities are strangely and wonderfully layered, and they often become previous incarnations of their present selves without wholly losing their present "identities." (The *Wake*-world has to be accepted from the first as a world where metempsychosis is continual, where characters blur and run together in that eerie–natural way which we can only describe as "dream-like.") But though their outlines are undefined and their comings and goings unpredictable, the gestures of the assistants at the *Wake* generally encompass a perfectly accessible pattern of wry and funny action. In short, swatches of the book can be read for simple delight by an altogether unprepared—though perhaps ideally tolerant—reader, as novels and short stories generally are read. From these little islands of familiar and at-least-partially-comprehended *Wake*-stuff, it is then possible for the adventurous reader to spread out, more assuredly, through a *terra* hitherto *incognita*, until he has formed little archipelagos or even subcontinents of understanding. Anyone whose present ambitions are global is in need of more help than this do-it-yourself instruction sheet can pretend to provide.

Well, but in general, who's who in Finnegans Wake *and why?* The entire book, in the first place, occupies the space of a single night and dawning in the subconscious mind of a single dreamer. It also occupies, simultaneously, a week, a year, and infinity. As *Ulysses*

is the book of a single day yet subsumes the full lives
of Bloom and Stephen, the long perspectives of Hebrew and Hellene—so *Finnegans Wake* is the book of
a single immense night and morning, yet includes
within itself perspectives on many days, many eras of
personal and national and ethnic history. Like Bloom,
the dreamer is no one less than Everybody. He enjoys
access to the collective unconscious, and so to the
entire reach and range of universal history; moreover,
his dream seems to have different levels, so that at
one stage he is dreaming about a second person's
dream about still a third person's dream. From the
mists of this universal subconscious a central figure
starts to emerge, who is at least partly molded into
the Dreamer, and who is of central importance to
Finnegans Wake. He has been in the past, and can at
any convenient time become again, Oliver Cromwell,
the Duke of Wellington, Shakespeare, Oscar Wilde,
the Hill of Howth, a big salmon in the Liffey, Finn
MacCool, God the Father, Adam, and Abraham.

In one of his major present incarnations, he is a
turn-of-the-century pub-keeper in the Dublin suburb
of Chapelizod; his name is Humphrey Chimpden Earwicker. His name is Humphrey because he is a bit of
a hunchback, having as a buried giant carried the Hill
of Howth on his shoulders for many years, and as
Adam carried a full load of guilt ever since the first
Fall. Chimpden perhaps suggests a simian background, though I must confess to not seeing the full
meaning behind this; and Earwicker derives from the
earwig, a cosmopolitan insect, gregarious and nocturnal, and fascinating to Joyce because an archetypal
character is in effect a bug in one's ear, an aural in-
truder, a persistent, inescapable interrupter of the
sense-continuum. Earwicker is not only an historical
stammer, a set of human ditto marks; he stammers
himself, he is introduced to us as "Bygmester [big
master, but also in Norse master-builder] Finnegan,

of the Stuttering Hand" (p. 4), and a name specially
associated with him because built from his initials is
"Hecitency Hec" (or "Hek").* Because the French
name for an earwig is *perce-oreille*, Joyce sometimes
refers to Earwicker as "Persse O'Reilly," and if one
knows that an earwig is *forfecchia* in Italian and
ørentvist in Danish, he will be able to recognize HCE
in still other contexts. Lastly, in the strange name
"Earwicker" Joyce united two metaphysical references
which were important to him: "wick" in a variety of
Scandinavian tongues means "place"—it survives in
nouns like Prestwick and bailiwick. "Ear" is a mild
anagram for era = time; Earwicker is a crossing of
time and space, of here and now.

Why is so much made of his initials, HCE? Joyce,
in a letter of March 24, 1924, explained to Miss
Weaver that his basic ideogram was E; by moving
this symbol around, Joyce declared, one could get
the three initials H and C and E. How one does this
is not altogether clear to me, but Joyce said it could be
done. More distinct and significant, perhaps, is the
fact of a certain instability in HCE's symbol.† In the
form ∃ it suggested to Joyce the Resurrection. ⊓
through its resemblance to ancient stone constructs,
as of Stonehenge, signifies heroic achievement and
prehistoric man; E represents civil life, as well as our
hero in his Earwicker manifestation; and ⊔ with
toes turned upward, represents his fall, death, and
burial. These four stages constitute one cycle of

---

* It was his misspelling of "hesitancy" that betrayed Richard
Piggott, the forger who attempted to ruin Parnell in the London *Times* trial of 1890.

† These signs or symbols, by which half-blind Joyce abbreviated his characters, are scattered intermittently through *Finnegans Wake* itself; but they are very frequent in all the MSS
which lie behind *Finnegans Wake* and in the correspondence
which annotates it; Joyce had them much in mind during
composition, and they point up on occasion significant charac-
teristics of the characters.

human history according to a system which Joyce freely adapted from the writings of Giambattista Vico, an eighteenth-century Neapolitan sociologist; the exact shape of this cycle, and the exact nature of Joyce's debt to Vico (which is clouded by the influence of several other cyclical theories of human life, among them the Buddhist and pseudo-Buddhist, i.e., theosophical) is less interesting than the fact of HCE's radical instability.* By contrast, the symbol of Earwicker's wife, Anna Livia Plurabelle, is a Greek delta or equilateral triangle, which is the same in every position and never off its bottom. Being a delta, she is intimately associated with rivers, especially the river Liffey and the river of time; the delta is also the letter D, which when tripled gives Dear Dirty Dublin, and is a traditional emblem of the female sex-organs. Naturally, if one can adjust to all HCE's simultaneous identities, one will not be distressed by ALP's relatively limited repertory; she is Eve, Lilith, Nora Joyce, the Liffey, Mrs. Noah, Ann Hathaway, and a few other fertile, continuous females. Finally, if one adds the initials HCE to those of ALP, one gets a useful anagram of the word CHAPEL—which, given the fact that the Earwicker family inhabits Chapelizod, may not be entirely accidental.

Earwicker, considered in artificial isolation for a moment, merely as himself, keeps a public house, the Mullingar, in the grubby little suburb Chapelizod, on the north bank of the Liffey just outside Phoenix Park. He is the host of the pub, a title which in addition to reaffirming his numerous plural identities, establishes him, like Bloom and Stephen, as the divine corpus in a public, i.e., catholic, religion of man. The

* By one of those coincidences with which Joyce's intellectual life is studded, there is a comet which returns cyclically to the neighborhood of the earth, known as Vico's comet; its period is 5.66 years, its least distance (in astronomical units) is 1.19, its greatest distance 5.01.

public part of his house contains, as a rule, twelve regular and often disagreeable customers, who may sometimes serve as a jury and sometimes as apostles; sometimes the topers divide up into three or six rann-singers; sometimes they include four suspicious, in-quisitional old men, who may be Matthew, Mark, Luke, and John; or they may be the Four Masters of Ireland, i.e., four Franciscan friars who wrote a famous history of Ireland while the depredations and decimations of sixteenth-century Ireland went on around them. In any case, the habitués of HCE's pub entertain themselves and are entertained by several skits, stories, radio or television programs, and ama-teur amusements, in which the landlord bears a help-ing hand. Most of them relate to the warfare between the generations, the struggle of sons with fathers.

Meanwhile, in the private part of Earwicker's public house are found the rest of his ménage, the publican's wife, variously known as Anna Livia Plurabelle or ALP, and their children. She has a hundred and eleven children (p. 201) or a thousand and one (p. 210), and he has three. The differences resolve pleasantly, how-ever, on at least two levels: 1001 illustrates the fruitful marriage of one with zero, something with nothing—a fruitful Hegelian intercourse, out of which all exist-ence springs; 111 shows that by the female system of counting all children are individuals and of equal value; finally, Hebrew letters have numerical values, according to which *aleph* = 1, *lamed* = 30, and *pe* = 80, therefore ALP = 111. They have in fact a daughter Isolde and twin boys named Shem and Shaun, i.e., Jim and John, but also known on occasion as Glugg and Chuff, Mutt and Jute, Old Nick and Saint Mick, Cain and Abel, Jerry and Kevin, Ishmael and Isaac, and numerous other pair-names.*

* The principle of duality which is so strong in *Finnegans Wake*, the insistent yoking of complementary opposites, owes something to Joyce's interest in the philosophy of Giordano

Shaun or John is a successful and businesslike extrovert, a bourgeois, common-sense, get-ahead, Apollonian fellow, a moralist, a hypocrite, a sentimentalist, and a braggart; he is at various times identified with Joyce's brother John Stanislaus Joyce, with his prudent friend John Francis Byrne, with gormandising John McCormack the tenor, with insensitive Oliver Gogarty, and with many historical characters. But he is also, on occasion, an aspect of the character of Joyce himself. By occupation, Shaun is a postman, partly because it is a get-around, cyclical occupation, partly by carry-over from the theatrical character Shaun the Post in Dion Boucicault's play *Arrah-na-Pogue*. Shem or James or Jim is a pariah, an outcast, an immoralist, a Dionysian, and a writer. His name too comes in part from a nineteenth-century play, *Jim the Penman*, by Sir Charles Young. Jim the Penman was a forger by trade, in historical fact as well as on the stage; and Joyce chose the name for his own representative in the book, because it suggested both the pride and the loathing which he felt for his occupation as a writer of fiction. Shaun hates and despises his brother Shem, primarily because they are brothers, but under the pretext that this particular brother is immoral in word and deed. In their boyish games, Shaun is Saint Mick and Shem is Old Nick. When they are working problems in the classroom, Shaun encourages the brainier Shem to solve a problem in triangular geometry, the answer to which reveals something about their mother's sexual nature (earth = mud = excrement = sex, and geometry measures it all), but when he sees what it is all about, Shaun is horrified at his wicked brother's lewd ideas. He himself could easily write better things than Shem does, and, what's more, they

Bruno, Renaissance heretical philosopher. Bruno came from the little town of Nola, in Italy, and Joyce derived great comfort from associating him with the Dublin bookstore of Browne and Nolan.

would be moral; but of course he hasn't bothered. Shaun is the native son who goes into exile, Shem is the foreign invader who turns out to be more Irish than the Irish themselves; Shaun is the Sun-Son; Shem is a moon or one of the wandering stars. Odious as he is, Shaun is the pre-ordained success, and it is inevitable that he will play Tristan to his romantically-attractive but inordinately-dumb sister Isolde, or Issy—who is also called "Nuvoletta" or "Little Cloud," because she is at once a diffusion and a foreshadowing of her mother the river Liffey.*

The five Earwickers, in their multiple-layered characters, are no doubt the central personages of *Finnegans Wake*; but they easily reduce to a couple, for Issy is simply a duplication and diffusion of her mother (as Milly Bloom was simply a watered-down Molly), and the two antithetical sons are merely two halves who go to make up one whole HCE. Shem's sign is ⊓; he is his father, minus the penis. Shaun's sign is ∧; he is his mother, without her bottom. Issy's sign is ⊣, which is said to represent Tristan turned topsy-turvy. The two essential characters of *Finnegans Wake*, to which the others are all reducible, are HCE, forever rising and falling, destroyed and reborn; and ALP, who flows and sustains. They are the Liffey and the Hill of Howth, the river and the mountain, a woman and a man, the subject of all romance.

Episodes, action? Hardly any. Some time in the past, it appears, HCE committed an indistinct and awful crime in the Phoenix Park; two young girls and three soldiers were witnesses of it. Whatever it was— heterosexual, homosexual, exhibitionistic, onanistic, or voyeuristic—it had sexual overtones; and from time to time charges based on it and rumors deriving from

---

* Shaun the Post is the successful wooer of Nora the heroine of Dion Boucicault's *Arrah-na-Pogue*. On the relation of Nuvoletta to Joyce's story in *Dubliners*, "A Little Cloud," the formulations are still to be made.

it revive in the popular mind. The populace riots, malicious gossip and satiric stories are repeated everywhere, there are investigations and reinvestigations, but nothing is ever settled. Like a loyal wife, ALP is intent on setting these rumors and agitations at rest, distributing placatory presents (many of which, like Pandora's, turn out badly) and scratching after evidence which will exculpate her husband, but in vain. The boys are involved in an intricate, interminable war of their own; they quarrel, combine, assert themselves against their father, and discover that they are merely repeating his repetitions of a primeval pattern. Empty-headed Issy is waiting endlessly for a Tristan who shows no signs of appearing. HCE dreams of "starting all over again," but never does so, for there is nothing really new. The choral customers at the bar are either indignant or apathetic about HCE, as their cycles move them, but they will not really change either. It is a condition of the world as Joyce sees it that nothing happens or, if something does, its happening is part of a cycle which has neither meaning nor direction, only an immemorial shape. *Plus ça change, plus c'est la même chose.* Thunder is important for Joyce and he was deeply afraid of it in his own person. Vico had a theory that primitive man learned to speak by imitating thunder, and a thunderclap always marks the onset of a Viconian cycle. The thunder speaks ten times in *Finnegans Wake,* always in a word just a hundred letters long—except for the last time, when the word is a hundred and one letters long.* That is Joyce's idea of incremental repetition, and it suggests a measure of the progress and importance of action in the book.

Something about the structuring of *Finnegans Wake* now. The book as a whole forms a circle or cycle, in

* Adaline Glasheen, *Second Census of Finnegans Wake* (Evanston Ill.: Northwestern University Press, 1963), p. xxv, footnote.

token of which the first sentence is merely the end of a sentence, beginning in the middle and proceeding to its period. The book is thus launched, and not until its last sentence is the cycle completed by the first half of the first sentence. So the book begins with an end and ends with a beginning; in between, it encompasses a cycle in four stages. The four books of *Finnegans Wake* may be conveniently labeled: I) the Book of the Parents, the Gods, Birth, or the Past; II) the Book of the Sons, the Heroes, Marriage, or the Present; III) the Book of the People, Men, Death, or the Future; and IV) the Book of *Ricorso*, Reconstitution, or the Great Silence, the timeless pregnant pause before the cycles all start again. Of course within these units there are all sorts of sub-cycles; Book II, for example, begins with a section of children's games, and progresses through two sections of intermediate development to a final fourth section portraying senility and second childhood. Book III, devoted to the Four Watches of Shaun, begins with an analysis of his prosperity and ends with his reduction to Yawn, his incorporation with the sleeping landscape, his return to and resumption into the identity of his father, HCE. The dream-patterning of the book allows all the characters to appear and disappear on cyclical schedules of their own, and the use of thematic repetitions (leitmotifs), as in *Ulysses*, allows for the stitching together of multiple cross-cyclical connections. Individual sentences are formed into cycles and even specific phrases and individual words may represent cycles and sub-cycles. On p. 99, HCE comes cycling furiously by: "A human pest cycling (pist!) and recycling (past!) about the sledgy streets, here he was (pust!) again!" On p. 19 someone cries: "Damadam to infinities!"—which, in addition to reading "Damn Adam to eternity" also presents a cyclical image of his damnation, Damadam being in effect a cycle of Adam begun in the middle and capable of infinite repetition. It is the overlaying and interweaving of these many cycles that makes the structure of the book hard to grasp or to represent with any fullness.

Backwards is a good way to approach the structure of *Finnegans Wake*. Book IV, the final soliloquy of Anna Liffey, is a single continuous sweep of fluid interior monologue in which all the previous themes of the book are caught up and resolved, as the themes of *Ulysses* are caught up and resolved in the life-giving flood of "Penelope." (To know this sort of thing doesn't make any particular passage more lucid, but at least it locates one's confusions within a framework.) Book III, comprising the Four Watches of Shaun, offers no particular structural complications. Though it is immensely difficult writing, especially in the fourth watch, for the decay and disintegration of Shaun take place on many intersecting, interpenetrating levels of time and space,* the structural outlines of Shaun's heroic-imaginary life are the structural principles of the book, and of course they complete a cycle.

Books II and I, where the dreaming is relatively superficial, and where the history of the Earwicker family is reported pretty much from the outside, seem to offer the greatest structural complications. Book II consists of four sections: 1) Mick, Nick, and the Maggies; 2) Studies and Contests, or The Eternal Triangle; 3) Pub and Festivities; 4) Mamalujo. Briefly, these sections grow out of the following concepts. The first section describes an innocent yet deeply revela-

* Joyce said in a letter to Miss Weaver that Shaun was cycling "backwards in the night through the events already narrated" (Stuart Gilbert, ed., *The Letters of James Joyce* [New York: Viking, 1957], p. 214), as the sun might seem to move backwards during the night to its point of rising. This might well be one source of confusion in the fourth watch. But the depth and locus of the dream are also unclear; if, as seems probable, it is a dream inside several other dreams, even a determined *Wake*-reader may consider it insufficiently defined.

tory guessing-game being played outside the pub by
Shem, Shaun, and some girls—Maggies—who are
simultaneously the seven colors—red, orange, yellow,
green, blue, indigo, and violet (Bloom's "roygbiv,"
Ulysses, pp. 376, 486)—and twenty-eight color-girls
from the story of "The Sleeper Awakened" in *Thous-
and and One Nights* (see Clive Hart, *Structure and
Motif in Finnegans Wake*, pp. 104–108)—plus Issy. In
this game, Shaun is an angel (Mick) and the protector
of the girls, Shem a devil (Nick) and their tempter-
seducer; in the course of the game, the girls praise
their angelic defender Shaun for his "puerity" (i.e.,
his purity and the fact that he is a harmless boy—
Latin, *puer*) though they really want Shem, their
demonic pursuer. The boys grow jealous of one another, and Shem in his frustration writes or contemplates writing libels on his whole family, parading
for his revenge the universal fact of sex. But neither
boy can really attract or hold the girls, and the section
ends with the children being called home by the
thunder of their father's voice and the reverberations
of his sexual authority.

The second section is patterned on a schoolchild's
exercise-book, with commentaries, relevant and irrelevant, by the boys, in both margins and on the bottom
of the page. (Since in addition to being a common
task, study is also a contest, the boys change position
at half-time [p. 293], Shaun moving from right to left
margin, Shem from left to right.) Issy knows her
letters (she can dirty a clean page, she is sexually
wise) but, not being the brainy type, she uses her
knowledge only to write an inane letter to a Maggy
(p. 280) and a love-letter to her unknown instructor
in "erringnesses in perfection class" (p. 279, footnote).
The boys study cosmology, ontology, history, government, literature, and finally geometry. Corrupt Shem
teaches stupid, innocent Shaun to draw a triangle on
Liffey mud (geometry is earth-measuring, the earth is

our common mother, mud is dirty, and the origins of geometry are said to have been the need for resurveying after the annual floods of the Nile). After the triangle finally dawns on Shem, or he on it (p. 287), the event is promptly discussed in the decent obscurity of a learned language, and there is a reassuring letter from the Liffey herself to the effect that she comprehends everything. But Shaun, momentarily intoxicated by his new knowledge, starts to write—his first letter, naturally, is D, delta, first letter of every letter ("Dear Herman") but also perhaps the "big D" of *H.M.S. Pinafore*, a blasphemy (p. 300). Then, overcome by remorse and shame, he knocks his brother down; far from being irritated, however, Shem thanks Shaun for insights received, and the two brothers unite to face their returning father. In answer to his questions, they provide virtuous, specious answers on their day's activities, contemplate a series of delirious topics for compositions, and write instead a letter to their parents, which seems to convey Christmas ("youlldied") greetings, but really expresses the wish that the old ones will soon be dead and buried.

The third section of Book II was (as A. Walton Litz points out, *The Art of James Joyce*, p. 99) one of the last to be written and, as one of the longest and loosest in *Finnegans Wake*, is analogous, in themes, structure, and function, to the "Circe" section in *Ulysses*. During a night's heavy drinking in Earwicker's pub, entertainment is provided by a machine, either radio or television, and by the customers themselves. The first story they tell is of a hunchbacked Norwegian captain who ordered a suit of clothes from Kersse the Dublin tailor; when it didn't fit, the captain denounced the tailor as an incompetent cloth-cutter, while the tailor cursed the captain as an impossibly-misshapen man. Outsiders and insiders never can agree; man is never well-suited by his philosophy; it is impossible to measure up to ideals, either one's own

or someone else's—these are some of the moral implications of the tailor story. But there is another one
woven into it of a suit, i.e., a wooing, in which Shem
as the Norwegian captain, or Tristan, seems to take
young Isolde away from HCE as Kersse the tailor or
King Mark; but, as so often, HCE seems capable of a
double role, and he may be (when envisaged as a
youth) the invading hunchback who steals ALP, as
well as the grudging husband–father who tries to hold
onto her.

Following this story, a pair of knockabout comedians appear; their names are Butt and Taff, but they
are really Shem and Shaun in disguise. After suitable
by-play, including an interesting reconstruction (probably on the box) of a horse race (pp. 349–350), they
proceed to recite the story of Buckley and the Russian
General. Buckley was an Irish soldier in the Crimean
War, assigned to duty as a sniper. A Russian general
coming under his sights, Buckley drew a bead on him,
but hesitated because impressed by his splendid uni-
form; then the Russian general let down his pants to
defecate, and again Buckley hesitated, overcome by
the sheer humanity of the situation. But when the
Russian general picked up a turf to wipe himself,
Buckley saw in the gesture an insult to Ireland, and
hesitated no longer. He shot the Russian general, in
the process killing an old Adam, an aboriginal father,
an outworn cycle, becoming thereby in an occult
sense, Bishop Berkeley, who slew the material universe with a thought. The silent humanity of a vulgar
predicament and the abstract logic of a metaphysical
hypothesis walk hand and hand in this episode of
Finnegans Wake. In this respect, the book is much of
a piece throughout.

Then comes a musical interlude, again probably on
the box (pp. 359–361), and a rather woozy discussion
of the shooting of the Russian general, which turns, as
a result of HCE's weak defense of the general, into an

increasingly-direct attack on the pub-keeper himself. His customers revive the old story of a misdeed in Phoenix (Fiendish) Park and hear from a soldier who claims to have witnessed the crime; they are only partially appeased by HCE's speech of uneasy explanation—he admits being guilty, but says so is everybody else. At last the mutter of a mob is heard in the distance; they arrive, singing a recognizable version of "The Ballad of Persse O'Reilly," invented by Hosty in Book I, section 2; and now the assault on HCE turns into a storm of abuse, in which his daughter and sons seem to take part. He is mocked and shamed and derided, he is disgraced and humiliated. Finally, he closes the pub, assumes the role of Roderick O'Connor, last native king of Ireland, drinks up the leftover liquor (symbolic hemlock), and falls in a stupor to the floor.

The last section of Book II describes Earwicker's deepest dream of sailing away to Nattenlaender (Nightlands) with Isolde, his pub being somehow transformed into a ship surrounded by screaming gulls. On board the vessel are four rather awful old men, Matthew, Mark, Luke, and John, who are always depressing HCE, trying to prevent his resurrection, moaning, groaning, and complaining. They conclude this cycle on a suitable note of senile impotence.

As for Book I, which we approach last in this reverse survey of the structure of *Finnegans Wake*, it comprises eight books, the first four dealing with HCE, the last four with his family. Section I (pp. 3–29) basically retells the ballad of "Finnegan's Wake," extending the import of the hero's fall by a visit to the museum of human history, of which Finnegan's body is an epitome and equivalent. The museum is full of relics of the battle of Waterloo, which is all the battles of the world, since it is the struggle of rising tyrant-sons (Lipoleums) against their fierce authoritative father (the Duke of Willingdone). Various rubble-heaps, junk-piles, and treasure-hordes are visited by hens and outlanders in this re-survey of historical accumulation; and the section ends with the spilling of whiskey over Finnegan, and his determination to rise again out of the kernel of the grave, despite objections by those four nasty old men who want to keep him down.

Section 2 (comprising pp. 30–47, and partially described above, pp. 175–176) recounts several stories about the origins of HCE and the source of his name. Here too we get a first hint of the crime he is alleged to have committed in Phoenix Park. While walking there, he met a Cad, who asked in Gaelic for the time of day. HCE misunderstood, thought it was a homosexual proposition,* and answered at cross purposes. Nothing, in other words, happened. But the story grows under a cloud of insinuation into a tale of vile, mysterious misdeeds, and culminates in "The Ballad of Persse O'Reilly." After the singing of this vicious and gleeful hate-paean, a variety of opinions are voiced (in section 3, pp. 48–74) as to whether HCE was really guilty of the crime which led to his downfall, and this discussion carries on, with multiplying points of view and increasing evidence both relevant and irrelevant. Three soldiers say he did something unseemly with young girls, but other witnesses suggest that the girls (Lupita Lorette and Luperca Latouche) were no better than they should be. In section 4 (pp. 75–103), the matter turns into a lawsuit, with four judges, numerous witnesses, limitless questions, and the whole business blowing up amid cries of Shame! Shame! or Shemus! Shemus! as one chooses (p. 93). Section 5 (pp. 104–125) turns from HCE to his wife;

* "What time is it?" in Gaelic would be *"Cad a chlog é?"* which doesn't make any obviously or specifically homosexual queries, but may help explain why the Cad was called Cad. Swift, who called himself "Cadenus," an anagram of *"Decanus,"* which is Latin for "dean" may also be included in the figure of the Cad.

she is a hen, scratching on the rubbish-heap of history and uncovering a letter from Boston, Massachusetts, which will (she hopes) make clear her husband's innocence. But the letter is hard to decipher and harder to interpret and the hen can't explain its message properly (all she gets are henscratches). Thus she gives it to her sons Shem the Penman to write up and Shaun the Post to deliver. But it doesn't seem likely that the message will get through. Section 6, questions and answers (pp. 126–168), comprises twelve questions asked by Shem, answered by Shaun, and offering portraits of the Earwicker family, their servants and surroundings. In order, the questions concern HCE, ALP, the pub, Dublin, Joe the manservant, Kate the slavey, the twelve customers, the Maggies, seven spectrum-girls, Issy, Shaun (at unbearable length), and Shem (in two words). Section 7 (pp. 169–195) is an extended denunciation of Shem by Shaun; but when Shem briefly defends himself, he is given an eloquent blessing from Anna Liffey herself, as well as a "lifewand" to make the dumb speak. In the last section of Book I (8, pp. 196–216), Anna Liffey becomes the theme as well as the great example of Joyce's speech. Chattering, flowing, swirling, shallow, devious, and rich, the talk of Anna Livia Plurabelle is the talk of two washerwomen who, as they kneel scrubbing by the darkening waters of the Liffey = Life, gradually metamorphose into a tree and a stone, elements of the permanent landscape, while the river flows unendingly by.

These then are the crudest structural outlines of what happens in *Finnegans Wake*; their use is the very simple one of providing a railing to hold onto when the language of the book seems to be giving way under one's feet. But the important thing that happens in *Finnegans Wake* is really that language itself, and precisely its giving-way; so that the difficulties from which the railing momentarily saves us are really the book's achievements. The language of *Finnegans Wake* is a dialect based primarily on English; it has, however, been compressed, twisted, and distorted by a variety of forces—twisted here into baby talk and there into pidgin, puffed up into multiple parodies, dragged in various directions by analogues, reduced to its roots, and occasionally torn violently apart into its component phonemes. Reading *Finnegans Wake* can be, if one isn't careful, a deeply disturbing experience because all the familiar conventions of English speech start to crumble and go to pieces within one's mind. It is a liberating experience, in a sense, but it may also be distressing; a basically destructive principle is set at large within one's head, and one finds oneself pouncing on random phonemes and wringing them into ridiculous, delightful meanings. If your mind is normally a pretty well-organized, friendly, clucking chicken-coop, *Finnegans Wake* may let loose a weasel in it. Confusion, feathers, and some bloodshed are almost sure to result.

Why did Joyce write Finnegans Wake *in an impossible pangloss of impacted lingos?* I think the reader wants an answer to this question before anything else and I fear the only answer to be offered is in the nature of the man as sketched throughout this entire study. He had come to see human history and human life in a certain visionary way; he had trained himself to see through the here and now; to seek (in Richard Ellmann's pregnant phrase) the remarkable in the commonplace. He could not bring himself to see things otherwise, or to express his vision in the two dimensions of ordinary English for mere reasons of convenience or convention. He needed a new dimension for speech and he created it.

It is curious to think what Joyce's reputation would be if *Finnegans Wake* had really been what it is often called, a piece of "experimental" prose. Had it been

50 pages long instead of 628, had it been a tentative venture to which he devoted six months instead of an anguished labor of seventeen years, had it been a stylistic game instead of a passionate vision, people would not have been so afraid of it. But in fact it is monolithic—a style of writing which answers to a style of vision, and that means a way of structuring reality. There is no getting away from the fact that the new structure, by its very existence, implies despair of the old ones. Tremendous bitterness lies just below the surface of the much and properly admired humor, tremendous cynicism behind the cyclical elaborations and verbal legerdemain. The creatures Joyce describes must be funny because their world contains nothing but seventh-hand folly, about which it is impossible to remain serious; Byzantine ingenuities of patterning can occupy the artist's whole attention because there are no moral or human or dramatic values to distract him. Moreover, Joyce seems altogether careless of "what he's saying," of the plain sense of his communication. He not only seems so, he is. To say just one thing at a time would be to emaciate and attenuate his view of reality; if confusion is the result of his vision, he accepts it. Certain sorts and degrees of control over his art he did not choose to exercise at all. A prudent artist wouldn't have done this. He might have written, like Joyce, in many languages at once, and with just as many cycles cycling, but he would have curbed and hedged his artistic statement and limited his intent as with a wiry bounding line. Joyce wrote in another way. If we as readers feel he is playing malicious jokes on us, we are badly wrong; we are also wrong if we imagine he is bending all the resources of his linguistic talent to impress or please us. He is not so much as aware of our existence. He is an artist in the presence of his materials (which are, in effect, the full deep, dark contents of his mind);

he is intent on seeing what can be made of them, what they insist on making of themselves.

Thus, reading *Finnegans Wake* is an endless and never-fully-satisfying process. One may read a single paragraph for weeks without ceasing to find new meanings in it and without ceasing to wonder if what one has found was really there or is only one's own importation. It is an unusual reader indeed who, facing *Finnegans Wake*, does not feel the need for more support (perhaps more catering) than Joyce has provided. If one takes this discomfort too hard, then before long one will probably give up on *Finnegans Wake* altogether. But a blend of relaxation and anxiety will keep one with it. It is a little like learning how to fall—a skill very necessary for acrobats, football players, and other athletes devoted to the science of balance. But practice at playing the *Wake*-game makes one better at it, resources of information build up, alternatives open out, some will-o'-the-wisps fade away, others solidify. The original feeling of impatience diminishes; the book takes its place in one's life. It is not like any other book, but it is more like books than any other experience.

I have deliberately refrained from saying anything about the advertised verbal music of *Finnegans Wake* because this seems too limited and misleading an approach to the book. Joyce's various melody is no more an object in itself than Milton's organ-voice. It is a vehicle of expression, as I have argued, organically bound up with a point of view. One can get a preliminary sense of Joyce's capacity for verbal music by listening to the well-known recording (made for C. K. Ogden and available until recently through the Gotham Book Mart in New York City) which he himself made of the ALP section. Other passages of sustained beauty, perhaps a bit less familiar, are the brother's denunciation and the mother's benediction

(Book I, section 7, toward the end), the final monologue of Anna Liffey (Book IV), and the children's
return home after play (Book II, section 1, toward
the end). But the true savor of any passage comes
out only in meditating its content; and this seems
like a useful way to live with the book, by taking it
in bite-size bits as the appetite invites and circumstances allow.

EXPLICATIONS OF TWO
WAKE-PASSAGES

Following are annotations for two *Wake*-
passages, presented not necessarily as
models of what ought to be done for the
whole book (for that would take more years than
any reader with a life of his own to be lived can
afford to give), but as evidence of the sort of problem that may occur in a close reading and the sort
of answer that will present itself. The first passage consists of 36 lines from pp. 15 and 16 (Book
I, section 1) in which we are introduced to Jute
and overhear a few words of his conversation with
Mutt. Jute is an island-aborigine, a dull-brained
primitive fellow and a born servant (son of Ham),
who in modern times is Joe, the handyman-serving-
boy at Earwicker's pub; Mutt is an invader, perhaps
a Dane, perhaps an Englishman; in any event, the
bloody struggle at Clontarf (in 1014) between Danes
and natives runs through both their minds as they
try to make one another's acquaintance. Wherever my
erudition and ingenuity broke down, I have left space
for the reader to supplement my efforts.

1   In the name of Anem this carl on the kopje in pelted thongs a parth a lone who the joebiggar be he? Forshapen his pigmaid hoagshead, shroonk his plodsfoot. He hath locktoes, this short-shins, and, Obeold that's pectoral, his mammamuscles most
5 mousterious. It is slaking nuncheon out of some thing's brain pan. Me seemeth a dragon man. He is almonthst on the kiep fief by here, is Comestipple Sacksoun, be it junipery or febrew-

1. **Anem:** anagram of "name"; also "amen" from Hebrew "truth"
   or "certainty"; also, as Ammon, an Egyptian god whom Milton and others connect with Ham—this fulfills the pig-imagery
   below. "A and M" would be short for "Adam"; **carl:** Old
   Norse, farmer, fellow = churl, Old English; **kopje:** hill or butte
   in Dutch and Afrikaans; **pelted thongs:** leather gaiters or
   sandals, like belts and with the fur-side out.

2. **a parth a lone:** a Parthian, apart and alone, with reference to
   Parthalon, Scythian giant who invaded Ireland after the
   deluge; **joebiggar:** Joseph Biggar, one of Parnell's lieutenants,
   a hunchback; **Forshapen:** foreshortened and misshapen; **pigmaid:** made like a pig, pigmy, and with reference to Grissel
   Steevens, Irish maiden of the eighteenth century supposed to
   have had features like a pig (*Ulysses,* p. 411).

3. **hoagshead:** "hogshead," a pig-image to reinforce our sense
   of a son of Ham; **shroonk:** "shrunk," but drawn out into a
   pig's oink; **plodsfoot:** "plodding foot" (he's a slow goer) plus
   plotz, Yiddish for "collapse"; **locktoes:** lacking in toes, or suffering from lockjaw of the toes, impeded either way.

3-4. **shortshins:**

4. **Obeold:** oh by all, oh behold; **pectoral:** his chest, breast, a
   cross worn on the breast, or (with the preceding "s") spectral;
   mammamuscles: the Finnegan stammer, plus mammary
   (chest–breast) muscles—Brian Boru won a victory at Glen
   Mama in 1000 A.D.

5. **mousterious:** "mysterious" with "mouse," "monster," and
   "moustache"; also "Mousterian" refers to an early form of
   paleolithic man; **slaking nuncheon:** "taking luncheon" and
   "slaking" his thirst with a "nuncheon" (dialect for a sip of
   liquor).

5-6. **brain pan:** prehistoric man is often preserved in skull-frag-
   ments, and the Jute is a cannibalistic drinker.

6. **dragon man:** a "dragoman," i.e., a professional interpreter,
   but also a backward element, a "drag on man"; **almonthst:**
   "always," or "almost always," and "every month"; **kiep:** *kip,*
   meaning "hut" in Danish, and "brothel" in English slang.

7. **fief:** a feudal estate—the **kiep-fief** = the premises of the kips plus
   the *qui-vive;* **Comestipple Sacksoun:** Constable (but also
   comestible) Saxon, i.e., of a race conquered by Normans, a
   servant; also, Sackerson, the famous baited bear of Elizabethan
   days (*Ulysses,* p. 188); "stipple" implies a spotted complexion,
   "comes-tiple" that drink is arriving, and Sacksoun = "the son
   of sack," a strong wine; **junipery:** June and January with
   juniper berries, whence gin; **febrewery:** February and a brewery.

ery, marracks or alebrill or the ramping riots of pouriose and froriose. What a quhare soort of a mahan. It is evident the mich-
10 indaddy. Lets we overstep his fire defences and these kraals of slitsucked marrogbones. (Cave!) He can prapsposterus the pillory way to Hirculos pillar. Come on, fool porterfull, hosiered women blown monk sewer? Scuse us, chorley guy! You toller-

8. **marracks:** March with arrack, an Indian punch; **alebrill:** April with ale; **ramping riots:** perhaps March coming in like a lion; **pouriose:** suggests **pluviôse**, rainy month (January–February) in the French Revolutionary Calendar, plus "pour" (either rain or beer) and furious.

9. **froriose:** past participle of German **frieren**, to freeze (*froren*) rhymed by force into the French Revolutionary Calendar; **quhare:** "queer" plus "hairy" plus "rabbit," also "hare" plus "mahan" below = Heremon, one of two sons of Miletus; **soort:** "sort" plus "sooty" plus perhaps "sewer" (no. 13 below); **mahan:** "man" plus "Mahon," brother of Brian Boru (see below, nos. 30 and 34) plus perhaps Alfred Mahan, nineteenth-century theorist of seapower.

9–10. **michindaddy:** (see also *Finnegans Wake*, p. 72, l. 13) "Mich" is an obsolete verb for "skulk" or "hide"; **miche is** French argot for "bottom"; **mishe** is Gaelic for "I am"; and "michin" includes the idea of a "machine" such as Mahan might want, plus German **mich-in-daddy**, i.e., myself in primitive form.

10. **fire defences:** fire outside a cave to keep animals away; fire-power as a preoccupation of Mahan, a modern caveman; **kraals:** from Dutch or Afrikaans, fold or pen, plus "crawls."

11. **slitsucked marrogbones:** archaeologists do in fact distinguish primitive cultures by the way they crack bones to suck the marrow; plus perhaps "rog" from Gaelic **rogha**, the best; **(Cave!):** English "cave" plus Latin "beware"; **prapsposterus:** "preposterous" and "perhaps post to us."

11–12. **pillory way:** the high way, a pillory being exalted, also perhaps "billowy wave."

12. **Hirculos pillar:** Hercules' pillar, Gibraltar; plus Latin hircus, a he-goat. Nelson's pillars, in Dublin and London, struck Joyce as emblems of rampant sexuality.

12–13. **Come on, fool porterfull, hosiered women blown monk sewer?** "Come here, you stupid drunk, have any women clad only in hosiery been blown ashore in this land of saints and sewers?" (or something like this) in English, plus, in French, *"Comment vous portez-vous aujourd'hui, mon blond monsieur?"* (How are you today, my blond sir?)

13. **chorley guy!:** Charley, my boy, fellow-churl; **tollerday:** talende in Danish = "speaking," plus "tolerate" and "today."

day donsk? N. You tolkatiff scowegian? Nn. You spigotty an-
15 glease? Nnn. You phonio saxo? Nnnn. Clear all so! 'Tis a Jute.
Let us swop hats and excheck a few strong verbs weak oach eather yapyazzard abast the blooty creeks.

Jute.—Yutah!

Mutt.—Mukk's pleasurad.

20 Jute.—Are you jeff?

Mutt.—Somehards.

Jute.—But you are not jeffmute?

Mutt.—Noho. Only an utterer.

Jute.—Whoa? Whoat is the mutter with you?

25 Mutt.—I became a stun a stummer.

Jute.—What a hauhauhauhaudibble thing, to be cause! How,
Mutt?

14. **donsk:** in and meaning Danish, *dansk;* **tolkatiff:** "talkative," plus the little stream Tolka which flows through Clontarf, plus talk with the idea of an accompanying drink, "tiff"; **scowegian:** Norwegian plus Scotch and perhaps scow = the invader's boats; **spigotty:** Italian–American dialect for "speak the," a spigot from a barrel, Richard Piggott (Parnell's libeler, see above p. 180, footnote), and spying on God; **anglease:** English, *anglais,* plus the idea of "easy" and a "lease" (Englishmen go where the living is easy and take a lease on it), also the island of Anglesea where the Druids made a last stand against invading Romans.

15. **You phonio:** euphonious (from Greek *phonē,* sound), plus phoney = fake; **saxo:** "saxophone," "Saxon," plus Saxo Grammaticus and sex and the solidity of a rock (Latin *saxum*); **Jute:** "Jew" plus "native of Jutland" plus "victim of a fall" (French *chute*).

16. **swop hats:** a custom in some primitive countries, with the overtone here of exchanging identities; **excheck:** check out, give one another checks which will be exchanged in the exchequer; **weak:** with, plus the grunt of a baby pig; **oach eather:** a Spoonerism for each other, plus either, plus "ouch!" (the exchange hurts a bit).

17. **yapyazzard:** yapping haphazardly, at random; **abast:** about, against; **blooty creeks:** "bloody creeks" (streams or Indians, see no. 18, Yutah) or Greeks, plus the idea of loot and booty. Maybe also "bleeding crooks."

18. **Yutah:** Utah, final destination of the Mormons, outsiders seeking a home in the wilderness; perhaps also an abridgment of "Jutes, hurrah!"

19. **Mukks pleasurad:** much pleased, much pleasure, to be sure; *muck* is Gaelic for "pig," and *rad* German for "wheel," hence, it's fun for pigs on the wheel of life.

20. **jeff:** "deaf," also "Are you your opposite?" (Mutt and Jeff).

21. **Somehards:** "somehow," "some hours," "sometimes but it's hard to say," "sometimes hard of hearing."

22. **jeffmute:** "deafmute" and "Jeff plus Mutt," i.e., both of them.

23. **Noho:** oh no, nohow; **utterer:** "spokesman," plus "stutterer," plus "other" and "outer-er," i.e., one from outside.

24. **Whoa?:** "who?" pronounced hoarsely, "stop" pronounced horsely. **Whoat:** "what?" plus oats; **mutter:** matter, mumble, mother.

25. **became:** German *bekommen,* got; **a stun:** through being stunned or stoned; **a stummer:** a stutter, a stammer, a mumble, and a stumble.

26. **hauhauhauhaudibble:** horrible, audible but the quadruple haw-haw sounds like laughter and the rumble of mocking thunder; **to be cause:** to be, what was the cause of it, with perhaps an echo from the thunder distorting the sentence.

Mutt.—Aput the buttle, surd.

Jute.—Whose poddle? Wherein?

30   Mutt.—The Inns of Dungtarf where Used awe to be he.

Jute.—You that side your voise are almost inedible to me. Become a bitskin more wiseable, as if I were you.

Mutt.—Has? Has at? Hasatency? Urp, Boohooru! Booru

35   Usurp! I trumple from rath in mine mines when I rimimirim!

The second passage introduces Shem (pp. 169–170), in a tone of heavy irony, as an exponent of forbidden knowledge. To his siblings he propounds a riddle, the answer to which condemns the asker. Two interesting sets of overtones in this passage are derived from the Elder Edda and its prediction of a final catastrophe for the world, a Ragnarok, and from the character of HCE as a great old salmon in the Liffey. This is used to suggest that there is something fishy about Shem.

1   Shem is as short for Shemus as Jem is joky for Jacob. A few toughnecks are still getatable who pretend that aboriginally he was of respectable stemming (he was an outlex between the lines

28. **Aput:** from Latin *apud*, amidst, among, plus English "about" and "abutting"; **buttle:** puddle, bottle, battle, particularly the Battle of Clontarf (Danes vs. Irish, 1014 A.D.); **surd:** "sir," "deaf" (via French *sourd*), a voiceless irrational.

29. **poddle:** puddle, poodle, bottle, battle, and the little stream called Poddle which flows through, or under, North Dublin and into the Liffey.

30. **Inns of Dungtarf:** the battle of Clontarf was between "ins" (Irish) and "outs" (Danes), *clon* means "field" in Gaelic, *tarf*, "bull," Dungtarf therefore = b.s.; **Used:**

    awe to be he: "ought to be he."

31. **voise:** "voice" plus French *voies*, ways; **inedible:** "inaudible," "uneatable"; hearing, like all social arrangements between invader and subject, is mixed up with eating and drinking throughout the passage.

32. **bitskin:** "a little bit," plus a pit and a skin; **wiseable:** visible, wise apple.

34. **Hasatency:** "has a tendency," hesitancy, a word on which see above, p. 180; **Urp:** a burp, up with an "R"; "Are you up?" was a key question for United Irishmen: **Boohooru!:** Brian Boru won the battle of Clontarf at the cost of his life, "boohoo" is a lament for him; **Booru Usurp:** up with us boors.

35. **trumple:** trumpet, trample; **rath:** "wrath" and a primitive Irish fortification; the passage has an echo from "The Battle Hymn of the Republic," "trampling out the vintage where the grapes of wrath are stored"; **mine mines:** "my mind."

36. **rimimirim:** remember him, murmuring, plus perhaps Urim and Thummim, which, besides their Biblical uses, were discovered by Joseph Smith when he found the book of Mormon.

1. **Shemus:** from Gaelic *Seamus*, James; **Jem is joky for Jacob:** Jem = Jim = James = Jacomus (Old French) = Jacobus (Latin); **joky:** jocular; Jacob and Esau are Shem and Shaun.

2. **toughnecks:** tough roughnecks; **getatable:** deliberately clumsy, joking speech; **aboriginally:** "originally" with an emphasis plus "aborigine," native.

3. **stemming:** "stem," "origin," plus German *Stimmung*, temper, humor; **outlex:** "outlet," "outlaw," "outcome," plus idea of illegitimacy.

of Ragonar Blaubarb and Horrild Hairwire and an inlaw to Capt.
the Hon. and Rev. Mr Bbyrdwood de Trop Blogg was among
his most distant connections) but every honest to goodness man
in the land of the space of today knows that his back life will
not stand being written about in black and white. Putting truth
and untruth together a shot may be made at what this hybrid
actually was like to look at.

Shem's bodily getup, it seems, included an adze of a skull, an
eight of a larkseye, the whoel of a nose, one numb arm up a
sleeve, fortytwo hairs off his uncrown, eighteen to his mock lip,

4. **Ragonar Blaubarb:** Ragnar Lodbrog is the hero of a Viking legend, *ragnarok* in Old Norse is the day of the downfall of the Gods; it means literally, "the rending of the rocks," see below nos. 47–48. Joyce could have learned, or been reminded, of a great deal of comparative mythology, combined with an immense and slightly loony theory of cosmic catastrophe and earthly cycles, from a book by Ignatius Donnelly, *Ragnarok: the Age of Fire and Gravel* (New York, 1884); **Blaubarb:** German for Bluebeard; **Horrild Hairwire:** Harold (plus horrid = bristling) Fairhair was the first king of Iceland, where many Irish settled. Harold Harefoot was the illegitimate son of King Canute, and a wirehair is a breed of terrier. It would be nice if one could figure out a way to use Hodgart and Worthington's reference to that grand old song, "There's Hair Like Wire Coming Out of the Empire," but I can't.

5. **Capt. the Hon. and Rev.:** military, political, and religious titles to suggest the universal man, also the three ages of a Viconian cycle—plus *Mr,* to represent the fourth age, or *ricorso.* **Bbyrdwood:**

   de Trop: in French, excessive, unwanted; **Blogg:** "blob," "log," plus the heavy, grotesque, ugly sound of a double "g" as in Swift's Luggnagg, etc.; **Bbyrdwood Blogg:** aristo- plus pleb, with an overtone of ancient forests, hardwood logs. Joyce parodies his own youthful pretensions to distinguished ancestry at Clongowes (cf. *Ulysses,* p. 39); **Trop Blogg:** true blue?

7. **in the land of the space of today:** time and space cross; the here and now; **back life:** past, in the backward part of time, but also backstairs, secret.

8–9. **truth and untruth together:**

11. **adze of a skull:**

12. **eight of a larkseye:**

   whoel of a nose: "whole," "wheel," "whale," "hole," plus Norse *oel,* oil and French *oeil,* eye; **one numb arm up a sleeve:**

13. **fortytwo hairs off his uncrown:** "off" substituted for "on," "uncrown" for "crown"—Shem is too low for a crown; **eighteen to his mock lip:**

a trio of barbels from his megageg chin (sowman's son), the
15 wrong shoulder higher than the right, all ears, an artificial
tongue with a natural curl, not a foot to stand on, a handful of
thumbs, a blind stomach, a deaf heart, a loose liver, two fifths of
two buttocks, one gleetsteen avoirdupoider for him, a manroot
of all evil, a salmonkelt's thinskin, eelsblood in his cold toes, a
20 bladder tristended, so much so that young Master Shemmy on
his very first debouch at the very dawn of protohistory seeing
himself such and such, when playing with thistlewords in their

14. **barbels:** fish-whiskers, carrying out the idea of a cold-blooded man; **megageg chin:** mega = big, plus a stammer; **sowman's son:** "salmon's son" (cf. *Finnegans Wake*, p. 297, 1. 3), also son of a sower (in the analogy of plowman), plus son of a sow (Stephen Dedalus said Ireland was the old sow that eats her farrow).

15. **wrong shoulder:** sinister = left, unlucky; **all ears:** attentive, with a reference to Joyce's auditory imagination.

15-16. **an artificial tongue:** the tongue of a liar, an artist, an artificer, with a reflection on the dialect of *Finnegans Wake* itself.

16. **with a natural curl:** normally used of hair; a curled lip denotes scornful or malicious speech; **not a foot to stand on:** adapted from the metaphor for "indefensible."

16-17. **a handful of thumbs:** all thumbs = clumsy.

17. **blind stomach:** like many salmon, caecal, blind, with no outlet; **deaf heart:** insensitive; **loose liver:** man who lives loosely, here given physiological meaning, like "all ears" above, by the context.

17-18. **two fifths of two buttocks:** perhaps implies no more than "meager."

18. **gleetsteen:** *gleet* = slime, mucous, discharge; *steen* = stein, stone (including kidney stone and a measure of weight); **avoirdupoider:** "weight," "*avoirdupois*," plus "avoider."

18-19. **manroot of all evil:** love of money is the root of all evil, Shem is a walking avarice; mandrake.

19. **salmonkelt:** a salmon that has spawned, and is therefore limp, tired, and unwholesome to eat; **thinskin:** sensitivity: **eelsblood in his cold toes:** a chilly fellow.

20. **tristended:** "sadly extended," "with a sad end," "thrice tended or tendered, like Tristan."

21. **debouch:** "pour fcrth" and "debauch"; **protohistory:** earliest form of history.

22. **such and such:**

thistlewords:

garden nursery, Griefotrofio, at Phig Streat 111, Shuvlin, Old
Hoeland, (would we go back there now for sounds, pillings and
25 sense? would we now for annas and annas? would we for fullscore eight and a liretta? for twelve blocks one bob? for fourtes-
ters one groat? not for a dinar! not for jo!) dictited to of all his
little brothron and sweestureens the first riddle of the universe:
asking, when is a man not a man?: telling them take their time,
30 yungfries, and wait till the tide stops (for from the first his day
was a fortnight) and offering the prize of a bittersweet crab, a
little present from the past, for their copper age was yet unminted, to the winner. One said when the heavens are quakers,
a second said when Bohemeand lips, a third said when he, no,

23. **Griefotrofio:** "grief" and "trophy" of course, but what else?;

Phig Streat: Pig Street or Fig Street with reference to the fig leaf of Adam and Eve, Pig's Treat or Retreat; **111:** the three Earwicker children, the multiple offspring of ALP; **Shuvlin:** Dublin, Shovelling, Scheveningen.

23–24. **Old Hoeland:** Holland, Lowland, oil-land (207, note 12), or Ireland.

24–25. **sounds, pillings, and sense;** pounds, shillings, and pence.

25. **annas and annas:** Indian coins plus *annus* = Latin for year.

25–26. **fullscore eight and a liretta:** threescore and ten, the traditional age of man; a score plus 8 = 28 (the 28 Maggies) plus liretta = Issy or a lorette or a little *lira* (Italian coin). ALP = 29 because A = 1, L = 12, P = 16 alphabetically. Perhaps with a remote echo from the Gettysburg Address.

26. **for twelve blocks one bob:** a bob is a shilling, which is twelve pence; but "block" is not an accepted term for "penny."

26–27. **for four testers one groat:** tester = shilling in the time of Henry VIII, sixpence in Shakespeare's day, a groat = fourpence. So it's a good deal to get four testers in exchange for a groat.

27. **not for a dinar!:** money of Iraq and Yugoslavia; **not for jo!:** a fourpenny piece (joe), but in the background, "I've Been Working on the Railroad" (cf. *Finnegans Wake*, p. 175, ll. 35–36, Dina and old Joe); **dictited:** dictated, indicted.

28. **brothron:** "brethren," "brothers"; **sweestureens:** "sweet sisters," "little sisters," "Swiss tureens," fit to hold broth.

29. **when is a man not a man?:** Hodgart and Worthington refer to the song, "When Is a Man Less than a Man?" but it's also an Oedipal question, as posed by the Sphinx.

30. **yungfries:** "young fries" or "fry" (HCE is the great Liffey salmon, his children are fry), also German *jungfraus,* maidens; **wait till the tide stops:**

30–31. **for from the first his day was a fortnight:**

31. **bittersweet crab:** crabapple, the tree in the Garden of Eden, of the knowledge of good and evil; *crab* = tree in Gaelic.

32–33. **their copper age was yet unminted:** copper = penny = money. The four ages of man are the ages of gold, silver, brass, and iron, so they are still in the ages of gold or silver, i.e., the infancy of mankind.

33. **when the heavens are quakers:** when the thunder sounds, man is not a man.

34. **when Bohemeand lips:** "Bohemian," with reference to "Then you'll remember me" (Hodgart and Worthington).

35 when hold hard a jiffy, when he is a gnawstick and detarmined
to, the next one said when the angel of death kicks the bucket
of life, still another said when the wine's at witsends, and still
another when lovely wooman stoops to conk him, one of the
littliest said me, me, Sem, when pappa papared the harbour, one
40 of the wittiest said, when he yeat ye abblokooken and he zmear
hezelf zo zhooken, still one said when you are old I'm grey fall
full wi sleep, and still another when wee deader walkner, and
another when he is just only after having being semisized, another when yea, he hath no mananas, and one when dose pigs
45 they begin now that they will flies up intil the looft. All were
wrong, so Shem himself, the doctator, took the cake, the correct
solution being—all give it up?—; when he is a—yours till
the rending of the rocks,—Sham.

35: **gnawstick:** "gnostic," with perhaps reference to skull and bones; **detarmined:**

36. **kicks the bucket:** dies.

37. **wine's at witsends:**

38. **lovely wooman stoops to conk him:** Goldsmith's poem with the title of his play, plus idea of a hit on the head. Woo + man = woman.

39. **littliest:** littlest plus bittiest; **pappa papared the harbour:** "painted the port red," "papered or prepared the harbor or arbor = tree."

40. **when he yeat ye abblokooken:** "when he eats (with a touch of Yeats) the apple cake" (German, *apfelkuchen*), but of course with a touch of Eden-apple.

40–41. **zmear hezelf zo zhooken:** and smears himself so shockingly (with sin, of course). The y's and z's in these lines probably mean something.

41–42. **when you are old I'm grey fall full wi sleep:** "When you are old and grey and full of sleep," first line of a poem by Yeats* (see above, no. 40).

42. **when wee deader walkner:** "when we (little) dead walk or wake," plus Ibsen's play, *When We Dead Awaken.*

43. **just only after having been semisized:** "half-sized," with an overtone from "seism," earthquake.

44. **yea, he hath no mananas:** the song, "Yes, We Have No Bananas," also, when we are dead and have no more Spanish *mananas* = tomorrows.

44–45. **dose pigs they begin now that they will flies up intil the looft:** "looft" = loft and German *luft* = air. "The Walrus and the Carpenter" proposes the questions, "Why the sea is boiling hot, / And whether pigs have wings," but I do not recognize the source of the specific phrases.

46. **doctator:** "doctor," "dictator."

47–48. **yours till the rending of the rocks:** *ragnarok,* the day of the downfall of the gods, see above, no. 4.

48. **Sham:** "Shem," "sham," i.e., fake, plus the idea of shame.

* "When You Are Old" in *The Collected Poems of W. B. Yeats* (New York: Macmillan, 1956).

EVALUATION

There are two wholly incompatible ways of estimating the future position of *Finnegans Wake* vis-à-vis *Ulysses*. Prudentially, it is clear, there are all sorts of reasons why *Finnegans Wake* will never be widely read or recognized as a great book: it is too long, too exasperatingly private and difficult, too far out of the common orbit. *Ulysses* is more accessible, more like a novel. It has characters as we are more or less used to seeing them, and the embryo of a plot. If people continue to seek in novels what they have always sought, it seems clear that *Finnegans Wake* is doomed to remain what is it presently considered, a vast *cul-de-sac* eccentricity of a wrong-headed genius. This is such an easy, unimaginative judgment that it is probably wrong. By this perverse logic I mean simply and seriously that literature by its very nature is committed to questioning yesterday's assumptions and today's commonplaces. Yesterday, *Ulysses* was a book so deliberately filthy and impossibly difficult that respectable and established critics rejected it with boisterous shouts of disgust and invocations to the nearest policeman. Today, it is a classic. I see many signs that the same process of change is under way with *Finnegans Wake*. Our minds are being stretched to encompass it. All the evidence on which to dismiss or diminish *Finnegans Wake*, including the built-in, semi-conscious rigidity of our minds, is already and easily to hand. We have only to stand pat in order to reject. But it is precisely that rigidity, that stand-pattism of which we should be suspicious. The sort of evidence on which the book's slow acceptance will be grounded is not yet available. It must be sought for and worked over. But the readiness to undertake this search and perform this work is making up in the intellectual weather of the age. Thus I will make bold to say that in the near future it is *Finnegans Wake* on which the major reputation of Joyce will depend. Nora Joyce herself understood this, and after the death of her husband would express impatience with people who talked about nothing but *Ulysses. Finnegans Wake*, for her, was the big book. There is no need to pretend that this big book doesn't have its tiresome and difficult, maybe even impossible, passages. But it carries to their logical conclusion the modalities of visionary insight and multiple imitation which we have learned to admire in *Ulysses* and *The Portrait*; it is an immense mine of verbal invention, from which artists will be quarrying for years to come. And it seems to me a prophetic book as well. If *Dubliners* summarized, as early as 1904, the condition of life in the last decade before World War I—if *Ulysses*, in 1922, described a shape of existence, a spiritual state which I recognize as culminating in 1939—then it seems equally conceivable that our world is just now entering into the phase of *Finnegans Wake*. There is no cause for jubilation here. It looks like an age of dark, anonymous, confused struggle, of infinite, blurred, blundering overlays and very short perspectives. But *Finnegans Wake* seems to me much closer to representing the full world in which real people live in 1966 than, say, the novels of E. M. Forster or those of J. P. Marquand (examples chosen at random). Conventional opinion will no doubt think this a bizarre judgment, but conventional opinion is busy day and night making sure that Finn remains buried. If one reflects a little on the real fabric of spiritual experience in the modern world, the idea may not seem so crazy. Putting matters very simply, *Finnegans Wake* answers to and expresses a fundamental bind in the modern consciousness, which, in becoming infinitely deep, complex, and cosmopolitan, has only shackled itself more terribly to the sense of universal meaninglessness.

What I have written above is prophecy, which, like all prophecy, can be ludicrously wrong. But, even supposing I am as wrong as can be imagined—that *Finnegans Wake* proves, over the years, to be a monadnock of perverse eccentricity—yet I think it will have had an immense influence on our perception of Joyce and his other books. In a world of flimflam and opportunism, his was a profoundly authentic voice; and the last proof of his authenticity is his readiness to fail big rather than succeed safe. Like Milton and Blake, his spiritual ancestors in so many ways, he followed the big reason of artistic conscience—his uncommon visionary sense—in preference to the petty reason of prudence and practicality, the common sense against which the artist can have no quarrel except that it is a bit too common. This is why we are already justified in talking of Joyce, not as the talented author of a couple of novels, but as a great and permanent complex, whose work will repay any attention we can afford to give it. He will be remembered as one of those rare and challenging figures whom the human race is perpetually rediscovering as it advances and hesitates and readvances toward the mirage of its own identity.

APPENDIX A

Time-Scheme of A PORTRAIT OF THE
ARTIST AS A YOUNG MAN

Pages	*Period Described*	*Period Elapsed*
	I	
1–2	Three episodes of a minute apiece	
		four to five years
3–7	Football game: ten minutes	
		overnight, a week, a month: indefinite
7–17	Class, teatime, study hall, bed: two hours	
		an hour
17–18	Dream of Christmas: instantaneous	
		overnight
18–22	Sickness and infirmary: a morning	
		three hours
23–26	Infirmary: afternoon and evening	
		seventy-five days
26–41	Christmas dinner: one hour	
		a month, two?
41–64	Pandying and complaint: one afternoon	
		a year of Clongowes; then vacation

II

65–71	Blackrock: June–September	three months? or fifteen?
71–73	Dublin at Christmas: two weeks	no way to estimate
73–74	At his aunt's house: five minutes	no way to estimate
74–75	Unknown house with two old women: five minutes	no way to estimate
75–77	Children's party: an evening	twenty-four hours
77–78	Writing the poem: an hour	some months
78–80	Entry into Belvedere: twenty minutes	two years
80–87	Whitsuntide play: half-hour	flashback one and a half years
87–91	Assault by Heron, Boland, Nash: fifteen minutes	return one and a half years
91–96	Complete Whitsuntide play: two hours	four months?
97–108	Trip to Cork: three days	three months? or 15?
108–109	Prize money (October): half-hour	continuous
110–114	Merrymaking, wandering, the whore: October, November	continuous

III

115–169 Retreat at Belvedere: four
days

continuous

IV

170–178 Piety: indefinite weeks,
months

some months

178–189 Talk with director, visit to
Dedalus home: one hour

months to leave
Belvedere and en-
ter UCD

190–201 Bird-girl: an afternoon

three years plus

V

202–211 Walk across town: half-
hour

flashback   (one
year?) to Davin's
story

211–213 Davin's story

return (one year?)

213–254 Dean of studies, lecture,
petition, esthetic talk with
Lynch: three hours

twelve hours

254–263 Composition of villanelle:
one hour

one night or thirty?

263–265 taking omens of birds: ten
minutes

flashback ten years

265–266 First night of *Countess
Cathleen:* ten minutes

return ten years

266–268 In the library: five minutes

flashback   forty
years

268   Incest with Davin: three
           minutes

                                        return forty years

269–292 In the library, talk with
           Cranly: one hour

                                        a few days

292–299 March 20–April 27: dated
           diary entries

APPENDIX B *Pattern-Outline of* ULYSSES

	Title	*Scene*	*Hour*	*Organ*	*Art*	*Colour*	*Symbol*	*Technic*
1.	Telemachus	The Tower	8 a.m.		Theology	White, gold	Heir	Narrative (young)
2.	Nestor	The School	10 a.m.		History	Brown	Horse	Catechism (personal)
3	Proteus	The Strand	11 a.m.		Philology	Green	Tide	Monologue (male)
4.	Calypso	The House	8 a.m.	Kidney	Economics	Orange	Nymph	Narrative (mature)
5.	Lotus-eaters	The Bath	10 a.m.	Genitals	Botany, Chemistry		Eucharist	Narcissism
6.	Hades	The Grave-yard	11 a.m.	Heart	Religion	White, black	Caretaker	Incubism
7.	Aeolus	The News-paper	12 noon	Lungs	Rhetoric	Red	Editor	Enthymemic
8.	Lestrygonians	The Lunch	1 p.m.	Esophagus	Architecture		Constables	Peristaltic
9.	Scylla and Charybdis	The Library	2 p.m.	Brain	Literature		Stratford, London	Dialectic
10.	Wandering Rocks	The Streets	3 p.m.	Blood	Mechanics		Citizens	Labyrinth

Pattern-Outline of ULYSSES *(Continued)*

Title	Scene	Hour	Organ	Art	Colour	Symbol	Technic
11. Sirens	The Concert Room	4 p.m.	Ear	Music		Barmaids	Fuga per canonem
12. Cyclops	The Tavern	5 p.m.	Muscle	Politics		Fenian	Gigantism
13. Nausicaa	The Rocks	8 p.m.	Eye, Nose	Painting	Grey, blue	Virgin	Tumescence, detumescence
14. Oxen of the Sun	The Hospital	10 p.m.	Womb	Medicine	White	Mothers	Embryonic development
15. Circe	The Brothel	12 midnight	Locomotor Apparatus	Magic		Whore	Hallucination
16. Eumaeus	The Shelter	1 a.m.	Nerves	Navigation		Sailors	Narrative (old)
17. Ithaca	The House	2 a.m.	Skeleton	Science		Comets	Catechism (impersonal)
18. Penelope	The Bed		Flesh			Earth	Monologue (female)

Reprinted from *James Joyce's Ulysses*, Stuart Gilbert (New York: Alfred A. Knopf, 1931), p. 28, by permission of the publisher.

FOR FURTHER STUDY

Additional Writings of Joyce, not discussed in this book

Collected Poems. New York: Viking, 1946.
Exiles, ed. Padraic Colum. New York: Viking, 1951.
Stephen Hero, ed. Theodore Spencer. New York: New Directions, 1963.
The Critical Writings of James Joyce, eds. Ellsworth Mason and Richard Ellmann. New York: Viking, 1959.

Bibliography

Beebe, Maurice and A. Walton Litz, "Criticism of James Joyce," in *Modern Fiction Studies* IV (Spring, 1958).
Magalaner, Marvin and Richard M. Kain, *Joyce, the Man, the Work, the Reputation.* New York: New York University Press, 1956.
Slocum, John J. and Herbert Cahoon, *A Bibliography of James Joyce.* New Haven, Conn.: Yale University Press, 1953.

Biography and Memoirs

Byrne, John F., *Silent Years.* New York: Farrar, Straus, & Cudahy, 1953.
Ellmann, Richard, *James Joyce.* London: Oxford University Press, 1959.
Gilbert, Stuart, ed., *Letters of James Joyce.* New York: Viking, 1957.

Joyce, Stanislaus, *My Brother's Keeper*. New York: Viking, 1958.

Sullivan, Kevin, *Joyce Among the Jesuits*. New York: Columbia University Press, 1958.

On *Dubliners* and *A Portrait of the Artist as a Young Man*

Connolly, Thomas, ed., *Joyce's Portrait*. New York: Appleton-Century, 1952.

Magalaner, Marvin, *Time of Apprenticeship*. New York: Appleton-Century, 1962.

Scholes, Robert E. and Richard M. Kain, *The Workshop of Daedalus*. Evanston, Ill.: Northwestern University Press, 1965.

On *Ulysses*

Gilbert, Stuart, *James Joyce's Ulysses*. New York: Knopf, 1931.

Hutchins, Patricia, *James Joyce's World*. London: Methuen, 1957.

Kain, Richard M., *Fabulous Voyager*. New York: Compass Books, 1959.

Noon, William T., *Joyce and Aquinas*. New Haven, Conn.: Yale University Press, 1957.

Schutte, William, *Joyce and Shakespeare*. New Haven Conn.: Yale University Press, 1957.

Stanford, William B. *The Ulysses Theme*. London: Blackwell, 1954, 1963.

On *Finnegans Wake*

Atherton, James S., *The Books at the Wake*. New York: Viking, 1960.

Campbell, Joseph, and Henry Morton Robinson, *A Skeleton Key to Finnegans Wake*. New York: Viking, 1944, 1961.

Glasheen, Adaline, *Second Census of Finnegans Wake*. Evanston, Ill.: Northwestern University Press, 1963.

Hart, Clive, *Structure and Motif in Finnegans Wake*.

Evanston, Ill.: Northwestern University Press, 1962.

Litz, A. Walton, *The Art of James Joyce*. London: Oxford University Press, 1961. Also has much material on the composition of *Ulysses*.

Critical Introductions

Givens, Seon, ed., *James Joyce: Two Decades of Criticism*. New York: Vanguard Press, 1948, 1963.

Levin, Harry, *James Joyce: A Critical Introduction*. New York: New Directions, 1941, 1960.

Strong, Leonard A. G., *The Sacred River*. London: Methuen, 1949.

Concordances and Scholarly Aids

Connolly, Thomas, *James Joyce's Scribbledehobble*. Evanston, Ill.: Northwestern University Press, 1961.
(Both Connolly and Hayman (see below) have been severely criticized for their transcriptions of *Finnegans Wake* manuscript-materials; yet both may be used with caution, though ultimate decisions on major matters will always have to depend on first-hand inspection of the original MSS.)

Hanley, Miles L., *Word Index to James Joyce's Ulysses*. Madison, Wisc.: University of Wisconsin Press, 1937, 1951.

Hart, Clive, *Concordance to Finnegans Wake*. Minneapolis, Minn.: University of Minnesota Press, 1963.

Hayman, David, *A First-Draft Version of Finnegans Wake*. Austin Tex.: University of Texas Press, 1963.

Hodgart, Matthew, J. C. and M. P. Worthington, *Song in the Work of James Joyce*. New York: Columbia University Press, 1959.

Scholes, Robert E., *The Cornell Joyce Collection*. Ithaca, N.Y.: Cornell University Press, 1961.

Spielberg, Peter, *James Joyce's MSS and Letters at the University of Buffalo*. Buffalo, N.Y.: University of Buffalo Press, 1962.

Periodical Publications

The Analyst, mimeographed periodically at North-western University.

James Joyce Miscellanies, ed. Marvin Magalaner, published from time to time (1957, 1959, 1962) by the Southern Illinois University Press.

The James Joyce Quarterly, presently edited at the University of Tulsa.

A Wake Newslitter, quarterly, eds. Fritz Senn, of Zurich, Switzerland, and Clive Hart, of Newcastle, New South Wales.

INDEX

Random House Studies in Language and Literature